María Teresa Sánchez Nieto (ed.)
Corpus-based Translation and Interpreting Studies/
Estudios traductológicos basados en corpus

Klaus-Dieter Baumann/Hartwig Kalverkämper/Klaus Schubert (Hg.)
TRANSÜD.
Arbeiten zur Theorie und Praxis des Übersetzens und Dolmetschens
Band 71

María Teresa Sánchez Nieto (ed.)

Corpus-based Translation and Interpreting Studies: From description to application

Estudios traductológicos basados en corpus: de la descripción a la aplicación

Frank & Timme

Verlag für wissenschaftliche Literatur

Umschlagabbildung: Puente de Piedra (Soria), España © Dgarcia29/Wikimedia

ISBN 978-3-7329-0084-8
ISSN 1438-2636

© Frank & Timme GmbH Verlag für wissenschaftliche Literatur
Berlin 2015. Alle Rechte vorbehalten.

Das Werk einschließlich aller Teile ist urheberrechtlich geschützt.
Jede Verwertung außerhalb der engen Grenzen des Urheberrechts-
gesetzes ist ohne Zustimmung des Verlags unzulässig und strafbar.
Das gilt insbesondere für Vervielfältigungen, Übersetzungen,
Mikroverfilmungen und die Einspeicherung und Verarbeitung in
elektronischen Systemen.

Herstellung durch Frank & Timme GmbH,
Wittelsbacherstraße 27a, 10707 Berlin.
Printed in Germany.
Gedruckt auf säurefreiem, alterungsbeständigem Papier.

www.frank-timme.de

Índice / Contents

María Teresa Sánchez Nieto
Introduction 7

María Teresa Sánchez Nieto
Introducción 19

Sara Laviosa
Corpora and Holistic Cultural Translation /
Los corpus y el enfoque holístico de la traducción cultural 31

Josep Marco
Taking stock: A critical overview of research on (universal) features of
translated language / A modo de balance: Una revisión crítica de la
investigación sobre propiedades (universales) de la lengua traducida 53

Esther Álvarez de la Fuente y Raquel Fernández Fuertes
A methodological approach to the analysis of natural interpreting: bilingual
acquisition data and the CHAT/CLAN tool / Un enfoque metodológico
para el análisis de la interpretación natural: los datos de adquisición
bilingüe y la herramienta CHAT/CLAN 77

Clara Pignataro
ELF pragmatics and interpreting /
Pragmática del inglés como lengua franca e interpretación 105

Miriam Seghiri
Determinación de la representatividad cuantitativa de un corpus *ad hoc*
bilingüe (inglés-español) de manuales de instrucciones generales de
lectores electrónicos / Establishing the quantitative representativeness of an
E-Reader Users' Guide *ad hoc* corpus (English-Spanish) 125

Índice / Contents

BELÉN LÓPEZ ARROYO y RODA P. ROBERTS
The use of a comparable corpus: How to develop writing applications /
Aplicaciones de ayuda a la escritura en L2 basadas en corpus comparables ... 147

INMACULADA SERÓN ORDÓÑEZ
Cómo crear y analizar corpus paralelos. Un procedimiento con *software*
accesible y económico y algunas sugerencias para *software* futuro /
How to build and analyse parallel corpora. A procedure with accessible and
affordable software and some suggestions for future software......................... 167

ANABEL BORJA ALBI and ISABEL GARCÍA-IZQUIERDO
Corpus-based knowledge management systems for specialized translation:
bridging the gap between theory and professional practice /
Sistemas de gestión del conocimiento basados en corpus para
traductores especializados: de la teoría a la práctica.. 191

ZURIÑE SANZ, NAROA ZUBILLAGA e IBON URIBARRI
Estudio basado en corpus de las traducciones del alemán al vasco /
Corpus based study of German-Basque translations...211

MARÍA TERESA SÁNCHEZ NIETO
Construcción de corpus virtuales comparables deslocalizados (DE/ES):
Análisis y comparación de recursos /
Building virtual delocalized comparable corpora (DE/ES).
Analysis and contrast of resources 235

Introduction

MARÍA TERESA SÁNCHEZ NIETO
Universidad de Valladolid

1. Overview of the volume

In this volume we have gathered a group of papers delivered at the *I Hermēneus Conference: Corpus-Based Translation and Interpreting Studies: from local to global*, which was held in Soria, on the 26th and the 27th March 2014 at the Faculty of Translation and Interpreting of the University of Valladolid. The selected contributions represent a well-balanced set of solid theoretical and applied proposals. The theoretical proposals give testimony to the conceptual development of the discipline, whereas the applied studies —all of them very inspiring— tackle challenging issues and fall into two main areas of corpus-based applied research: corpus-based translator and interpreter training and aids for the professional translator.

The volume opens with a paper delivered by Sara Laviosa, entitled "**Corpora and holistic cultural translation**", in which Laviosa offers a description of the trends she observes in the evolution of Corpus-based Translation Studies (CBTS) during their last decade of existence (2003-2013). Laviosa's observations will help us to give a brief panorama of the contents of this book. In sections 2 to 5 the individual chapters will be presented in greater depth.

According to Laviosa, the continued interest in universals of translation and in the characterization of translated language has resulted in a growing body of research that has focused mainly on translators' behaviour, and particularly on that of literary translators. An example of this kind of research is found in the contribution by Sanz et al., which includes descriptive data based on translations from German literary and philosophical texts into Basque, both as direct and indirect translation —the latter using a Spanish pivot text. Marco, for his part, reviews the criticisms issued on the concept of *translation universal*, and proposes three axes along which the research on (universal) features of translated language can be (re)organised.

Another outstanding issue pointed out by Laviosa in her analysis of the last decade of Corpus-based Translation Studies is the creation of the first corpora for research in interpreting. The chapters by Pignataro and Álvarez de la Fuente and

Fernández Fuertes represent this area of research. Clara Pignataro focuses on how English as a Lingua Franca has an influence on the decisions and strategies adopted by consecutive interpreters, whereas Álvarez de la Fuente and Fernández Fuertes detail the methodology they employ for research on Natural Interpreting, which draws on the CHAT transcription and codification system.

A third trend noticed by Laviosa in Corpus-based Translation and Interpreting Studies from the 2003-2013 decade is the establishment of a strong relationship between the latter and Corpus-based Contrastive Studies (p. 34). The chapter by Roberts and López is a testimony to this trend. They develop a writing application for Spanish-speaking users based on their findings about lexis and rhetorical structure in wine tasting notes (a specialized genre in the domain of wine production) in an EN/ES specialized comparable corpus.

Still regarding the Applied branch of Corpus-Based Translation and Interpreting Studies, Laviosa stresses that since the 2000s corpora have contributed to developing "a culture of research in education" (p. 35). In this vein, Pignataro shows how the corpus of interpreted interactions in literature festivals provides valuable materials for her students, who through autonomous observation can infer the norms and strategies on which interpreters rely, thus preparing themselves for their professional lives. Seghiri's paper can also be subsumed under the Applied branch, as the protocol she designs for compiling DIY corpora that are qualitatively as well as quantitatively representative can be adopted by professional translators. Furthermore, translator trainers who adapt their teaching to market demands will find Seghiri's proposal useful as well.

Two contributions to this volume relate to the fifth characteristic that Laviosa observes in Corpus-based Translation and Interpreting Studies between 2003 and 2013: the creation of many new corpora which are, according to Marco, "invaluable documentation resources" (pág. 67). Our volume includes three contributions that are related to this area of research: those by Sanz et al, Borja and García-Izquierdo and Sánchez Nieto. Borja and García-Izquierdo present two web platforms that serve as knowledge management systems and include corpus-based and additional resources. Sánchez Nieto, for her part, analyses and compares several reference corpora on the basis of a methodology specially developed for this purpose.

The last tendency noticed by Laviosa in the first part of her chapter is the use of corpora as resources for the development of Computer Assisted Translation-Tools. Inmaculada Serón's contribution represents a complementary line: in a sort of "back and forth" process, she shows how some software tools used by professional translators can also be employed to build complex parallel corpora such as those that include an original text and multiple translations of the same.

2. Analysis of the achievements of Corpus-Based Translation and Interpreting Studies in their Descriptive and Applied branches: perspectives for the future

In his chapter, entitled "**Taking stock: A critical overview of research on (universal) features of translated language**", Josep Marco analyses and classifies the criticisms that have been launched against the notion of *translation universal* during the last years by researchers pertaining to the field of Corpus-based Translation and Interpreting Studies. In a second step, he selects those aspects of the criticisms that may serve as a guide for future research on the characterization of translated language. Marco groups the critical stances taken with respect to so-called translation universals as follows: (i) criticisms concerned with the notion of *universal* itself (probably the most widespread); (ii) criticisms concerned with the methodology employed to research the alleged universals — especially Becher's (2010) critical stance against the explicitation hypothesis; (iii) those criticisms questioning the list of features of translated language that are candidates for translation universals, and (iv) criticisms which reject how these universals are defined —with Becher (2010) and Halverson (2003) as representative examples. Marco draws our attention to Halverson's *gravitational pull hypothesis*. This hypothesis "pertains to a higher level of generalisation" than the translation universals put forward so far because it aims at giving a cognitive explanation to the latter, which, in the end, points out regularities in human behaviour. Marco reports on Hareide's (2013) findings; she, for the first time, operationalizes the *gravitational pull hypothesis*. He concludes that, in the last years, research on regularities of translated language has become much more refined and sophisticated.

In the rest of the chapter, Marco devotes himself to analysing and weighing the aforementioned criticisms. For the purpose of this introduction, just one idea of

Marco's analysis will be highlighted, as well as his synthesis at the end of the chapter. The idea he stresses is that it is worthwhile, and even necessary, to invest our efforts in the research of the general features of translated language, be they universal or not, as they make up the main object of study of our discipline: translated texts. Nevertheless, Marco insists on the need to avoid lingering at the descriptive level and try to advance towards the level of explanation (if possible by looking for cognitive or socio-communicative explanations) in order to explain the results of our descriptions of the properties of translated texts. In his final synthesis, certainly one of the most striking elements of his paper, Marco designs a diagram which can serve as a guide for future research on the characterization of translated language. In this new map, the hypothesis or alleged universals are arranged in pairs or groups along three axes (or dialectic oppositions). This allows him to overcome the rather linear approach represented in the traditional list of translation universals, and, moreover, to subscribe to Corpas' (2008) suggestion of investigating universals not in an isolated way but rather in matrixes which group several of them.

If Josep Marco sketches a map for future research in the Descriptive branch of this discipline, Sara Laviosa (p. 48) shares with us her vision of the target towards which the discipline as a whole has to move. Laviosa suggests keeping on promoting the "culture of research in translator education" (p. 3535) and in the training of language specialists. The author is convinced that these good means will help to bring theory and practice closer together in Descriptive Translation Studies, an issue already addressed by Tymoczko (1998: 652, 658, in Laviosa, 2011: 21). Laviosa makes the case for the action-research methodology. Projects of this kind (i) are solidly based on theoretical findings in the Descriptive branch of the discipline, (ii) are undertaken in the classroom; (iii) emerge from problem areas identified by the students themselves regarding issues in the professional exercise of translation; and (iv) allow the students "to gain a deep and critical understanding of the process, product and function of translation" (pág. 36), as well as to understand what is expected of them as "experts of human translation" (Kujamäki 2004: 199, in Laviosa, p. 36) and "self-reflexive, responsible meaning makers" (p. 42). For Laviosa, who follows Tymoczko (2007), a "responsible meaning maker" has to understand that translating is a complex phenomenon that implies *transculturation* —i.e., creating "new cultural phenomena in the target culture" (p. 37), at the same time as representing an original text through a target text and reproducing its content, language, function and form. *Transculturation* is only possible if the translator perceives and analyses the differences between the original and the target culture. In the fourth section of her chapter, Laviosa lists a set of elements in which culture crystallizes in texts. These elements, as they are linguistically codified, can be researched in corpora by students. In her case study (p. 44 ff), the author observes that when students begin to work with corpora they become professionally empowered by combining techniques of Data Driven Learning and Descriptive Translation Studies. (p. 4848).[1]

3. Corpus-based Interpreting Studies

The aim of the chapter by Álvarez de la Fuente and Fernández Fuertes, entitled **"A methodological approach to the analysis of natural interpreting: Bilingual acquisition data and the CHAT/CLAN tool"** is to present a free access tool for the computer-aided interpreting analysis (p. 77): the CHAT transcription and codification system and its associated software, CLAN. In order to show the potential of the methodology they have developed with the aid of the tools mentioned, the authors present a set of data obtained from a couple of bilingual twins (EN/ES). This data is included in the FerFuLice corpus, a corpus transcribed and codified with CHAT and located in *CHILDES*, a subproject of *Talkbank* (http://talkbank.org). The authors stress that the CHAT/CLAN system has never been used previously in Corpus-based Interpreting Studies (pág. 78). Along with this methodological innovation, the description of the linguistic and contextual variables that the authors use for the study of Natural Interpreting should be highlighted (table 1, p. 87 and table 2, p. 87), as well as the valuable reference that Álvarez and Fernández make to the project *Talkbank* and its bilingual datasets for the study of the acquisition of a second language or a foreign language (*BilinBank* and *SLABank*). These corpora could probably be employed

---

[1] In an earlier article (Laviosa 2010), the author explains the essence of corpus-based translator training, specifically the theoretical approach, the design of training and the procedures used. The case study in the present volume complements, thus, Laviosa's (2010) article, as here she offers an example of the concrete forms which can be taken by approach, design and procedures in corpus-based translator training.

for descriptive or applied interpreting studies in foreign language or second language acquisition contexts as well (see Álvarez and Fuertes, p. 88 note 7).

Clara Pignataro's contribution, entitled "**ELF pragmatics and interpreting**", revolves around a series of examples extracted from a corpus of consecutive interpretations from English to Italian in literature festivals. In those settings, Italian interpreters use English as a Lingua Franca (ELF). The author proves that the pragmatics of ELF "impact on the interpreter's work where he/she acts as an active participant in the co-construction of meaning" (p. 106). Pignataro's work is particularly original because, as the author herself remarks, the influence of ELF on the performance of interpreters is a field of study that only very recently has begun to be taken into account by researchers in Corpus-Based Interpreting Studies. The primary goal of Pignataro's research is of an applied nature: have students transcribe and study the interpretations included in the corpus with the aid of a special software (*Transana*) so they can detect intercultural phenomena present in interpreter-mediated ELF conversational interactions and observe the skills and strategies that an interpreter needs in those special communicative settings. The inductive (*corpus driven*) methodology employed by the author is closely related to the "culture of research in education" in corpus-based translator and LSP training put forward by Laviosa (see section 2 above).

4. Applied research

The chapter by Miriam Seghiri, entitled "**Establishing the quantitative representativeness of an E-Reader Users'Guide *ad hoc* corpus (English-Spanish)**", is a research paper focused this time on professional translation practice. Nevertheless, Seghiri's proposal can also be directly applied in competence-based, market-oriented translator training settings; as the author herself observes (p. 131), the construction and validation of DIY corpora is a skill pertaining to translation competence. In this chapter, which adopts the form of a case study, Seghiri first gives a step-by-step account of the compilation process of a corpus of user's guides for e-readers. Secondly, she explains how we can determine *a posteriori* if the corpus is quantitatively representative, along with a brief —yet very focused— account of the discussion about the question of representativity in Corpus-Based Translation Studies. This chapter complements other studies by the same author or collaborations with other authors which are focused on different textual genres and various domains (see Seghiri 2011, unpaginated). Seghiri proves that her parameters allow her to design and compile DIY corpora for any genre of specialized communication. The main accomplishment of her methodology lies in the fact that the representativeness of the corpus can be simultaneously assured on two different levels. On the one hand, the design and compilation protocol in five steps assures the qualitative representativeness, whereas, on the other hand, the *a posteriori* analysis of the corpus with the program ReCor allows one to determine exactly when a corpus is quantitatively representative. Thanks to the ReCor software program, the size of a corpus is neither determined *a priori* by the availability of the texts nor by intuition.

It is true that many studies in the field of Contrastive Rhetorics, including those focused on languages other than English, limit themselves to the identification and contrast of the rhetoric structure of examples of the same genre in two or more languages. Nevertheless, Roberts and López, in "**The use of a comparable corpus: How to develop writing applications**", go a step further and show that basic knowledge can be implemented in applied proposals. This occurs especially when working with genres that have highly standardized textual parts, such as the wine tasting note, for which the writing application is developed. The authors' analytic efforts and their ability to progress from an analytic to an applied environment become evident in the concept of *model line*. Another very original decision consists of grouping the *model lines* by their complexity, so that the user of the writing application can decide which degree of grammatical and/or thematic complexity he/she prefers for the English text.

Inmaculada Serón's contribution, "**How to build and analyse parallel corpora. A procedure with accessible and affordable software and some suggestions for future software**", has the merit of offering a solution to two important drawbacks in the most widespread computer programs for parallel corpus concordancing: the impossibility of aligning more than four texts at a time, and the limited context offered for each concordance line. Based on her experience as a professional translator, Serón develops a personal and creative procedure that allows her to align one original text and as many translations as desired, as well as to show as much context as needed —with the complete text as the maximal context. To that end, she uses a translation memory management system on the one hand, and a text file search utility that is used by professional translators when performing terminological queries in their glossary files on the other hand (p. 171). The process of building parallel corpora with multiple target texts is highly detailed therefore facilitating the way for those researchers who decide to adopt these procedures to their own research projects. The parallel corpus used by the author to exemplify the corpus building process is the one the author used when doing her doctoral research, and consists of one play by Shakespeare and several (as many as 5) translations of the same into Spanish. This devised system allowed Serón to align the corpus by response and to include metadata to identify —among other elements— acts, scenes and responses. Notwithstanding, she stresses that her procedure can be adapted to other literary genres (lyric, narrative) or to include the most variegated metadata for the identification of texts or textual parts in the corpus.

5. Corpus set-up and reflection on existing corpora

The contribution by Borja and García-Izquierdo (GENTT group), entitled "**Corpus-based knowledge management systems for specialized translation: bridging the gap between theory and professional practice**", straddles the border between sections 4 and 5, as the authors deal with the creation of a resource that, nevertheless, clearly constitutes an achievement in the Applied branch of Corpus-Based Translation Studies centred in professional translation. This area of research is progressively gaining momentum, as the results by Orozco (2014) and Bestue (2014) also show. Borja and García-Izquierdo describe comprehensively the newly developed MEDGENTT and JUDGENTT web platforms, designed for highly-specialized translators working with genres from concrete medical and legal domains. Thanks to solid field work, the researchers from the GENTT group could identify the socio-professional habits of these highly-specialized translators and their needs (p. 197 ff). In these web platforms professional translators can easily access sources of specialized knowledge —vital for the phase of understanding the source text and also for the documentation phase— and integrate the linguistic resources of the platforms in their translation memories or just use those resources to construct their own DIY corpora.

In the chapter entitled "**Corpus-based study of German-Basque translations**", Zuriñe Sanz, Naroa Zubillaga and Ibon Uribarri describe the process of setting up the ALEUSKA corpus along with its composition. This corpus includes philosophical and literary (narrative) texts written originally in German as well as the corresponding Basque target texts, but also in some cases Spanish texts that have mediated the translation process between German and Basque. It should also be highlighted that the authors give a detailed account of their research context, not only in the map of Corpus-based Translation Studies (Xiao and Yue, 2009), but also in the highly complex translation situation in which the Basque texts of their corpus appear: a situation in which diglossic translators translate for diglossic readers (utilising diglossic translation tools) (p. 216). Moreover, the authors expand the inventory of Toury's (1995) theoretical tools with the concept of *assumed direct translation* (p. 219). In the second part of their chapter, Sanz et al. present the main findings of the research they have carried out so far on the basis of the ALEUSKA corpus.

In his study, Marco declares that efforts invested in investigating the features of translational language "inevitably lead to practical applications into the bargain" (p. 67), one of these being the corpora themselves. These are described by the author as "invaluable documentation resources" (ibid.). Laviosa, for her part, pointed out the compilation of big parallel corpora in the decade between 2003 and 2013. Such corpora are *translation-driven* in nature (Zanettin, 2012). Nevertheless, theoretical and applied advances in Corpus Linguistics have made it possible that many and important corpora for many world languages have been compiled, in some cases since the 1960s. Researchers in Corpus-Based Translation and Interpreting Studies or Contrastive Studies usually draw on the data from *reference corpora*, with different purposes. These can include, in the case of Translation and Interpreting Studies, contrasting the results obtained in the exploitation of small DIY parallel corpora, and, in the case of Contrastive Studies, searching for broader evidence to confirm the observation of a similar phenomenon in two different languages.

So, reference corpora in two languages do not necessarily have to be comparable to each other. Maybe they do not offer evidence directly comparable with that which is included in a small DIY corpus for a specific project. In view of this fact, María Teresa Sánchez Nieto puts forward a model that makes it possible to compare on-line reference corpora among themselves, and, also, to analyse, describe and classify them. Her model is described in the chapter entitled "**Build-**

ing virtual delocalized comparable corpora (DE /ES). Analysis and contrast of resources", and comprises three groups of parameters: (i) parameters for the analysis of the subsets that make up the textual base of each corpus; (ii) parameters for the comparison of the way each corpus offers information about the subsets selected by the user (number of types and tokens), and (iii) parameters for the comparison of the possibilities that the search engine of each corpus offers to the user in order to interact with the information included in the corpus. These groups of parameters are applied to the analysis of two reference corpora in German and two in the Spanish language. The author detects important similarities and differences among the textual bases, their annotation, the statistical information offered by the systems and the export possibilities of the four resources. These results make even more evident the recommendation to devote the necessary efforts to become familiar with the configuration of each on-line reference corpus before extracting data for specific research projects.

6. References

Bestué, Carmen. 2014. El corpus global como fuente de creación de corpus especializados de géneros jurídicos (vídeo). @ *I Coloquio Hermēneus. Los estudios de Traducción e Interpretación basados en corpus: de lo local a lo global.*Soria, 26 y 27 de marzo de 2014. Available at <http://coloquiohermeneus.blogs.uva.es/programa-del-coloquio/ponencia-carmen-bestue/>. [Last accessed 30/10/2014].

Corpas Pastor, Gloria. 2008. *Investigar con corpus en traducción: los retos de un nuevo paradigma.* Frankfurt: Peter Lang. ISBN 9783631584057.

Laviosa, Sara. 2011. Corpus-based translation studies: Where does it come from? Where is it going? @ A. Kruger, K. Wallmach & J. Munday, eds. *Corpus-Based Translation Studies. Research and Applications.* ISBN 9781441115812, pp. 13-32.

Laviosa, Sara, 2010. A transcultural conceptual framework for corpus-based translation pedagogy. Keynote lecture pronounced at *Using Corpora for Constrastive and Translation Studies*, Edge Hill University, 27-29 July 2010.

Orozco Jutorán, Mariana. 2014. El concepto de "corpus revisado" para uso profesional (vídeo) @ *I Coloquio Hermēneus. Los estudios de Traducción e Interpretación basados en corpus: de lo local a lo global.*Soria, 26 y 27 de marzo de 2014. Available at <http://coloquiohermeneus.blogs.uva.es/programa-del-coloquio/ponencia-mariana-orozco-jutoran/>. [Last accessed 30/ 10/2014].

Seghiri, Miriam. 2011. Metodología protocolizada de compilación de un corpus de seguros de viajes: aspectos de diseño y representatividad @ *RLA. Revista de lingüística teórica y aplicada (RLA)*, 49 /2: 13-30.

Varantola, Krista. 2000. Translators, dictionaries and text corpora. @ S. Bernardini & F. Zanettin, eds. *I corpora nella didattica della traduzione*. Bologna: CLUEB, pp. 117-133. ISBN 8849115598

Xiao, Richard & Ming Yue. 2009. Using Corpora in Translation Studies: The State of the Art. @ P. Baker, ed. *Contemporary Corpus Linguistics*. London/New York: Continuum. ISBN 9780826496102, pp. 237-261.

Zanettin, Federico. 2012. *Translation-Driven Corpora. Corpus Resources for Descriptive and Applied Translation Studies*. Manchester: St. Jerome. ISBN 9781905763290.

Introducción

MARÍA TERESA SÁNCHEZ NIETO
Universidad de Valladolid

1. Panorámica general del volumen

En el presente volumen reunimos una serie de trabajos que fueron presentados en el *I Coloquio Hermēneus: Los estudios de traducción e Interpretación basados en corpus: de lo local a lo global*, celebrado en Soria entre el 26 y 27 de marzo de 2014 en la Facultad de Traducción e Interpretación de la Universidad de Valladolid. Estos trabajos han sido seleccionados por representar un conjunto equilibrado de sólidas propuestas teóricas y aplicadas. Las propuestas teóricas dan cuenta del desarrollo conceptual de la disciplina y proponen vías para el avance futuro de la misma. Las propuestas aplicadas, valientes, originales e inspiradoras, se adscriben principalmente a dos de las ramas de los estudios aplicados: la formación de traductores e intérpretes y la labor del profesional de la traducción o de la interpretación.

El volumen se inaugura con una aportación de Sara Laviosa, titulada «**Corpora and holistic cultural translation**», que comienza con una descripción de las líneas de evolución de los estudios traductológicos basados en corpus durante la última década (2003-2013). Las observaciones de Laviosa nos ayudarán a ofrecer una breve panorámica de los contenidos del libro. A continuación, en las secciones 2 a 5 presentaremos con mayor detalle cada uno de los trabajos.

Según Laviosa (p. 34), en esta última década, el interés por los **universales de la traducción** y la caracterización de la lengua traducida ha seguido generando una importante cantidad de investigación, prestando especial atención al estudio del comportamiento de los traductores, y sobre todo de los traductores literarios. Un ejemplo de este tipo de investigaciones lo encontramos en la aportación de Sanz et al., que contiene datos descriptivos del euskera traducido a partir de originales alemanes en traducciones directas e indirectas (mediadas estas últimas por un texto español). Marco, por su parte, pasa revista a las críticas vertidas sobre la noción de universal de traducción y esboza los ejes en torno a los que (re)organizar la investigación sobre los rasgos supuestamente universales de la lengua traducida.

Otro de los hechos destacables para Laviosa en esta última década de investigación en estudios traductológicos basados en corpus es la aparición de los primeros corpus para el estudio de la interpretación. Las aportaciones de Pignataro y Álvarez de la Fuente y Fernández Fuertes se insertan dentro de este ámbito. No obstante, cada uno de estos dos trabajos gravita en torno a un interés diferente: Mientras que Pignataro está interesada en observar cómo el inglés como lengua franca influye en el comportamiento del intérprete que trabaja en modalidad consecutiva, Álvarez de la Fuente y Fernández Fuertes ponen el acento en la metodología que utilizan para investigar la interpretación natural ayudándose del sistema de transcripción y codificación CHAT.

Una tercera tendencia advertida por Laviosa en la década 2003-2013 es la consolidación de la relación entre los estudios traductológicos basados en corpus y la lingüística contrastiva (p. 34). En esta línea se sitúa la aportación de Roberts y López: Las autoras estudian la estructura retórica y el léxico de la nota de cata (un género especializado del dominio de la vitivinicultura) en un corpus comparable (EN/ES) y desarrollan una herramienta de ayuda a la escritura en inglés para hispanohablantes.

Dentro ya de la rama aplicada de los estudios traductológicos basados en corpus, Laviosa subraya cómo desde la década de 2000 los corpus han contribuido a crear «una cultura de la investigación en educación» (pág. 35, nuestra traducción). Un buen ejemplo de ello es el capítulo de Clara Pignataro, donde la autora demuestra que el corpus de interpretaciones recopilado en su proyecto de investigación permite a sus estudiantes inducir, mediante un trabajo autónomo de observación, las normas y las estrategias utilizadas por los intérpretes y prepararse así para su vida profesional. Dentro de la rama aplicada se ubica también el trabajo de Seghiri: El protocolo diseñado por la autora para compilar corpus *ad hoc* representativos cualitativa y cuantitativamente tiene una aplicación directa tanto al ejercicio profesional de la traducción como a la formación de traductores basada en competencias demandadas por el mercado.

Dos trabajos de este volumen se relacionan con una quinta característica que Laviosa observa en la evolución de los estudios traductológicos basados en corpus durante la última década: la creación de nuevos y numerosos corpus, que, en palabras de Marco, son «invaluable documentation resources» (pág. 67). El volumen contiene tres aportaciones relacionados con esta línea de trabajo, a cargo de Sanz et al., Borja y García-Izquierdo y Sánchez Nieto. Mientras Borja y García-Izquierdo presentan una plataforma de gestión del conocimiento especializado integrada por corpus y otros recursos informativos, Sánchez Nieto propone una metodología para analizar y comparar corpus de referencia.

La última tendencia señalada por Laviosa en la primera parte de su capítulo es el uso de los corpus como recursos para el desarrollo de las herramientas de traducción asistida por ordenador. En este volumen, el trabajo de Inmaculada Serón representa una línea complementaria. En una suerte de camino de vuelta, esta autora muestra cómo algunas herramientas informáticas propias del ejercicio profesional de la traducción sirven para construir corpus paralelos de un nivel importante de complejidad como son los formados por un texto original y múltiples traducciones del mismo.

2. Análisis de los logros de los estudios traductológicos basados en corpus en su ramas descriptiva y aplicada y perspectivas para el futuro

Josep Marco, en su capítulo titulado **«Taking stock: A crítical overview of research on (universal) features of translated language»** analiza y clasifica las críticas que ha recibido la noción de «universal de traducción» por parte de los investigadores en estudios traductológicos basados en corpus, para, en un segundo paso, seleccionar aquellos aspectos de las críticas que pueden ayudar a reorientar la investigación en el terreno de la caracterización de la lengua traducida. Marco agrupa las objeciones hechas a la noción de universal de traducción en cuatro grupos: (i) las centradas en el propio concepto de «universal» (quizá las más conocidas); (ii) las formuladas acerca de la metodología empleada para investigar los supuestos universales (más recientes, destacado las de Becher (2010), sobre la hipótesis de la explicitación); (iii) las que cuestionan la amplitud de la lista de rasgos del lenguaje traducido candidatos a universales y (iv) las que rechazan la manera en la que se definen los universales, resultando aquí especialmente relevantes las aportaciones de Becher (2010) y Halverson (2003). Marco reclama atención para la «hipótesis de la fuerza gravitacional» de esta última autora: Esta hipótesis pertenece a un nivel epistemológico superior que los universales de traducción, pues intenta dar una explicación de corte cognitivo para estos últimos, que, al fin y al cabo, remiten a regularidades de un comportamiento humano. El autor informa también de los resultados de Hareide (2013), que por primera vez operacionaliza la hipótesis de la fuerza gravitacional, y concluye que en los últimos años la investigación sobre las regularidades de la lengua traducida ha ganado en sofisticación y refinamiento.

El resto del trabajo recoge la posición de Marco ante las críticas mencionadas. Por razones de espacio, destacaremos únicamente una idea y su ejercicio final de síntesis. La idea es que merece la pena seguir investigando las propiedades generales de la traducción, ya sean estas universales o no, puesto que atañen al propio objeto de la disciplina. No obstante, Marco insiste en que hemos de hacer un esfuerzo por no quedarnos en la descripción y avanzar hacia la explicación (a ser posible de carácter cognitivo o socio-comunicativo) de los resultados de las descripciones. En su síntesis final, sin duda uno de los elementos más llamativos del trabajo, Marco diseña un esquema que ha de servir para orientar la investigación futura en torno a la caracterización de la lengua traducida. En este nuevo mapa, las hipótesis o supuestos universales se organizan por parejas o incluso grupos en torno a tres ejes (o continuos u oposiciones dialécticas). Así, supera el planteamiento linear de la lista de supuestos universales y recoge la sugerencia de Corpas (2008) de investigar matrices de universales y no universales aislados.

Si Josep Marco esbozaba una hoja de ruta para la investigación futura en la rama descriptiva de la disciplina, Sara Laviosa (pág. 48) nos participa su visión de hacia dónde deben dirigirse los esfuerzos del conjunto de la disciplina de los estudios traductológicos basados en corpus. Laviosa propone seguir alentando la cultura de la investigación en la formación de traductores y estudiantes de lenguas para fines específicos. La autora se muestra convencida de que estas prácticas contribuirán a cerrar el hueco que separa a la teoría de la práctica en los estudios descriptivos de traducción, un aspecto advertido ya por Tymoczko (1998: 652, 658, en Laviosa, 2011:21).Laviosa defiende aquellas investigaciones que, cimentadas sólidamente en resultados de la rama descriptiva de la disciplina, se llevan a cabo en el aula, nacen de inquietudes de los propios estudiantes con respecto al ejercicio profesional de la traducción, permiten a los estudiantes «to gain a deep and critical understanding of the process, product and function of translation» (pág. 36), así como entender qué se espera de ellos como «expertos en traducción humana» (nuestra traducción) y «self-reflexive, responsible meaning makers» (pág. 42). Para esta autora, que sigue a Tymozcko (2007), un «responsible meaning maker» tiene que tener claro que traducir es un hecho complejo que implica *transculturar* — es decir, crear «nuevos fenómenos culturales en la cultura meta» (pág. 37, mi traducción) —, además de lograr que un texto origen quede representado por medio de uno meta y de transmitir sus contenidos, su lenguaje, su función y su forma. Para *transculturar* es imprescindible que el traductor perciba y tenga en cuenta las diferencias entre la cultura origen y la meta. En el cuarto apartado de su trabajo (pág. 36 y ss.), Laviosa expone un inventario de elementos en los que la cultura cristaliza en los textos y que, al estar codificados lingüísticamente, pueden ser investigados en los corpus por los estudiantes. En su estudio de caso (pág. 44 y ss.) la autora observa que al poner a los estudiantes a trabajar con corpus, combinando técnicas del aprendizaje guiado por datos (*Data Driven Learning*) y de los DTS, se consigue empoderarlos profesionalmente (pág.48).[1]

3. Estudios de interpretación basados en corpus

El objetivo de la aportación de Álvarez de la Fuente y Fernández Fuertes, titulada **«A methodological approach to the analysis of natural interpreting: Bilingual acquisition data and the CHAT/CLAN tool»**, consiste en presentar «a tool available for the computerized analysis of interpretation that has not been previously considered» (pág. 77): el sistema de transcripción y codificación CHAT y el programa informático asociado, CLAN. Para demostrar el potencial de la metodología que han desarrollado a partir de estas herramientas, las autoras presentan datos de unos gemelos bilingües inglés/español (analizados en profundidad en otro lugar). Estos datos están comprendidos dentro de un corpus transcrito y codificado con CHAT y recogido en subproyecto *CHILDES* dentro de *Talkbank* (<http://talkbank.org>). Las autoras subrayan que el sistema CHAT/CLAN no ha sido utilizado previamente en los estudios de interpretación basados en corpus (pág. 78). Además de esta innovación metodológica, destaca

---

[1] En un trabajo anterior (Laviosa, 2010), la autora explica en qué consisten las propuestas de la formación de traductores basada en corpus (*Corpus-Based Translator Training*), concretamente el acercamiento teórico que hay detrás, cómo se diseña la formación y qué procedimientos se utilizan en ella. Al contener un caso práctico, entendemos que el trabajo que contiene este volumen complementa al de 2010, puesto que aquí Laviosa demuestra cómo se concretan el acercamiento, el diseño y los procedimientos en la formación de traductores basada en corpus.

la descripción que hacen las autoras de las variables lingüísticas y contextuales con las que estudian la actividad de interpretación natural (tablas 1 y 2, págs. 87 y 87), descripción que puede inspirar a otros autores para diseñar sus propios estudios. Nos parece asimismo muy valiosa la referencia que Álvarez y Fernández hacen al proyecto *Talkbank* y sus conjuntos de datos bilingües para el estudio de la adquisición de la segunda lengua o de la lengua extranjera (*BilinBank* y *SLABank*). Estos corpus quizá podrían fundamentar también estudios descriptivos o aplicados de interpretación en contextos de adquisición de lenguas (pág.88, nota 7).

La aportación de Clara Pignataro, «**ELF pragmatigs and interpreting**», gira en torno a una serie de ejemplos extraídos de un corpus de interpretaciones consecutivas del inglés al italiano llevadas a cabo en festivales de literatura, en las que los interlocutores utilizan el inglés como lengua franca. La autora demuestra cómo las convenciones comunicativas propias del inglés como lengua franca «afectan el trabajo del intérprete donde este actúa como un participante activo en la co-construcción de significado» (pág. 106, nuestra traducción). El trabajo de Pignataro reviste una originalidad especial, pues, como subraya la autora, la influencia del ELF en la interpretación es un campo de estudio muy joven, que sólo en los últimos años ha comenzado a atraer el interés de la investigación en estudios de interpretación basados en corpus. La motivación del estudio es de carácter aplicado: lograr que mediante la transcripción y estudio de las interpretaciones del corpus (con un software especial, *Transana*), los estudiantes detecten los fenómenos interculturales en la comunicación con inglés como lengua franca y observen las habilidades y estrategias necesarias en determinados contextos comunicativos. La metodología inductiva (*corpus-driven*) empleada por la autora entronca perfectamente con la cultura de investigación en la formación basada en corpus propuesta por Laviosa (v. sección 2 de esta introducción).

4. Estudios aplicados

El capítulo de Miriam Seghiri, «Determinación de la representatividad cuantitativa de un corpus *ad hoc* bilingüe (inglés-español) de manuales de instrucciones generales de lectores electrónicos», constituye un estudio aplicado a la práctica traductora, que, no obstante, también tiene aplicaciones directas para la formación de traductores centrada en competencias, ya que, como la propia autora subraya con Varantola (2000), hoy en día la construcción y validación de corpus *ad hoc* forma parte de la competencia traductora (pág. 131). Adoptando la forma de estudio de caso (la compilación de un corpus de manuales de instrucciones de lectores electrónicos y la posterior determinación de su representatividad cuantitativa), este capítulo complementa otros estudios realizados con la misma metodología por la misma autora o por otros autores, si bien con diferentes géneros textuales y en diferentes dominios (turismo, seguros turísticos y contratos de viaje, salud y belleza, resúmenes de artículos científicos, v. Seghiri 2011).

Seghiri demuestra así cómo sus parámetros permiten diseñar y compilar corpus *ad-hoc* para cualquier género textual especializado. El principal logro de esta metodología consiste en que el diseño y protocolo de compilación en cinco fases asegura la representatividad cualitativa, mientras que el análisis con el programa ReCor permite fijar cuándo se logra su representatividad cuantitativa. Gracias a la herramienta ReCor, el tamaño del corpus ya no queda determinado por la disponibilidad de los textos o por la intuición.

Es cierto que muchos trabajos de retórica contrastiva, también para otros idiomas diferentes del inglés, se limitan a la identificación y el contraste de la estructura retórica de ejemplos de un mismo género en varios idiomas. Sin embargo, Roberts y López, en «**The use of a comparable corpus: How to develop writing applications**», demuestran que se puede ir un paso más allá e implementar esos saberes básicos en propuestas de aplicación, especialmente cuando se trabaja con géneros que tienen partes textuales estandarizadas, como la nota de cata, para la que se diseña la aplicación en cuestión. El concepto de *model line* cristaliza el esfuerzo analítico de las autoras, a la vez que deja patente su habilidad para aplicar los resultados del análisis. Otra decisión muy original consiste en agrupar las *model lines* por niveles de complejidad, de modo que el usuario de la herramienta pueda decidir qué grado de complejidad gramatical y/o temática quiere para su texto en inglés.

El capítulo de Inmaculada Serón Ordóñez, titulado «**Cómo crear y analizar corpus paralelos. Un procedimiento con software accesible y económico y algunas sugerencias para *software* futuro**», tiene el mérito de ofrecer una solución a dos de las desventajas que presentan los programas de alineación de corpus paralelos más extendidos: la imposibilidad de alinear más de cuatro textos paralelos y las limitaciones con respecto a la muestra del contexto. A partir de su experiencia como traductora, Serón desarrolla un sistema personal y creativo que le permite alinear un original y tantos textos meta como se desee, así como ampliar el contexto mostrado hasta la totalidad del texto si fuera necesario. Para ello, la autora se sirve de un gestor de memorias de traducción y de «una aplicación de búsqueda en archivos que los traductores utilizan para realizar búsquedas terminológicas en glosarios» (pág. 171). El proceso de creación de corpus paralelos con múltiples textos meta está descrito con un nivel de detalle importante, que facilita la labor a aquellos investigadores decididos a adaptarlo a sus propios proyectos. El corpus paralelo cuya creación se describe es el que sirvió a Serón como base para su investigación doctoral, en la que analizaba un original y cinco traducciones de un texto dramático. El sistema le permitió alinear por réplica e incluir metadatos que le ayudaron a identificar, entre otros elementos, actos, escenas y réplicas. No obstante la autora subraya que su procedimiento puede adaptarse a otros géneros literarios (líricos, narrativos) o a casos en los que el investigador necesite incluir otros metadatos para la identificación de textos o partes textuales.

5. Creación de recursos y reflexión sobre corpus

La aportación de Borja y García-Izquierdo (grupo Gentt) se encuentra a caballo entre las secciones 4 y 5, puesto que se centra en la creación de recursos que, no obstante, representan claramente un logro de la rama de los estudios de traducción basados en corpus aplicados a la profesión del traductor, ámbito al que se dirigen cada vez mayores esfuerzos, como demuestran también Orozco (2014) y Bestué (2014). Las autoras llevan a cabo una presentación comprehensiva de las plataformas MEDGENTT y JUDGENTT, los nuevos recursos creados por el grupo GENTT para traductores altamente especializados en dominios muy concretos de la medicina y del derecho. El desarrollo de estos novísimos entornos de gestión del conocimiento descansa sobre un sólido trabajo de campo para el estudio de los hábitos socio-profesionales de la los traductores y sus necesidades (pág. 197 y ss.). En las plataformas el profesional de la traducción puede acceder fácilmente a fuentes de conocimiento especializado —vitales para la fase de comprensión del texto origen y para la fase de documentación— e integrar los recursos lingüísticos de la plataforma en sus memorias de traducción o construirse con ellos sus propios corpus *ad hoc*.

En el capítulo «**Estudio basado en un corpus de las traducciones del alemán al vasco**», comentado más arriba, Zuriñe Sanz, Naroa Zubillaga e Ibon Uribarri describen el proceso de creación y la composición interna del corpus ALEUSKA, creado para su investigación, formado por textos originales alemanes (filosóficos y literarios, concretamente narrativos), textos meta en euskera y, en una parte de los casos, por textos intermedios españoles. Destaca el detalle con el que los autores contextualizan su investigación, no solo en el mapa de los estudios de traducción basados en corpus (Xiao y Yue, 2009), sino también en la situación de traducción, altamente compleja, en la que surgen los textos meta vascos de su corpus: Una situación en la que traductores diglósicos traducen para lectores diglósicos con herramientas diglósicas o intermedias (pág. 216). Además, los autores amplían el inventario de las herramientas teóricas de Toury (1995) con el concepto de *supuesta traducción directa* (pág. 219). En la segunda parte del artículo Sanz et al. presentan algunos resultados de investigaciones concretas realizadas sobre la base de ALEUSKA.

En su estudio, Marco indicaba que uno de los «efectos colaterales» de la investigación de las características de la lengua traducida, sean estas universales o no, ha sido la compilación de un gran número de corpus, que califica como «invaluble documentation resources» (pág. 67). También Laviosa señalaba la aparición en la década entre 2003 y 2013 de grandes proyectos de corpus paralelos. Estos corpus a los que se refieren Marco y Laviosa son *translation-driven* por naturaleza (Zanettin 2012). No obstante, los avances teóricos y aplicados en lingüística del corpus han posibilitado, en algunos casos desde los años 60 del siglo pasado, la recopilación de importantes corpus de referencia para muchas lenguas del mundo. Los investigadores de los estudios traductológicos basados en corpus o de los estudios contrastivos basados en corpus a menudo recurren también a los corpus de referencia con diferentes propósitos, p. ej.: la comparación de resultados obtenidos en la investigación de pequeños corpus paralelos *ad-hoc* para proyectos específicos (en el caso de los estudios traductológicos) o la observación de hechos lingüísticos similares en dos lenguas y el posterior contraste de resultados (en el caso de los estudios contrastivos).

Ahora bien, los corpus de referencia de dos lenguas no tienen por qué ser directamente comparables entre sí, y puede que no ofrezcan tampoco evidencia directamente contrastable con la contenida en un pequeño corpus *ad hoc* de un proyecto específico. Ante esta realidad, María Teresa Sánchez Nieto, en su contribución titulada «**Construcción de corpus virtuales comparables deslocalizados (DE/ES): Análisis y comparación de recursos**» propone un modelo de análisis de corpus de referencia en línea que permite comparar entre sí (y, secundariamente, analizar, describir y clasificar) corpus de referencia en línea. El modelo de Sánchez Nieto comprende tres grupos de parámetros: (i) el análisis de los subconjuntos en los que está organizada la base textual de cada corpus, (ii) la comparación de la manera en la que cada corpus ofrece información sobre el número de palabras y formas de los subconjuntos seleccionados por el usuario, y (iii) las posibilidades de interacción con los subconjuntos que el motor de búsquedas ofrece al usuario. Estos grupos de parámetros se aplican al análisis de dos corpus de referencia de la lengua alemana y dos de la lengua española. La autora detecta importantes similitudes y diferencias entre las bases textuales, en la codificación, en la información estadística ofrecida y en las prestaciones de exportación de los cuatro recursos. Estos resultados hacen si cabe más urgente la recomendación de dedicar el esfuerzo necesario a familiarizarse con la configuración de cada corpus antes de extraer datos del mismo para investigaciones concretas.

6. Bibliografía

Bestué, Carmen. 2014. El corpus global como fuente de creación de corpus especializados de géneros jurídicos (vídeo). *@ I Coloquio Hermēneus. Los estudios de Traducción e Interpretación basados en corpus: de lo local a lo global*.Soria, 26 y 27 de marzo de 2014. Disponible en <http://coloquiohermeneus.blogs.uva.es/programa-del-coloquio/ponencia-carmen-bestue/>. [Última consulta 30/10/2014].

Corpas Pastor, Gloria. 2008. *Investigar con corpus en traducción: los retos de un nuevo paradigma*. Frankfurt: Peter Lang. ISBN 9783631584057.

Laviosa, Sara. 2011. Corpus-based translation studies: Where does it come from? Where is it going? @ A. Kruger, K. Wallmach y J. Munday, eds. *Corpus-Based Translation Studies. Research and Applications*. ISBN 9781441115812, pp. 13-32.

Laviosa, Sara, 2010. A transcultural conceptual framework for corpus-based translation pedagogy. Keynote lecture pronounced at *Using Corpora for Constrastive and Translation Studies*, Edge Hill University, 27-29 July 2010.

Orozco Jutorán, Mariana. 2014. El concepto de "corpus revisado" para uso profesional (vídeo) *@ I Coloquio Hermēneus. Los estudios de Traducción e Interpretación basados en corpus: de lo local a lo global*.Soria, 26 y 27 de marzo de 2014. Disponible en

<http://coloquiohermeneus.blogs.uva.es/programa-del-coloquio/ponencia-mariana-orozco-jutoran/>. [Última consulta 30/ 10/2014].

Seghiri, Miriam. 2011. Metodología protocolizada de compilación de un corpus de seguros de viajes: aspectos de diseño y representatividad @ *RLA. Revista de lingüística teórica y aplicada* (*RLA*), 49 /2: 13-30.

Varantola, Krista. 2000. Translators, dictionaries and text corpora. @ S. Bernardini y F. Zanettin, eds. *I corpora nella didattica della traduzione*. Bologna: CLUEB, pp. 117-133. ISBN 8849115598

Xiao, Richard y Ming Yue. 2009. Using Corpora in Translation Studies: The State of the Art. @ P. Baker, ed. *Contemporary Corpus Linguistics*. London/New York: Continuum. ISBN 9780826496102, pp. 237-261.

Zanettin, Federico. 2012. *Translation-Driven Corpora. Corpus Resources for Descriptive and Applied Translation Studies*. Manchester: St. Jerome. ISBN 9781905763290.

Corpora and Holistic Cultural Translation

[Los corpus y el enfoque holístico de la traducción cultural]

SARA LAVIOSA
University of Bari Aldo Moro (Italy)
saralaviosa@gmail.com

> **Abstract:** This paper first traces the development of corpus studies of translation from 1993 to the present day. Next, it proposes that corpora be used to foster the holistic approach to cultural translation (Tymoczko 2007) in two interrelated ambits of the discipline, namely descriptive research and pedagogy.
>
> **Keywords**: corpus-based translation studies; translation universal; holistic cultural translation; holistic pedagogy

1. Introduction

Corpora have come of age in Translation Studies as in other fields of scholarship as varied as historical linguistics, documenting endangered languages, language acquisition, lexicography, comparative grammar, to name just a few. Over the past two decades corpora have changed the way we understand and study languages within and across cultures. Given this premise, the aim of my presentation is first to examine the development of Corpus-based Translation Studies (CTS) from its advent to the present day and then point to future directions. The analysis will underscore the role that corpora have played and will continue to play in pushing the discipline towards empiricism, opening a fruitful dialogue between pure and applied translation studies and forging strong links with neighbouring disciplines, thus fostering interdisciplinarity.

2. Introducing corpora in translation studies: 1993-2003

The introduction of corpora in the discipline was conceived within an empirical paradigm and came to be as a result of the convergence between the discovery and justification procedures put forward by Gideon Toury (1995/2012) for the study of translation and the data-driven approach developed by Corpus Linguistics for the study of languages. The synergy between Descriptive Translation Studies and Corpus Linguistics acted as a stimulus to the creation of a variety of corpus resources, the development of a descriptive research methodology and the growth of a line of enquiry that had been put forward in the 1980s and gathered momentum thanks to the availability of corpora. This body of research is known as the quest for translation universals. I will now give some details about each of these achievements of CTS.

One of the first corpus resources that were designed for contrastive linguistics and translation studies was the bidirectional *English-Norwegian Parallel Corpus* (ENPC) designed at the University of Oslo under the direction of Stig Johansson. The ENPC served as a model for the bidirectional parallel corpus of English and Portuguese, COMPARA.[1] Another corpus design is the monolingual comparable corpus. The first one was created at the University of Manchester under the direction of Mona Baker. It is the *Translational English Corpus* (TEC).[2] The second one is the *Corpus of Translated Finnish* (CTF) compiled at the Savonlinna School of Translation Studies by Anna Mauranen's research group. The methodology adopted by CTS involved a helical progression from the elaboration of descriptive, interpretive and explanatory hypotheses to inferences about the non-observable culturally-determined norms that govern translators' choices.

Translation universals were posited as probabilistic laws of translational behaviour (Toury 1995/2012). Initially, research focused on four universals: simplification, explicitation, normalization and the law of interference. Simplification is "the process and/or result of making do with less words" (Blum Kulka & Levenston 1983: 119). Explicitation is "an observed cohesive explicitness from SL to TL texts regardless of the increase traceable to differences between the linguistic and textual systems involved" (Blum Kulka 1986: 19). Normalization (also known as the law of growing standardization) posits that "in translation, textual relations obtaining in the original are often modified, sometimes to the point of being totally ignored, in favour of [more] habitual options offered by a target repertoire" (Toury 1995/2012: 304). The law of interference states that "in translation, phenomena pertaining to the make-up of the source text tend to force themselves on the translators and be transferred to the target text" (Toury 1995/2012: 310). In sum, during the first decade of its life, CTS built upon, refined, extended and diversified previous research into the regularities of translational language.

---

[1] Available at: <http://www.linguateca.pt/COMPARA/Welcome>.

[2] Available at: < http://www.llc.manchester.ac.uk/ctis/research/english-corpus/>.

Meanwhile, corpora were making inroads into Applied Translation Studies. In this area of research and practice, corpora were used as translation aids and formed an integral part of translator training. As translation aids, corpora were utilized as repositories of data for retrieving translation equivalents, acquiring content knowledge about specialized subject fields and developing stylistic fluency and terminological accuracy in the target language. Translation pedagogy drew on Data-Driven Learning (DDL), developed by Tim Johns for the teaching of languages (Johns 1991a, 1991b), and on constructivist principles, which constitute a dominant paradigm in contemporary educational philosophy and "serve as a strong cornerstone for the development of student- and praxis-relevant teaching methods" (Kiraly 2003: 8).

More specifically, the DDL approach adopts the principles of Corpus Linguistics and involves carrying out small-scale projects where students identify problem areas arising from translation practice, suggest hypotheses and then test them with their own tutor who has the role of "director and coordinator of student-initiated research" (Johns 1991a: 3). The approach adopted by the collaborative-constructivist method combines social constructivism with modern functionalist theories and expertise studies. The design involves collaborative learning and project-based activities. The procedure requires that students engage in an authentic or realistically simulated translation project together with peers (Kiraly 2000, 2003). Summing up, within the empirical paradigm, which can be regarded, in line with Andrew Chesterman (1998), as the most important trend that characterized translation studies in the 1990s, corpora engendered a number of novel syntheses in the pure and applied branches of the discipline.

3. Consolidating corpora in translation studies: 2003-2013

The second decade in the life of CTS is marked by two international conferences entirely devoted to corpora and Translation Studies. The first was held in Pretoria in 2003, it was entitled *Corpus-based Translation Studies: Research and Applications* (Kruger, Wallmach & Munday 2011). The second was hosted in Shanghai in 2007, *Conference and Workshop on Corpora and Translation Studies*. As regards Descriptive Translation Studies, many new corpora have been created in the last ten years or so, as amply testified by Richard Xiao's corpus survey online and Federico Zanettin's web page.[3]

A novelty is the design of corpora of interpreted speeches and the consequent growth of a new body of research named Corpus-based Interpreting Studies (CIS) (see Setton 2011 for a review). Its main goal is to unearth the specificity of interpreting vis-à-vis original oral discourse and written translation in the same target language, a line of enquiry that was first proposed by Miriam Shlesinger (1998). The creation of new corpus resources goes hand in hand with the development of methodology. This is enriched by historical and sociolinguistic data and is becoming more and more sophisticated thanks to the advancement of technology. As for the range of research endeavours, we can say that the quest for translation universals goes on. In addition to the four universals mentioned earlier, a new one emerged, namely the Unique Items Hypothesis. It states that target-language-specific elements, which do not have equivalents in the source language, tend to be under-represented in translated texts, since "they do not readily suggest themselves as translation equivalents" (Tirkkonen-Condit 2004: 177-178). Other research projects involved the study of literary translators, the role of ideology in determining translation strategies and the study of Anglicisms as an example of transculturation, of which more later.

This decade is characterized by the establishment of a strong partnership between contrastive and translation studies, in line with the research programme initiated by Stig Johansson in the 1990s and pursued in several interdisciplinary collected volumes such as Granger, Lerot & Petch-Tyson (2003). The cooperation between these two disciplines finds its voice in a series of biennial international conferences, *Using Corpora in Contrastive and Translation Studies* (UCCTS). The first conference was held at Zhejiang University in Hangzhou, China, on 25-27 September 2008 (Xiao 2010), the second, jointly organized by Edge Hill University, the University of Bologna and Beijing Foreign Studies University, took place at Edge Hill University in Ormskirk, UK, on 27-29 July

---

[3] Richard Xiao's corpus survey can be found at the following URL address: <http://www.lancaster.ac.uk/fass/projects/corpus/cbls/corpora.asp> and Federico Zanettin's web page is at: <https://sites.google.com/site/federicozanettinnet/cl-htm#TOC-Translation-driven-Bilingual-and-Multilingual-Corpora>.

2010. The third one was hosted at Lancaster University, UK, from 24 to 26 July 2014.

In Applied Translation Studies corpora continue to be used to retrieve and examine lexical, terminological, phraseological, syntactic and stylistic equivalents. They are also essential components of Computer-Aided Translation (CAT) technology and are utilized in Translation Quality Assessment (TQA) (Bowker 2003a, 2003b). So, corpora are being increasingly incorporated in the curricular design of postgraduate translator training programmes to satisfy the exigencies of today's increasingly technologized language industry (Koby & Baer 2003; Kelly 2005; Ulrych 2005; Olohan 2007; Beeby, Rodríguez Inés y Sánchez-Gijón 2009). In sum, we can affirm that a coherent interdisciplinary theory combined with the professional and institutional recognition of corpora as linguistic resources and CAT tools has given rise to an effective partnership that is playing a crucial role in engendering a culture of research in education.

The question I wish to address next is the extent to which corpora have provided "an opportunity to reengage the theoretical and pragmatic branches of Translation Studies, branches which over and over again tend to disassociate, developing slippage and even gulfs" as was envisaged by Maria Tymoczko (1998: 658). My view is that the relationship between corpus-based descriptive and applied studies has been open and reciprocal to a degree. Let me explain what I mean by this with two examples taken from the quest for translation universals. As we saw earlier, this line of enquiry was conceived as a descriptive endeavour. Its findings were then projected into Applied Translation Studies where the Unique Items Hypothesis was tested and confirmed experimentally in the translation classroom to raise awareness among students of what translation entails (Kujamäki 2004). Also, simplification and explicitation were tested as possible indicators of translation quality with a view to improving teaching methods and assessment criteria. Simplification was found to correlate with lower-scoring translations and explicitation was found to correlate with higher-scoring ones (Scarpa 2006).

I believe that these studies, which engage in classroom-based investigations inspired by the insights provided by the pure branch of the discipline, represent the beginning of a new trend in Translation Studies. I also believe this new direction to be a promising one not only because it aims to replicate descriptive investigations and make translation teaching more effective and evaluation more rigorous, but because it empowers students to gain a deep and critical understanding of the process, product and function of translation. It is reasonable to predict that, thanks to this inside knowledge, translators will be capable of adhering to or innovating culturally-determined norms in an informed, conscious and responsible way. As Pekka Kujamäki contends, theories, models, concepts and experimentation with students should have an essential role in translation pedagogy "not only in research seminars but also and above all in the translation class: they open a way to novices' better understanding of their future status as experts of human translation" (Kujamäki 2004: 199).

In line with this envisioned direction for CTS, I propose that the holistic approach to translating culture elaborated by Tymoczko (2007) be adopted as a theoretical framework within which corpora can reengage the pure and applied branches of the discipline for the benefit of both of them in unison. So, in the second part of my paper, I will first expound the notion of holistic cultural translation and then I will put forward the idea that corpora be used to foster this approach in two interrelated ways, i.e. through research and pedagogy. The latter includes translation education, language teaching, translator trainer training and language teacher training.

4. Looking to the future: corpora and holistic cultural translation

The holistic approach to translating cultural difference presupposes that translation be conceived as an open, cluster concept with blurred edges. This notion of translation, which Tymoczko calls the 'cluster concept translation' (or 'translation with an asterisk'), is defined in terms of resemblances between translation and three forms of cultural interface, i.e. representation, transmission and transculturation. I shall now define each of these large superordinate categories that partially encompass, impinge on and illuminate translation.

As a form of representation, translation stands in place of a source text. Almost all translations are forms of representation, with a few exceptions such as pseudotranslations (or fictitious translations) (Toury 1995/2012: 47-59). As a form of transmission, translation involves different types of transfer from one language and culture to another. Translations typically relay the content, language, function or form of the source text. The variability of methods adopted by translations that privilege transfer is very wide. It ranges from close textual fidelity to various degrees of manipulation of the linguistic features of the original. Many factors influence the vast array of transmission procedures adopted in translation practices, e.g. linguistic asymmetries, translation technologies, literacy practices, economic conditions, cultural sufficiency or enclosure, receptiveness to difference, aesthetic norms, taboos about certain types of content, asymmetries in power and cultural prestige as well as ideology (Tymoczko 2007: 119).

Transculturation is the transmission and uptake of borrowed cultural forms in the receptor environment and the consequent creation of new cultural phenomena. Transculturation includes such elements as verbal materials, religious beliefs and practices, social and political organization, artistic forms as well as aspects of material culture including technology and tools, agricultural and industrial practices, clothing, food, housing, transport and media (Tymozcko 2007: 120). In textual domains transculturation often entails transposing elements of a literary system, e.g. poetics, genres, tale types. It also involves the uptake of such textual technologies as literacy, printing and electronic media and of the elements expressed in or carried by language such as discourses and world views (2007: 121). Lexical borrowing from a donor to a receptor language is also an example of transculturation. Anglicisms have been investigated extensively through corpora, particularly in Europe where this linguistic and socio-cultural phenomenon has attracted the interest of a growing number of scholars (Anderman & Rogers 2005; Furiassi, Pulcini & Rodríguez Gonzáles 2012).

The cluster concept translation rests on the assumption that language and culture are closely intertwined and "culture is the domain where human differences are most manifest" (Tymoczko 2007: 221). When communicating across cultural differences, argues Tymoczko, it is not sufficient to approach the representation of culture in a linear, piecemeal fashion and resolve the problems incorporated in surface elements of the text one by one, sentence by sentence until the translation is complete (Tymoczko 2007: 233). What is needed instead is a holistic approach. As Tymoczko explains, "a holistic approach to translating culture will begin with the largest elements of cultural difference that separate the source culture and the target culture as a framework for coordinating the particular decisions about culture that occur as the text is actually transposed into the target language" (Tymoczko 2007: 235).

In order to help translators accomplish such a complex task, Tymoczko offers a partial repertory of cultural elements that might be taken into account as a guide for interpreting the source text and for determining the overall representation of culture in the target text. The inventory comprises:

- Signature concepts of a culture
- Key words
- Conceptual metaphors
- Discourses
- Cultural practices
- Cultural paradigms
- Overcodings
- Symbols.

I will now define each of these large cultural elements in turn and illustrate them with examples from various languages and genres. As we shall see, many of these examples are offered by corpus research. Signature concepts express key values in the social and economic organization of a culture. The words denoting them are highly connoted and rich in cultural associations. In early medieval Irish texts, for instance, words belonging to the semantic field of heroism, such as *honour*, *shame*, *taboo*, fall under the category of signature concepts (Tymoczko 2007). The signature concepts of contemporary American society correspond to the values that American citizens cherish and are encouraged to promote. These are "hard work and honesty, courage and fair play, tolerance and curiosity, loyalty and patriotism", as we read in the letter that the President of the United States of America sends to every new American citizen. On the other side of the Atlantic, the liberal values held by British people today are *openness*, *tolerance*, *compassion* and *strength*, as stated by the Deputy Prime Minister, Nick Clegg in his speech delivered at the Liberal Democratic Party Conference held in York on 9 March 2014.

Key words are words that may point either to the signature concepts of a culture or to the thematic cultural elements chosen by a writer or speaker to structure a given text or a corpus of texts. For example, the strongest key words analyzed by Norman Fairclough (2000) in the corpus of New Labour texts, which contains a variety of texts produced under the New Labour Government led by the British Prime Minister Tony Blair from 1994 to 1999, are: *New Labour, new deal, new Britain, business and partnership, welfare reform* (Fairclough 2000: 17-20).

Drawing on the work of cognitive linguists such as George Lakoff and Mark Johnson (1980), conceptual metaphors shape the mental representations of a given group as well as its perspectives on the world. An example of variation in conceptual metaphors across languages is offered by Ding, Noël & Wolf (2010). Their corpus-based analysis of the metaphorical representation of the topic FEAR and its Chinese equivalent KONGJU, reveals that Chinese does not have the English conceptual metaphors FEAR IS A SUPERNATURAL BEING/A DISEASE/A SHARP OBJECT/A POISON/A LEGACY/A MACHINE. Moreover, the shared metaphor FEAR IS AN OPPONENT tends to be used in English to conceptualize the state of falling victim to fear, whereas in Chinese it is usually used to conceptualize an attempt to control it.

Ideological discourses are representations and visions of the social world and as such they motivate action and cultural practice. They are the object of study of Critical Discourse Analysis, an area of research which has been investigated extensively through corpora. An example of such analysis is offered by Fairclough's research into the political discourse of the 'Third Way' in Tony Blair's speeches from 1998 to early 1999. The Third Way signifies a programme that was defined by centre and centre-left British governments as being neither old left nor 1980s right. It was built upon the notion of "the new global economy", that was accepted "as an inevitable and unquestionable fact of life" upon which politics and governments were to be premised (Fairclough 2000: 15,150). In the European Union the discourse of 'unity in diversity', which first came into use in 2000, "signifies how Europeans have come together, in the form of the EU, to work for peace and prosperity, while at the same time being enriched by the continent's many different cultures, traditions and languages."[4]

Cultural practices such as naming practices, forms of address and titles, the naming of kinship relationships play an important role in constructing personal and social identities and achieving social cohesion. They too may vary across lan-

---

[4] <http://europa.eu/about-eu/basic-information/symbols/motto/index_en.htm>.

guages. In English, for example, the word *grandfather* means 'father of one's father or mother' and the word *grandmother* means 'mother of one's father or mother'. The Italian equivalents are: *nonno* and *nonna* respectively. But in Thai the word ปู่ (po) means 'father of one's father', the word ตา (ta) means 'father of one's mother', the word ย่า (ya) means 'mother of one's father', and the word ยาย (yay) means 'mother of one's mother'. Similarly, in Swedish *farfar* = father's father, *morfar* = mother's father, *mormor* = mother's mother and *farmor* = father's mother. In Chinese there are five equivalents of the English word *uncle*, i.e. *shushu, bobo, jiujiu, guzhang*, and *yizhang*, each referring to a specific family relationship.

Cultural paradigms pertain to humour, argumentation, logical sequencing in a text or the use of tropes. They tend to vary from language to language and within the same language over time. For example, a corpus-based study carried out by Niu & Hong (2010) on rhetorical repetition in English and Chinese print ads published in two leading newspapers in Singapore shows different patterns. The four most frequent repetition types found in English are: alliteration, rhyme, assonance, anaphora, while in Chinese they are: assonance, anaphora, alliteration, rhyme. So, it was found that English used more alliteration and rhyme than Chinese and Chinese used more assonance and anaphora than English.

Overcodings are "linguistic patterns that are superimposed on the ordinary ranks of language to indicate a higher-order set of distinctions in language practices" (Tymoczko 2007: 243). They signal specific literary genres (e.g. poetry or narrative) and modes of communication (e.g. spoken or written). They also comprise rhetorical devices such as intertextuality, quotation and allusion. For example, the literary style of Latino writers in the United States is characterized by a constant code-switching from English to Spanish. As Francisco Díaz Pérez (2012: 171-172) observes, "[b]y introducing Spanish words, phrases or syntactic constructions into their English texts, they try to evoke the feeling of living on a *frontera*, of inhabiting two worlds which can be conflicting and complementary at the same time."

Within the category of overcodings we also find forms of textual structuring pertaining to aspects of register, dialects and languages for special purposes. An excellent example of corpus-based research that throws light into the relationship between overcodings and cultural context is Meng Ji's investigation of the lexico-grammatical features that characterize scientific language in early modern Chinese. This specialized register was developed by translating scientific texts from Western languages, most notably English, French and Dutch from the mid-nineteenth century to the turn of the twentieth century. This was a time characterized by the expansion of capitalism and imperialism in Asia. Two types of overcodings were unveiled by Ji's study: a) dysillabic word structure, i.e. words created by combining two existing characters, and b) functional particles. Functional particles were created in Chinese to relay the meanings and functions expressed by the prefixes and suffixes of Latin and Greek origin that characterized Western scientific writing.

Ji's study reveals two groups of functional particles: grammatically modified and semantic-cognitive functional particles. An example of the former is *de*, which identifies an adjective and was retrieved from ancient Chinese literary fiction. An example of the latter is *zhe*, an abstract term for things, agents or concepts, which was retrieved from ancient phylosophical and historical texts as well as biographical essays. As Ji observes, while the original affixes "reflect the systematicity and continuity of the development of modern scientific language based on ancient Latin and Greek cultures and thoughts" (Ji 2012: 255), the development of equivalent functional particles in early Chinese scientific language "involved a thorough and painstaking re-examination of the target language body, searching for expressions of metaphorical references parallel to their Western counterparts" (Ji 2012: 255).

Finally, symbols are related to the identity of an individual, family, class, nation or deity (Tymoczko 2007: 145, fn.28). Indeed, flower symbolism varies from language to language. Lilacs stand for light and early summer in Sweden but in Italy they represent envy. In some English villages a lilac branch may signify a broken engagement (Anderman 2007: 3). Folklore provides many other symbols and icons. In Indian mythology the word *naga* describes any kind of semi-divine serpent associated with water and fluid energy. *Nagas* are ambivalent deities, they are believed to bestow wealth and assure abundant crops but revoke these blessings if offended.

As Tymoczko maintains, considering all the above cultural elements helps translators compare their own culture with the source culture as it is reflected in texts. In order to make these cross-cultural comparisons translators need to develop self-reflexivity. Indeed, it is through self-reflexivity that they will be able to identify those elements of cultural difference that need to be mediated. To sum up, "a holistic approach to cultural translation rather than a selective focus on a limited range of cultural elements enables greater cultural interchange and more effective cultural assertion in translation, allowing more newness to enter the world" (Tymoczko 2007: 233). And, I wish to add, corpora can play an important role in fostering holistic cultural translation since they can fruitfully be used "to illuminate both similarity and difference and to investigate in a manageable form the particulars of language-specific phenomena of many different languages and cultures" (Tymoczko 1998: 657).

4.1. Towards a corpus-based holistic pedagogy

How can corpora be used to unearth cross-cultural differences and similarities in research as in practice? I think an effective way of achieving this goal is to work towards a pedagogy that is underpinned by the tenets of holistic cultural translation and incorporates corpora not only as tools for acquiring technical skills, but also as resources for developing vital translingual and transcultural competences that enable translators to act as self-reflexive, responsible meaning makers in late modern societies. In such envisioned pedagogy I recommend that comparable and parallel corpora be explored through discovery and justification procedures (Toury 1995/2012) so as to infer culturally determined norms on the basis of empirical evidence.

What follows is an example of how this teaching methodology was adopted to investigate the degree of equivalence between the lexical Anglicism *business* in Italian and its English etymon in the specialized language of business and economics. Polysemic loan words are problematic in translation as their range of meanings does not always match across donor and receptor languages. An Anglicism may, for example, convey only a subset of the senses expressed by the English etymon. Hence, translator trainees often find it difficult to decide when to use Anglicisms in Italian texts translated from English. Before moving on to report on the findings of a small-scale research project conducted in the postgraduate translation classroom, I will outline the procedural steps we adopted in keeping with the methodology elaborated by Toury (1995/2012) for discovering regularities in translational behaviour.

4.2. Toury's discovery and justification procedures

The methodology proposed by Toury (1995/2012: 31-34) for descriptive translation studies is articulated in three phases. The first phase starts with the selection of individual translations or a corpus of translations within the target culture. Toury's perspective is target-oriented: translations are texts that belong to the target culture, they are texts in their own right, not just mere representations of their source texts. The analysis carried out in the first phase involves the initial assessment of the acceptability of the individual translations or corpus of translated texts without reference to the source texts. Acceptability is the extent to which a translated text adheres to the linguistic and cultural norms prevailing in the target language for a particular text genre. The opposite concept is that of adequacy. An adequate translation is one which leans towards the norms of the source language and culture and contains traces of the textual features of the source text.

The second phase starts with the identification of the source texts and proceeds to comparing the target texts and their sources in parallel, that is sentence by sentence, paragraph by paragraph. The aim is to determine target-source relationships, translation problems, translation solutions and shifts. According to Toury they can be of two kinds: obligatory, which are caused by systemic differences between the source and target languages, and non-obligatory, which are motivated by literary, stylistic or cultural considerations.

In the third phase of the analysis, the relationships established between the target texts and their sources become the basis of first-level generalizations about the initial norm underlying the concrete way in which equivalence is realized. The initial norm governs the basic choice which can be made between adequacy (which involves adhering to source norms) and acceptability (which involves subscribing to norms originating in the target culture). Adequacy and acceptability are to be considered as two poles of a continuum where the target text can be positioned on the basis of its linguistic features examined vis-à-vis the source text and comparable original texts produced in the target language (Toury 1995/2012: 79-85). Equivalence is not conceived as an a-priori notion which is based on an absolute criterion of adherence to the source text. This means that in a descriptive study the researcher will always assume that equivalence exists. What s/he will unveil is the actual way in which it is realized in terms of the balance between invariance and transformation. This type of equivalence in turn constitutes a stepping stone for discovering the concept of translation that informs the target texts examined, this being defined in terms of the acceptability-adequacy continuum.

At each stage of this process of gradual discovery of facts about the nature of translation and translating, hypotheses are formulated on the basis of empirical descriptions and then verified through further procedures that are applied to an expanding corpus to achieve higher and higher levels of generalization. The procedures elaborated by Toury are largely compatible with the Data-Driven Learning approach developed by Johns (1991a, 1991b) in foreign language education, which, as we discussed earlier, is also employed in corpus-based translator training, particularly in the field of Language for Specific Purpose (LSP). The notion of 'discovery' plays an important role in Toury's and Johns' methodologies. They both require the student and researcher alike to progress from empirical data to generalization. The basic corpus-based procedure adopted by Johns is, in fact, "Identify – Classify – Generalise" (Johns 1991a: 4) the lexico-grammatical features associated with words that are particularly problematic for advanced learners, through the examination of KWIC concordance lines. What follows is an illustration of how Toury's and Johns' methods of enquiry were integrated in a corpus-based methodology devised for the student-centred, professionally-oriented translation classroom.

5. Case study

A corpus-based investigation was performed by the students attending a 60-credit postgraduate course in specialized translation at the University of Bari Aldo Moro during the 2008-2009 academic year. As part of the module devoted to the language of business and economics, I designed a teaching unit on Anglicisms. The learning objectives were: a) to become familiar with corpora as one of the computer-aided translation tools and resources available to the professional translator; b) to discover the textual-linguistic norm underlying the translation of polysemic lexical Anglicisms; c) to discover Italian native equivalents of well-established English loan words.

The sources of data consist of a corpus of 71 translated and non-translated comparable articles taken from the Italian weekly magazine *Economy* and a corpus of 71 English articles from *The Economist* and their translations in *Economy*. In the first phase, the lexical Anglicisms contained in the translational subcorpus were identified. By Anglicism we intend "a word or idiom that is recognizably English in its form (spelling, pronunciation, morphology or at least one the three), but is accepted as an item of the vocabulary of the receptor language" (Görlach 2003: 1). The most frequent Anglicism was *business*, a well-established English loan word, having been introduced in the Italian lexicon in 1895 as attested by the *Vocabolario della lingua italiana di Nicola Zingarelli* (2004).

Out of nearly 60,000 running words, 37 occurrences of *business* were retrieved. The analysis of the KWIC concordance lines revealed five discrete meanings of *business*.

I. the work of producing or buying and selling goods or services for money.
II. a high profile area of business where more than one company operates.
III. a) a highly profitable business activity undertaken by a company;
b) investment, deal or transaction made by a company.
IV. a large organization that provides services, or that makes or sells goods.
V. volume of business.

For each of the above meanings the collocation, colligation and semantic preference were identified as follows.

I. *Business* occurs with words that refer to other human activities, (*turismo e business*), the geographical place where business is carried out, and the people of different nationalities that are in business; it forms multi-word-units (*business hub, area business, segmento business, aree consumer e business*).

II. *Business* occurs with nouns that identify a particular business sector and the position gained in the market, nouns referring to the major players that operate in or impact on it, adjectives describing its qualities, such as diversity, profitability or importance.

III. *Business* occurs with words that refer to the company undertaking a particular business activity and to the type of activity undertaken, verbs referring to the changes undergone by a business, adjectives and nouns describing its main features, such as novelty, solidity or volatility; it forms one compound (*core business*).

IV. *Business* occurs with words referring to the people owning or running a company or to the way in which a company organizes its activities; it forms multi-word-units (*business model, modello di business, business manager, business partner*).

V. *Business* occurs with words that refer to the monetary value (or turnover) of a company or business sector:
Al 73enne Ecclestone è rimasto il 25% del gruppo che gestisce il business da 800 milioni di dollari.
Per contrastare il cambiamento del clima anche gli ambientalisti riscoprono il nucleare. Un business da 125 miliardi di dollari.

Next, *business* was examined in the comparable subcorpus of non-translated articles. The number of occurrences was nearly double, 74 against 34. The meanings identified were the same, except for senses II and V, which also referred to illegal business activities. The analysis of the KWIC concordance lines revealed sameness and difference (examples of the latter are highlighted in bold):

I. *Business* occurs with words that refer to other spheres of human activity (*business & società, sport e business, musica & business, business & genetica*), the geographical place where business is carried out, and the people of different nationalities that are in business; it forms multi-word-units (*business information, aree di business, clienti business, utenti business*). ***Business* is used in creative collocations:** *Il business resta in porto; Titanic del business; Il business non è l'unico quadrante su cui far girare le lancette della vita.*

II. *Business* occurs with nouns that identify a particular sector and the position gained in the market, nouns referring to the major players that operate in or impact on it, adjectives describing its qualities, such as diversity, profitability or importance. ***Business* forms compounds:** *business travel, social business, business online. Business* **refers to illegal sectors:** *il business dei falsi; i business si chiamano droga, prostituzione, racket. Business* **is used in creative collocations:** *un business che si chiama sconto; un business duro come il teak.*

III. *Business* occurs with words that refer to the company undertaking a particular business activity and the type of activity undertaken, verbs referring to the changes undergone by a business activity, adjectives and nouns describing its main features, such as novelty, **as well as importance, competitiveness, credibility or profitability; it forms various compounds:** *core business, business continuity, business case, business plan.* **It strongly collocates with:** *possibilità, opportunità, occasioni, fare.* **It is used in creative colloca-**

tions and puns: *il business in una cannuccia; ora faccio business col cuore*; *un Tornado di business*; *ho più di un business per capello*.

IV. *Business* occurs with words referring to the people owning or running a company or to the way in which a company organizes its activities; it forms multi-word-units (*business unit, unità di business, business development manager*). **Business is used in creative collocations and puns:** *un business fatto di nuvole*; *l'Enav e quel business che è caduto dal cielo*; *il business lievita alla luce del sole*.

V. *Business* occurs with words that refer to the monetary value (or turnover) of a company or business sector. **It is used in creative collocations:** *Quel business da 2,5 milioni di sacchi di caffè*. **It refers to illegal activities:** *Il business [dei falsi] vale almeno 7 miliardi di euro all'anno*; *Cibo Nostro. La Mafia nell'alimentare. Quasi 20 miliardi di incassi per la criminalità organizzata: tanto vale oggi il business mafioso nell'agroalimentare, nelle sue varie declinazioni.*

The results show that the collocation, semantic preference and colligation of *business* in translational and non-translational Italian appear to be divergently similar. Moreover, translators seem to have resisted the influence of English by limiting the use of *business*.

The next phase involved mapping the Italian target texts onto the English source texts. For each of its five meanings, the following native Italian equivalents of *business* were retrieved:

I.   il mondo degli affari, gli affari, affari, l'attività, attività commerciali
II. il settore, l'industria, le industrie
III. un'attività commerciale, l'attività, le attività delle aziende
IV. un'azienda.
V.   generating the business → cedendo i prestiti.

The textual-linguistic norm that was inferred from these findings is a preference for native Italian equivalents. There is also one example (see meaning V above) where the original non-finite verb phrase, *generating business*, was translated with an equivalent expression, *cedendo i prestiti* (relinquishing loans), which explicates the original sense. Interestingly, the preference for 'domestic competitors' (Görlach 2003) of *business* in translational Italian is consistent with Maria Teresa Musacchio's (2005:76) study of a parallel/comparable corpus of economics articles, which shows a lower percentage of lexical borrowings in translational versus non-translational business Italian.

The final phase of the analysis, which was carried out with the subcorpus of original English articles vis-à-vis the subcorpus of comparable non-translated Italian articles, involved identifying the lexico-grammatical shifts in the use of *business* across the donor and the receptor language. Unlike in English, *business* appeared to have pejorative overtones in Italian when it conveyed meanings II and V. Also, while in English *business* was found to refer to a small or medium enterprise, in Italian it was found to denote a large company (meaning IV). Finally, in Italian *business* was sometimes used in creative expressions, which usually appeared in titles or subtitles and fulfilled the pragmatic function of attention-getting devices.

The case study presented here focuses on an authentic problem raised by the students themselves, namely the norm governing the translation of polysemic Anglicisms in a specific subject domain and text type: the language of business and economics in periodicals articles. Students' evaluations at the end of the course show that their learning experience aided by corpora and inspired by a holistic pedagogy was perceived as 'professionally empowering' (Kiraly 2003). Indeed, they stated that learning through corpora had equipped them with the specialized knowledge, self-reliance, authentic experience and expertise they need to acquire in order to become language professionals with highly developed intercultural communicative competences. Moreover, as a teacher, I felt professionally empowered too, because I learnt from my students as much as I taught them about translation and language for specific purposes. Also, I was able to engage in what Kiraly (2003) calls 'action research', which is carried out by teachers in their own classroom with a view to bringing about long-term changes in pedagogy.

6. Conclusion

The agenda I wish to set for corpus studies of translation is to engage the pure and applied branches of the discipline so as to stimulate a continuous process of mutual exchange between theory, research and practice. By this I mean undertaking empirical investigations that are firmly grounded in theory and are driven by concerns arising in practice, promoting practice that is underpinned by the insights of empirical research and developing theory that is substantiated and refined by the findings of empirical studies. For those who are interested in pursuing this long-term scholarly endeavour, I am pleased to announce the launching of a new editorial venture, *Translation and Translanguaging in Multilingual Contexts* (TTMC), published by John Benjamins. This journal provides a forum for interdisciplinary research aimed at creating synergies within the discipline and between translation studies and neighbouring fields of applied linguistics.

7. References

Anderman, Gunilla. 2007. Introduction. @ G. Anderman, ed. *Voices in Translation. Bridging Cultural Divides*. Clevedon: Multilingual Matters. ISBN 9781853599828, pp. 1-5.

Anderman, Gunilla & Margaret Rogers, eds. 2005. *In and out of English: For Better, for Worse?* Clevedon: Multilingual Matters. ISBN 1853597880.

Beeby, Allison, Patricia Rodríguez Inés & Pilar Sánchez-Gijón, eds. 2009. *Corpus Use and Translating*. Amsterdam: John Benjamins. ISBN 9789027224262.

Blum-Kulka, Shoshana. 1986. Shifts of Cohesion and Coherence in Translation. @ J. House & S. Blum-Kulka, eds. *Inter-lingual and Inter-cultural Communication: Discourse and Cognition in Translation and Second Language Acquisition Studies*. Tübingen: Gunter Narr. ISBN 9783878082729, pp. 17–35.

Blum-Kulka, Shoshana & Eddie A. Levenston. 1983. Universals of Lexical Simplification. @ C. Faerch & G. Kasper, eds. *Strategies in Interlanguage Communication*. London: Longman. ISBN 9780582553736, 119–139.

Bowker, Lynne. 2003a. Towards a Collaborative Approach to Corpus Building in the Translation Classroom. @ B.J. Baer & G.S. Koby, eds. *Beyond the Ivory Tower: Rethinking Translation Pedagogy*. Amsterdam: John Benjamins. ISBN 9027231885, pp. 193–210.

Bowker, Lynne. 2003b. Corpus-based Applications for Translator Training: Exploring the Possibilities. @ S. Granger, J. Lerot & S. Petch-Tyson, eds. *Corpus-based Approaches to Contrastive Linguistics and Translation Studies*. Amsterdam: Rodopi. ISBN 9042010460, pp. 169-183.

Chesterman, Andrew. 1998. Causes, Translations, Effects. @ *Target* 12/1: 200–230.

Díaz Pérez, Francisco. 2012. Writing and Translating on the *Frontera*: Language and Identity in Liliana Valenzuela's Translations of *Latina* Writers in the United States. @ C. Iliescu Gheorghiu, ed. *Traducción y (A)culturación en la Era Global/Translation and (Ac)culturation in the Global Era*. Alicante: Editorial Agua Clara. ISBN 9788480183635, pp. 171-180.

Ding, Yan, Dirk Noël & Hans-Georg Wolf. 2010. Patterns in Metaphor Translation: Translating Fear Metaphors between English and Chinese. @ R. Xiao, ed. *Using Corpora in Contrastive and Translation Studies*. Cambridge: Cambridge Scholars Publishing. ISBN 9781443817554, pp. 40-61.

Fairclough, Norman. 2000. *New Labour, New Language?* London: Routledge. ISBN 0415218276.

Furiassi, Cristiano, Virginia Pulcini & Félix Rodríguez Gonzáles, eds. 2012. *The Anglicization of the European Lexis*. Amsterdam: John Benjamins. ISBN 9789027211958.

Görlach, Manfred. 2003. *English Words Abroad*. Amsterdam: John Benjamins. ISBN 9789027275226.

Granger, Sylviane, Jacques Lerot & Stephanie Petch-Tyson, eds. 2003. *Corpus-based Approaches to Contrastive Linguistics and Translation Studies*. Amsterdam: Rodopi. ISBN 9042010460.

Ji, Meng. 2012. Translation and Scientific Terminology. @ M.P. Oakes & M. Ji, eds. *Quantitative Methods in Corpus-Based Translation Studies*. Amsterdam: John Benjamins. ISBN 9789027203564, pp. 251-273.

Johns, Tim. 1991a. Should you be Persuaded: Two Examples of Data-Driven Learning. @ T. Johns & P. King, eds. *Classroom Concordancing. ELR Journal* 4: 1-16.

Johns, Tim 1991b. From Printout to Handout: Grammar and Vocabulary Teaching in the Context of Data-Driven Learning. @ T. Johns & P. King, eds. *Classroom Concordancing*. Special Issue. *English Languate Research Journal* 4: 27-46.

Kelly, Dorothy. 2005. *A Handbook for Translator Trainers*. Manchester: St. Jerome. ISBN 1900650819.

Kiraly, Donald C. 2000. A Social Constructivist Approach to Translator Education. Empowerment from Theory to Practice. Manchester: St. Jerome. ISBN 9781900650328.

Kiraly, Donald C. 2003. From Instruction to Collaborative Construction: A Passing Fad or the Promise of a Paradigm Shift in Translator Education? @ B.J. Baer & G.S. Koby, eds. *Beyond the Ivory Tower: Rethinking Translation Pedagogy*. Amsterdam: John Benjamins. ISBN 9042010460, pp. 3–27.

Koby, Geoffrey S. & Brian James Baer. 2003. Task-Based Instruction and the New Technology. Training Translators for the Modern Language Industry. @ B.J. Baer & G.S. Koby, eds. *Beyond the Ivory Tower: Rethinking Translation Pedagogy*. Amsterdam: John Benjamins, ISBN 9042010460 pp. 211–227.

Kruger, Alet, Kim Wallmach & Jeremy Munday, eds. 2011. *Corpus-Based Translation Studies: Research and Applications*. London: Continuum. ISBN 9781441115812.

Kujamäki, Pekka. 2004. What Happens to "Unique Items" in Learners' Translations? "Theories" and "Concepts" as a Challenge for Novices' Views on "Good Translation. @ A. Mauranen & P. Kujamäki, eds. *Translation Universals: Do they Exist?* Amsterdam: John Benjamins. ISBN 9789027216540, pp. 187-204.

Lakoff, George y Mark Johnson. 1980. *Metaphors We Live By*. Chicago: The University of Chicago Press. ISBN 0226468011.

Musacchio, Maria Teresa. 2005. The Influence of English on Italian: The Case of Translations of Economics Articles. @ G. Anderman & M. Rogers, eds. *In and Out of English: For Better, For Worse?* Clevedon: Multilingual Matters. ISBN 1853597880, pp. 71-96.

Niu, Guiling and Huaqing Hong. 2010. Repetition Patterns of Rhetoric Features in English and Chinese Advertisements: A Corpus-based Contrastive Study. @ R. Xiao, ed. *Using Corpora in Contrastive and Translation Studies*. Cambridge: Cambridge Scholars Publishing. ISBN 1443817554, pp. 433-456.

Olohan, Maeve. 2007. Economic Trends and Developments in the Translation Industry. @ *The Interpreter and Translator Trainer* 1/1: 37-63.

Scarpa, Federica. 2006. Corpus-based Specialist-Translation Quality Assessment: A Study Using Parallel and Comparable Corpora in English and Italian. @ M. Gotti y S. Šarčević, eds. *Insights into Specialised Translation*. Bern: Peter Lang. ISBN 3039111868, pp. 155-172.

Setton, Robin. 2011. Corpus-Based Interpreting Studies. @ A. Kruger, K. Wallmach & J. Munday, eds. *Corpus-Based Translation Studies: Research and Applications*. London: Continuum. ISBN 9781441115812, pp. 33-75.

Shlesinger, Miriam. 1998. Corpus-Based Interpreting Studies as an Offshoot of Corpus-Based Translation Studies. @ *Meta* 43/4: 486–93. Retrieved on April 14, 2014, from <http://www.erudit.org/revue/meta/1998/v43/n4/>.

Tirkkonen-Condit, Sonia. 2004. Unique Items – Over- or Under-Represented in Translated Language?. @ A. Mauranen & P. Kujamäki, eds. *Translation Universals. Do they Exist?* Amsterdam: John Benjamins. ISBN 902721654, pp. 177-186.

Toury, Gideon. 1995/2012. *Descriptive Translation Studies and Beyond*. Amsterdam: John Benjamins. ISBN 9789027224491.

Tymoczko, Maria. 1998. Computerized Corpora and the Future of Translation Studies. @ *Meta* 43/4: 652–60. Retrieved on April 14, 2014, from <http://www.erudit.org/revue/meta/1998/v43/n4/>.

Tymoczko, Maria. 2007. *Enlarging Translation, Empowering Translators*. Manchester: St. Jerome. ISBN 9781900650663.

Ulrych, Margherita. 2005. Training Translators: Programmes, Curricula, Practices. @ M. Tennent, ed. *Training for the New Millennium*. Amsterdam: John Benjamins. ISBN 9027216665, pp. 3-33.

Vocabolario della Lingua italiana di Nicola Zingarelli. 2004. Undicesima Edizione. Bologna: Zanichelli. ISBN 8808233006.

Xiao, Richard, ed. 2010. *Using Corpora in Contrastive and Translation Studies*. Newcastle upon Tyne: Cambridge Scholars Publishers. ISBN 9781443817554.

Taking stock: A critical overview of research on (universal) features of translated language[1]

[A modo de balance: Una revisión crítica de la investigación sobre propiedades (universales) de la lengua traducida]

JOSEP MARCO
Universitat Jaume I (Castelló, Spain)
jmarco@trad.uji.es

Abstract: The first aim of this study is to provide an overview of the criticisms that have been levelled against so-called translation universals. These criticisms may be said to fall under four headings: the concept of universal itself, the methodology employed in many studies, the list of universal candidates, and how those universals are defined. A personal response to those criticisms is then articulated with a view to clearing the ground for future research. Special attention is paid to Becher's (2010) reformulation of the explicitation hypothesis and Halverson's (2003, 2010) gravitational pull hypothesis. It is tentatively concluded that hypothesised features of translation could be arranged along three axes: over-representation of target language features – interference; explicitation – implicitation; and simplification – complication.

Key words: translation universals; normalisation; simplification; explicitation; interference; criticism; gravitational pull hypothesis

1. Introduction

The idea that translated language is different from the language used in non-translations is not new. It is quite explicit in the term *translationese*; it is perhaps not so explicit but present nevertheless in the concept of translation as a *third code*, put forward by Frawley (1984) – a code "in its own right, setting its own standards and structural presuppositions and entailments, though they are necessarily derivative of the matrix information and target parameters" (1984: 168-169). However, this idea did not open up new paths for research until it was taken up by Mona Baker in the mid-nineties of the last century and held up for scrutiny with the aid of corpus-based methodology. Baker (1993, 1995, 1996) operationalised it by first turning it into a fact and then breaking it down into a series of allegedly universal features, or properties, of translated text (1993:

---

[1] This article has received financial support from research project FFI2012-35239, funded by the Spanish Ministry of Economy and Competitiveness.

234): "The starting point of this paper is that translated texts record genuine communicative events and as such are neither inferior nor superior to other communicative events in any language. They are however different, and the nature of this difference needs to be explored and recorded". Difference is assumed, and it is the nature of that difference that needs to be explored. This is where so-called *translation universals* come into play.

The notion of translation universal was advanced by Toury (1977) in a very tentative, cautious sort of way, and more fully developed in later works (e.g. 1995). In order for a property of translations to qualify as universal, a lot of cumulative empirical evidence needs to have been collected from many different quarters, i.e. involving a large number of language pairs, translation briefs, genres, historical periods, etc. A property which is shown to be sensitive to one or more of these factors will have *norm* (not universal) status, as it will signal patterns occurring in a particular place at a particular time under particular circumstances. If a norm cuts across the boundaries imposed by these categories (if it is observable in different periods, in different communities and/or across different genres), then it may be said to approach *law* status. But for a law to become a universal, massive support from empirical data is required. And even so, the only tenable sense of the concept is a relative one, according to which a would-be translation universal is defined as a "probabilistic explanation" of features observed in translations (Toury 2004: 24). Translation is such a multi-faceted phenomenon that no such thing as absolute universals can be expected to occur in its environment.

Baker (1993: 243-245) provided the first attempt at a list of universal candidates, which included the following:

   a). "A marked rise in the level of explicitness compared to specific source texts and to original texts in general", which may involve adding connectives, replacing pro-forms with full lexical items or providing cultural information;
   b). "A tendency towards disambiguation and simplification", signalled, for instance, by less complex syntax or by elements of punctuation;
   c). "A strong preference for conventional 'grammaticality'", whereby translators and interpreters tend to avoid deviations from grammatical norms even if they featured in source texts;

d). "A tendency to avoid repetitions which occur in source texts, either by omitting them or rewording them";

e). "A general tendency to exaggerate features of the target language", as in the well-known case of Hebrew binomials composed of synonyms or near-synonyms, mentioned by Toury (e.g. 1995);

f). "it has been shown that the process of mediation often results in a specific type of distribution of certain features in translated texts vis-à-vis source texts and original texts in the target language"

Three years later two further categories were added to the list (Baker 1996: 183-184): normalisation/conservatism, which "is a tendency to exaggerate features of the target language and to conform to its typical patterns", and levelling out, which "concerns the tendency of translated text to gravitate towards the centre of a continuum". The latter is new, but the former seems to be a blend of the tendency to exaggerate features of the target language and of the preference for conventional 'grammaticality' – two tendencies which may converge but which are different in principle. This point will be taken up again in section 3.

It is not the aim of this study to provide a detailed account of research on translation universals as conducted within the field of corpus-based translation studies. That has already been done, and very competently indeed, by such scholars as Laviosa (2002), Olohan (2004), Corpas Pastor (2008) and Zanettin (2012). What I set out to do here is to review the criticisms that have been levelled at the notion of translation universal, at some of the universals themselves and the way they are formulated, and then to explore how criticisms, qualifications and reformulations could inform future research on the specificity of translated texts.

2. Translation universals under fire: criticism, counter-criticism and hypothesis reformulation and refining

Criticisms launched against translation universals might be said to fall at least under four headings or groups: the concept of universal itself, the methodology employed in many studies, the list of universal candidates, and how those universals are defined. In what follows these groups of criticisms will be dealt with in turn.

It is highly significant that the 1998 special issue of *Meta* devoted to "The Corpus-based Approach", edited by Sara Laviosa, which did so much to promote and disseminate such an approach, should include contributions calling into question the very notion of translation universal, which featured largely in the volume. Tymoczko's (1998) article is a case in point. She starts from the assumption that translation manifests itself in such a large variety of ways over space and time that it is impossible to define its prototype. As a result (1998: 656),

> To discover general laws of translation, if indeed such laws exist, [...] at the very least what will be needed are corpora representing as many types of translations as are known from the whole of human history. It may be, however, that such a quest is a positivist chimera, the commonalities so restricted for a category like translation that the effort is unlikely to provide the field of Translation Studies with much information of lasting value or transferable worth and, therefore, would not be worth the effort.

The objection is, thus, of an epistemological nature: the very object of research, "commonalities" of translation, may recede farther into the researcher's background the harder s/he attempts to grasp them and bring them to the fore.

Malmkjær (2008) does not deny the possibility of translation universals, but limits their scope and posits strict conditions for their existence. The starting point of her argument is that there is a certain tension between the concepts of norm and universal. Norms are socio-cultural in nature, they are assimilated by individuals in the process of their socialisation, and their existence can only be assumed "in situations which allow for different kinds of behaviour" (Toury 1995: 55). On the other hand, universals, by definition, allow for no variation in behaviour. However, Malmkjær seeks parallels in other social sciences and finds that, in linguistics, a distinction is made between absolute universals, which admit of no exceptions, and non-absolute universals, which adopt the form of statistically significant tendencies (akin to Toury's "probabilistic explanations"). The former are cognitively determined, whereas the latter are cognitively constrained – cognition being the only possible reason underlying (allegedly) universal features in any kind of linguistic behaviour. When Baker's list of universal candidates is brought face to face with these considerations, Malmkjær (2008: 55) observes that, even if their formulation "seems to suggest a purely cognitive source and explanation of translation universals", "the examples she [*i.e. Baker*] uses to illustrate what a translation universal might be are strongly suggestive of explanation in terms of the kinds of norm that might guide translational behaviour". The candidates on the list, then, would not qualify as universals, according to Malmkjær's criterion; but there is one, paradoxically not put forward by Baker but by Tirkkonen-Condit (2002, 2004), which would – the so-called *unique items hypothesis*. (This hypothesis will be dealt with later in this section.) Malmkjær (2008: 57) concludes that "if the concept of the universal is to retain any theoretical bite in our discipline, we would do well to reserve it for use in connection with phenomena such as this [*the unique items hypothesis, just mentioned*], for which it makes sense to produce a cognitively based explanation".

House (2008) shows no patience for nuances and "quite bluntly" (2008: 11) denies the possibility for translation universals to exist. She pronounces the quest for them "in essence futile" (2008: 11) and adds that if many translation scholars have embarked on such a quest it is only because it has been made technically feasible by the advent of corpus-based methodology. Thus, technical feasibility has overridden the more basic question of whether the quest was justifiable or worth undertaking. House substantiates her claim on five reasons (2008: 11-12): translation is an operation on language and therefore language universals, as identified in the functional-typological approach to the study of language, are enough to account for regularities in translation; translation is a language-pair specific practical activity, but detailed comparative analysis of the languages involved often fails to be carried out by scholars searching for evidence of translation universals; translation is sensitive to directionality (what is the case for, say, translation from English into German may not be so for translation from German into English); translation is sensitive to genre (a feature observed in the translation of scientific texts may not obtain in the translation of economic texts); and, finally, texts belonging to a given genre undergo diachronic development. House (2008: 15) summarises her objections to the concept of translation universal, which ultimately stem from "the complexity of translation as a performative act" (2008: 15), in a diagram including variables not previously mentioned (translator, situational and translator task variables) which complicate matters further. In that same diagram, candidate universals (explicitation, simplification, etc.) are mapped onto the three language metafunctions identified by Halliday and the systemic-functional tradition – ideational, interpersonal and textual – although links are very tentatively set up, not carefully spelt out. Even so, the point remains clear: there is nothing special about translation which justifies talk of translation universals; language universals will do, as translation is no more than a linguistic operation.

Tymoczko, Malmkjær and House, then, engage with the notion of the universal in translation as a whole. A second group of criticisms finds no fault with the notion but with various aspects of the methodology employed by scholars searching for evidence of universals in translation. In other words, these criticisms are not epistemological but methodological in nature. A case in point is Bernardini's (2005) argument that the methodology for the study of potential translation universals delineated by Baker (1993), based solely on comparable corpora, might turn out to be inadequate because a crucial factor impinging on the make-up of translated texts, i.e. their corresponding source texts, is deliberately left out of the picture. Baker's (1993: 245-246) suggestion is well-known:

> Take a corpus of translations into L from a large number of languages and compare it with a corpus of texts originally written in L, looking for evidence of feature F. Do this for as many Ls as possible. If it is found, for each pair of translation corpus and non-translation corpus, that evidence for F occurs more frequently in the corpus of translated text, then we will have cause to believe that it does so as a result of the translation process and not because of any relationship between any language pair. We may then be justified in calling F a translation universal.

This method is explicitly intended to address "the elucidation of the nature of translated text as a mediated communicative event". But it is precisely this definition of translated text that Bernardini (2005: 6) takes issue with: "it is the very nature of translation as a mediated communicative event (Baker, 1993) that makes an exclusively target-oriented approach to translation analysis methodologically questionable". This author calls for the balance to be redressed, so that the standard methodology combines comparable with parallel and reference corpora. The data furnished by comparable corpora may well be supplemented and sometimes even accounted for by an analysis based on parallel corpora, as many translation decisions derive from the make-up of the source text.

Corpas Pastor (2008), for her part, offers comprehensive, often scathing criticism of the methodology used in most corpus-based studies on alleged translation universals. Firstly, she argues, most corpora are small and unbalanced. Their composition is biased, as literary texts often prevail. Bias also affects language combinations, English featuring in most of them. There are very few corpora in which English is not either the source or the target language. In addition, most studies are centred on a single universal, which does not help establish relationships and balances between different features. And, for each universal, a small number of indicators are brought under scrutiny. By implication, the kind of study Corpas favours should comprise more than one translation universal and, for each universal, a set of related indicators (what she calls a "matrix of features") should be put to the test in order to validate (or otherwise) a given hypothesis. By way of conclusion, she claims that most corpus-based analyses of alleged universals of translation lack an experimental design which is robust and can be replicated and automated. Some of these issues will be taken up again below.

A third group of criticisms concerns the list of universal candidates itself. In section 1 Baker's original proposal (1993) was presented, together with some slight changes introduced in a later publication (1996). It is only fair to remark that such a proposal was advanced in a tentative way, with a view to opening up paths and avenues for research – which it most certainly did. It did not aim at being exhaustive, and it is only natural that later research should have uncovered other potential candidates for the category of universals. Perhaps the most conspicuous absence from the list was that of interference – an absence which can logically be put down to the kind of methodology advocated by Baker, based on comparable corpora alone.[2] But interference has regained its former prominent position among scholars' interests since then.

Interference was presented by Toury as a law, formulated as follows (1995: 275): "In translation, phenomena pertaining to the make-up of the source text tend to be transferred to the target text". Every translator knows that the source text exerts pressure on the profile finally adopted by the translated text. But the extent of that pressure and the strength of the translator's resistance to it may vary, as always in translation, in accordance with different factors. Therefore, when put to the test of empirical research, the interference hypothesis will have to be operationalised through specific indicators and tools, and data analysis may yield different results.

The second candidate universal put forward in recent years is the so-called *unique items hypothesis*, first formulated by Tirkkonen-Condit (2002, 2004).

---

[2] Both these aspects (the absence of interference and its presumable relationship to Baker's method) are made abundantly clear by Pym (2008: 320 ff.).

While searching for evidence of Baker's hypothesis that translations show a general tendency to exaggerate features of the target language, Tirkkonen-Condit found just the opposite, i.e. that in Finnish translations some typical features of Finnish were under-represented as compared to Finnish originals. She called these features *unique*, but uniqueness must here be understood in a relative sense, since it does not imply that such elements do not exist in any other language, but rather that they exist in Finnish (or in any other target language) but not in the corresponding source language in a given language pair. As to possible explanations of this phenomenon, it is argued that typical target language features are under-represented in translations for lack of stimulus across the source/target language divide. If the target language features lack straightforward, readily available, *prima facie* equivalents in the source text, their use is not triggered by any source text segment and they remain underused. Therefore, the unique items hypothesis might be regarded as a kind of negative interference.

The fourth, and last, group of criticisms against translation universals concerns the way hypotheses have been formulated and possible interaction, or interdependence, between them. Two major attempts at re-defining well-known alleged translation universals will be discussed in what follows: Becher (2010) on the explicitation hypothesis and Halverson's (2003, 2010) *gravitational pull hypothesis*, which aims to reconcile two apparently opposing tendencies – over- and under-representation of typical target language features in translations.

Becher (2010) takes as his starting point Blum-Kulka's (1986: 19) often-quoted formulation of the explicitation hypothesis, "which postulates an observed cohesive explicitness from SL to TL texts regardless of the increase traceable to differences between the two linguistic and textual systems involved". Blum-Kulka further claims (1986: 21) that "explicitation is a universal strategy inherent in the process of language mediation". Blum-Kulka's formulation has been so influential in Translation Studies that the translation-inherent conception of explicitation has found its way even into Klaudy's (2008) classification of explicitness, which includes four types: obligatory, optional, pragmatic and translation-inherent. Obligatory explicitation is caused by differences between the source and target linguistic systems; optional explicitation is due to differences in stylistic preferences between the two languages involved; pragmatic explicitation takes place when relevant differences in world knowledge shared by members of the source and target cultures are perceived; and translation-inherent explicitation is due to "the nature of the translation process itself" (2008: 107). Translation-inherent explicitation is taken for granted in most, if not all, of the studies on explicitation, both within and without corpus-based translation studies.

Becher (2010), in what may strike some as a rather radical move, suggests (2010: 1) abandoning the explicitation hypothesis altogether because "it is unmotivated, unparsimonious and vaguely formulated". It is unmotivated because it remains to be proved that any increase in the level of explicitness perceived in translated texts vis-à-vis non-translated texts in the target language or source texts stems from the nature of the translation process. No direct causal link should be postulated between the two phenomena because correlation is not the same as causation. There might be other reasons for the observed increase in explicitness, such as the translators' urge to simplify, which "raises the level of explicitness by resolving ambiguity" (Baker 1996: 182). It is unparsimonious because it flouts the scientific maxim (also known as Occam's Razor) that explanations should be kept as simple as possible, so that an explanation with fewer elements is always to be preferred to a more complex one. Becher (2010: 7-8) argues that assuming the existence of translation-inherent explicitation is an unnecessary step, as higher explicitness in translated texts could be explained on the basis of Klaudy's other three types of explicitation alone. Finally, the explicitation hypothesis is badly formulated because, as seen above, explicitation is defined as "a universal strategy inherent in the process of language mediation" (Blum-Kulka 1986: 21) but it is never specified whether, as a strategy, it is conscious or sub-conscious, so that different researchers understand it differently.

As a result of all this, Becher argues (2010: 17) that "a slightly extended and motivated version of Klaudy's (2009) Asymmetry Hypothesis can serve as a more useful and plausible guide for further research on explicitation". The Asymmetry Hypothesis claims (Klaudy and Károly 2005: 14) that

> explicitations in the L1→L2 direction are not always counterbalanced by implicitations in the L2→L1 direction because translators – if they have a choice – prefer to use operations involving explicitation, and often fail to perform optional implicitation.

Becher finds this formulation partly unsatisfactory for three reasons: the types of explicitation meant are not specified; the term "prefer" seems to point to a conscious strategy, whereas he would like to contemplate sub-conscious explicitation too; and "fail" has a "prescriptive flavour to it" (2010: 17). Becher's modified version of the Asymmetry Hypothesis reads as follows (2010: 17): "Obligatory, optional and pragmatic explicitations tend to be more frequent than the corresponding implicitations regardless of the SL/TL constellation at hand". Then he goes on to motivate this new hypothesis on the general grounds that translation acts are above all acts of communication and, as such, they are ruled by the same general principles as rule human communication. These principles are the Q Principle ("Say as much as you can!") and the R Principle ("Say no more than you must!"), the former leading to explicitness and the latter to implicitness. Participants in communication are said to be torn between these two extremes and expected to find the best trade-off point between them, depending on the situation. Now, the communicative situation underlying translation is characterised, according to Becher (2010: 18-20), by two properties: cultural distance between SL author and TL reader, and a great deal of communicative risk (Pym 2005). Both properties will tend to push the translator towards the explicitness end of the scale, as a way of both bridging the cultural gap and avoiding the risk of a potential breakdown in communication, which an excess of implicitness might bring about.

Becher's discussion of the explicitation hypothesis has been dealt with at length here because it is a very healthy exercise in not taking concepts for granted. The fewer assumptions a researcher makes, the better. What types of explicitation they have in mind, whether explicitation is taken to be conscious, sub-conscious or both, are aspects that need to be built into the hypothesis; otherwise, we do not know what we are talking about, and communicative breakdowns may well occur among translation scholars. The initial formulation of a hypothesis is bound to be approximative, tentative in nature; the need for refining it will be suggested by the data and their analysis. This might turn out to be a long journey which is nowhere near its final destination yet, as far as alleged universals of translation are concerned.

Halverson's gravitational pull hypothesis constitutes a good example of the point just raised. Halverson (2003: 197-198) sets out to show that "the various lexical/semantic patterns that have been subsumed under the heading 'translation universals' may be explained with reference to general characteristics of human cognition". There is no space here to provide even a brief summary of the cognitive theoretical assumptions that lend support to her approach to universals. Suffice it to say, then, that according to cognitive linguistic theory linguistic units are integrated into higher-order structures, such as schematic networks, made up of nodes and links between nodes. The different meanings of a particular word, for instance, may be said to constitute a schematic network. An important aspect of networks is that they are characterised by asymmetry: not all nodes are equally prominent (or *salient*, to put it in cognitive terms), some are more salient than others. The most salient elements in a schematic network are usually the high-level schema (on account of its high level of generality) and the prototype (because it is regarded as the best representative of a category). In the bilingual brain, as has been attested by empirical research, there are two layers of representation: the lexical memory, where the forms of spoken and written lexical items are stored, and the conceptual level, where word meanings are stored. Links between words in different languages are set up through connections at the conceptual level, although such connections may rest upon total or partial overlap, the latter being very often the case.

The implications of all this for translation are spelt out by Halverson (2003: 218) as follows:

> The basic idea is straightforward: in a translation task, a semantic network is activated by lexical and grammatical structures in the ST. Within this activated network, which also includes nodes for TL words and grammatical structures, highly salient structures will exert a gravitational pull, resulting in an overrepresentation in translation of the specific TL lexical and grammatical structures that correspond to those salient nodes and configurations in the schematic network.

According to this author, the gravitational pull exerted by salient structures (high-level schemas and prototypes) would lie at the basis of such apparently heterogeneous features of translation as simplification, normalisation, exaggeration of target language items and others. But the opposite may also be true (2003: 222). When the schematic networks activated do not contain highly salient structures, no over-representation of salient nodes will be found in translations; "[i]nstead, a range of translation selections will be found". And, Halverson claims, this accounts for the under-representation of typical target language features, also known as unique items hypothesis.

The consequences of all this for the study of translation universals are far-reaching. In a nutshell, it is no longer possible to approach universals without taking into account the degree of salience of the structures involved within each individual language and the degree of linkage, or overlap, between related structures from both languages in a given schematic network. Since this is a crucial point, it may be worth quoting Halverson at length (2003: 224-225):

> Analyses aimed at the investigation of translation universals must be contingent on the type of semantic network that is tapped into in any given instance. In short, different effects may be expected dependent on the structure of the network, including the types of connections within it, their varying strengths, the number of nodes shared and resulting distance between L1 and L2 items, the question of activation from one or the other language and the existence of any type of asymmetry within the network. As we have seen, both over and underrepresentation of TL items may be expected, depending on the structure of the network in question. Thus, attempts at verification or falsification of hypothesized translation universals must be specified at this level, and, crucially, must take into account the two languages involved, as well as the direction of translation.

Be it noted that the gravitational pull hypothesis pertains to a higher level of generalisation than the various hypotheses subsumed under the heading of translation universals. Simplification, normalisation, etc. attempt to capture patterns and regularities shown by translations, whereas the gravitational pull hypothesis purports to provide a cognitive explanation for them. But part of the explanation lies in *specifying the conditions* under which a given feature obtains. Thus, the two levels of generalisation do not remain parallel and apart but in fact touch each other and end up producing a more refined hypothesis. Halverson (2009: 93-102) suggests ideas for testing her hypothesis with different indicators, tools and methods. In a recently defended PhD dissertation, Hareide (2013) puts the gravitational pull hypothesis to the test, together with the opposing over- and under-representation of typical target language items hypotheses. In order to do that, Hareide uses P-ACTRES, an English-Spanish parallel corpus already in existence, compiled at the University of León in Spain, and builds herself the Norwegian-Spanish Parallel Corpus, which is assumed to be comparable to P-ACTRES in all relevant respects. The reason for having two parallel corpora with Spanish as target language is that the whole study was to pivot around two grammatical structures, the Spanish gerund and the *estar* + gerund construction, which may be said to be unique items for the Norwegian-Spanish language pair, since Norwegian lacks straightforward equivalents for those structures, but not for the English-Spanish language pair, since there is a high degree of linkage or overlap between the Spanish structures, on the one hand, and the English gerund and the be + *-ing* form.

Hareide (2013: 36 and ff.) draws on Halverson (2010) to formalise the gravitational pull hypothesis as follows. There are three potential causes of translational effects: patterns of prototypicality, which are target language internal (factor 1); conceptual structures/representation of the source language item, which are related to the structure of the source language (factor 2); and patterns of connectivity, which reflect relationships between the source and the target languages (factor 3). One effect is predicted for each potential cause, or factor. The effect of factor 1 will be over-representation, as prototypical or frequent target language elements exert gravitational pull. The effect of factor 2 will be over-representation too, as salience or prototypicality in some part of the source language network may impact choice in the target language. And the effect of factor 3 may be over- or under-representation, as a result of the degree of linkage between the related concepts in the bilingual's mental lexicon.

Hareide's findings (2013: 268-270) are extremely interesting and informative. The Spanish gerund was found to be significantly more frequent both in Spanish translated from English and in Spanish translated from Norwegian than in original Spanish, which provides support for the over-representation of target-language specific features hypothesis and for factor 1 of the gravitational pull hypothesis. Therefore, in the case of the Spanish gerund in translations from Norwegian, prototypicality and frequency (factor 1) outweigh the lack of corresponding structures in the source language (factor 3 of the gravitational pull hypothesis). The unique items hypothesis is thus disproved. Moreover, the Spanish gerund was found to be significantly more frequent in translations from English than in translations from Norwegian, thereby providing support for the gravitational pull hypothesis. As to the *estar* + gerund construction, it is found to be significantly more frequent both in Spanish translated from English and in Spanish translated from Norwegian than in original Spanish. In the case of the English-Spanish language pair, this finding lends support to the over-representation of target-language specific features hypothesis and to factors 1 and 2 of the gravitational pull hypothesis. In the case of the Norwegian-Spanish combination, the over-representation hypothesis and factor 1 of the gravitational pull hypothesis receive support from the findings. Again, as in the case of the gerund just mentioned, the unique items hypothesis is refuted, as factor 1 (prototypicality and frequency) seems to exert a stronger pull than factor 3 (lack of corresponding structures in the source language). Finally, contrary to expectations, the *estar* + gerund construction is found to be more frequent in Spanish translated from Norwegian than in Spanish translated from English, even if in the former language pair there is only one factor at play (factor 1) and in the latter all three factors pull in the direction of over-representation. According to Hareide (2013: 270), this finding does not contradict the gravitational pull hypothesis as a whole but runs counter to one of its predictions, namely, that several factors pulling in the same direction will have a cumulative effect.³

It is quite obvious that we have gone a long way from the somewhat crude formulations hypothesised universals received a couple of decades ago and (alas) too often still receive nowadays. But attempts at reformulation are there, and much more sophisticated pieces of research stem from them. They may not be enough in themselves, but they certainly clear the ground and point the way for future developments.

3. Where do we go from here?

It may strike some as pretentious to try and make general statements on the vast body of research on translation universals already in existence, and even more so to attempt to answer the question heading this section. Much more humbly, my purpose here is to try and digest the criticism reported on in the previous section and, if possible, to arrange it into a coherent picture.

As to the first group of criticisms, I would like to assume that general properties of translation, whether universal or not, are worth investigating because they are intrinsic to one of the primary objects of study in our discipline – translated

---

[3] However, Halverson (personal communication) is wary of making predictions about possible interactions between factors. She thinks it highly likely that the factors interact, and one possible interaction pattern is a cumulative one, but this is only one of many possible patterns. She thinks it is premature to make predictions at this stage.

texts. Are astronomers not justified in trying to find out what the universe is, or what its defining characteristics are? Or, on a much smaller, human scale, are literary scholars not justified in trying to determine what literariness is, over and above their more immediate concerns (e.g. studying a certain author)? If we answer these questions in the affirmative, then it is only logical that translation scholars should attempt to determine what it is that makes translated texts different from non-translated texts in the target language and/or their source texts. It is basic research and, as such, needs no further justification. But it is basic research that will inevitably lead to practical applications into the bargain. Let us think of corpora themselves, to begin with, which are invaluable documentation resources regardless of what they were initially compiled for. And let us think of translator training, by all means, as we need to know what *is* the case before we give students our version of what *should be* the case.

That said, of course many of the reservations about the concept of translation universal voiced by different scholars must be taken into account and their implications for research explored. The concept is always used in a relative sense, i.e. translation universals are "probabilistic explanations", as claimed by Toury (2004: 24); but even so Malmkjær (2008) argues that most universals put forward so far do not qualify as such, and would like to see the category restricted to such cases of translation (or translator) behaviour as can only be accounted for by cognitive constraints. Pym (2008) is not so keen on restricting the category but is equally willing to offer comprehensive grounds for translation universals – in his case, translators' *aversion to risk*, a motive which may sound psychological but is ultimately social in nature. Translators are averse to running risks in their work because risk does not pay off in societies that see translators as subservient figures and translations as derivative texts. Since there is no reward for risky options, translators tend to make conservative decisions which rest on two kinds of authority – that of the source text, which leads to interference, and that of the target language, which leads to normalisation, simplification and explicitation. Halverson (2003), even if her assumptions are based on cognitive linguistic theory, is less restrictive than Malmkjær and states (2003: 232-233) that "the cognitive factors that I have described are by no means the only external factors that may be posited. Indeed […] there are also social/cultural factors that must come into play". (But then she goes on to add that "for the universals thus far posited and investigated, I believe that the cognitive factors are far more important than the social ones".) It must be, then, one or the other or both: translation universals, if they are to qualify as such, must be shown to rest on general principles related to human cognition or social communication or both. Some links in the chain of causality that binds description and explanation are missing. It is an important task for research to provide those links.

From the second group of criticisms, having to do with methodological shortcomings in corpus-based studies on translation universals, I would like to pick up and subscribe to the views expressed by Bernardini (2005) and Corpas Pastor (2008). Bernardini's point about the need for parallel and reference corpora alongside comparable corpora is worth considering and adopting. In fact, it has already been adopted in most ambitious research projects carried out nowadays. Since the reasons underlying many instances of translation behaviour are to be found in source texts, we leave them out of the picture at our peril. Corpas Pastor, for her part, argues that research aiming to test hypothesised universals should move from small-scale studies, centring on a single feature or indicator, to sets, or matrixes, of features. This is a very valuable suggestion if one considers that the results and conclusions of small-scale studies will tell us more about the indicator in question (e.g. creative collocation for normalisation, optional *that* for explicitation, etc.) than about the more general hypothesis, since they do not reveal whether other possible indicators would point in the same direction or not. In fact, it is an observable tendency that the more indicators are included in a study, the more mixed the evidence. When dealing with universals, indicators are no more than necessary elements to operationalise a given hypothesis. But the analyst, while (passionately) engaged with data, is apt to forget that and to equate the indicator with the alleged universal. A broader perspective will always be (methodologically) welcome.

The third and fourth groups of criticisms dealt with in the previous section will be lumped together in this section, as the shape the list of would-be universals may finally take and issues of (re)formulation of hypotheses are inextricably united.

Let us begin with the couple *exaggeration of target language features/normalisation*. As remarked in section 1, Baker (1993: 244) included "exaggeration of target language features" in her original list, side by side with "[a] strong preference for conventional 'grammaticality'", but then in a later work (1996) both tendencies were blended into *normalisation/conservatism*, which was defined (1996: 183) as "a tendency to exaggerate features of the target language and to conform to its typical patterns". However, there might be good reasons for keeping these two notions apart. In some pieces of empirical research (e.g. Kenny 2001) normalisation has been taken to highlight and prioritise the preference-for-conventional-grammaticality ingredient, already present in Toury's *law of growing standardisation*, which postulates that in translation source-text textemes tend to be replaced by target-language repertoremes (1995: 267-268). Textemes are elements which, even if they need not always be creative, play a stylistically significant role in the make-up of the source text, whereas repertoremes are standard elements of the target language system, or repertoire, which give the target text a lower stylistic profile. This is more akin to *flattening* (Lefevere 1992: 107; Chesterman 1997: 71-72; target texts are flatter, less expressive, than their corresponding source texts) than to mere overuse of target language resources. It might be argued then that normalisation and over-representation of typical target language elements are different processes, even if their end-product is the same.

The second proposed universal that needs to be addressed is the unique items hypothesis. As remarked above, *uniqueness* is understood in the context of this hypothesis as a relative notion, dependent on the particular language pair involved. But, even in this relative sense, in most cases it might be a matter of degree, not kind. The Spanish gerund in the Norwegian-Spanish combination, analysed by Hareide (2013), is a case in point. It is firmly established in that work right from the outset that, for the Norwegian-Spanish language pair, the gerund is a unique item, Norwegian not having any structure which could be regarded as a straightforward equivalent, and expressing such meanings as duration or progressive aspect by other means. However, as the dissertation progresses the reader learns (2013: 170) that there is such a thing as the Norwegian present participle, which may be said to account for 43 instances of use of the Spanish gerund in the Norwegian-Spanish Parallel Corpus. If some degree of formal overlap were postulated for the Spanish gerund and the Norwegian present participle, the uniqueness of the Spanish gerund would not be so neat but rather a matter, precisely, of degree. Therefore, in light of the gravitational pull hypothesis, the whole notion of *unique item* might well be superseded by Halverson's notion of *degree of linkage* (paraphrased as "distance" or "degree of overlap") between related concepts across the two languages involved in the bilingual's mental lexicon. In fact, the latter notion accommodates the former, for, if the degree of linkage between a certain target-language item and related items in the source language is close to zero, then the item in question may be said to qualify as a unique item. What research has shown so far, though, is that the unique items hypothesis works particularly well for language combinations made up of typologically diverse languages, such as Finnish plus an Indo-European language, and not so well for language pairs within the Indo-European family. And, at any rate, this hypothesis has been regarded by several scholars (Eskola 2004: 96, Corpas Pastor 2008: 119-121) as a negative kind of interference, so that it could always be subsumed under this more general notion.

The third alleged universal on Baker's list that I would like to discuss is avoidance of repetition, which conveys a sort of paradox, since translations are often claimed to contain more repetition than non-translations. That is implicit in several hypotheses, such as explicitation, simplification, levelling out and exaggeration of target language features. The kind of repetition referred to in Baker's hypothesis is repetition that constitutes a relevant feature of the source text. In other words, even if translators are in general more prone to repetition than original authors, they avoid relaying source text repetition. If source text repetition is regarded as a texteme, in Toury's sense, the avoidance of repetition hypothesis would be no more than a particular case of a more general statement, i.e. normalisation. Therefore, it would be unnecessary as an independent category.

Fourthly, the third-code hypothesis mentioned by Baker, according to which "it has been shown that the process of mediation often results in a specific type of distribution of certain features in translated texts vis-à-vis source texts and original texts in the target language" (Baker 1993: 245), might be marred by excessive breadth of scope and degree of generality (or lack of specification). This hypothesis differs from explicitation, simplification or normalisation, for instance, in that it does not refer to any particular feature exhibited by translations, but to the more general (alleged) fact that translations are different from non-translations. In other words, it seems to be co-extensive with the idea that lies at the basis of translation universals, and therefore cannot be a universal itself.

Finally, I would like to touch upon the cluster *simplification – levelling out – normalisation/exaggeration of target language features*, a set of concepts which are different in principle but show some overlapping.[4] In purely quantitative terms, levelling out, or the tendency of translated texts to gravitate towards the centre of any continuum (and to avoid its edges, it might be added), implies simplification, since, out of the full range of possibilities offered by the continuum (i.e. the linguistic system), fewer will be used in translated than in non-translated texts, the former thus taking a simpler, more schematic shape than the latter. By the same token, both levelling out and simplification imply normalisation/exaggeration of target language features, since the fewer the items used, the more often they will be repeated, the most frequent items being those which are most typical of the target language (pending cognitive factors such as degree of linkage between related concepts across languages, as predicted by the gravitational pull hypothesis). To complicate matters further, some degree of overlap has also been posited (e.g. by Pym 2008: 316-320, Becher 2010: 7) between explicitation and simplification, as translation solutions resulting in explicitation make for more readable, easier-to-process texts – i.e. simpler texts. As a way out of this conundrum, I would suggest maintaining all these proposed universals as separate entities (perhaps with the exception of levelling out, which could be subsumed under simplification in many cases, pending further research), since they are different in principle, while keeping a watchful eye on their areas of overlap. A crucial aspect of research where special caution must be used is choice of indicators in hypothesis operationalization, as a given indicator may point to more than one hypothesis (a warning already issued by Baker 1996: 180).

4. Concluding remarks

What are we left with, then? After reviewing criticisms in section 2 and attempting to integrate them into mainstream research in section 3, in this concluding section I would like to suggest that research on translation universals (under that

---

[4] As argued by Pym (2008: 316-320), who claims that these three, together with explicitation, can be "more or less fitted into Toury's law of standardization" (2008: 320).

or a different name) could be arranged along three clines, or axes, as shown in Figure 1.

The rationale for this arrangement is that alleged (universal) features of translation are better accounted for by means of dialectic oppositions than mere lists. The latter result in dispersion and isolation, whereas the former make for dynamic integration. There are examples of research into universals where this

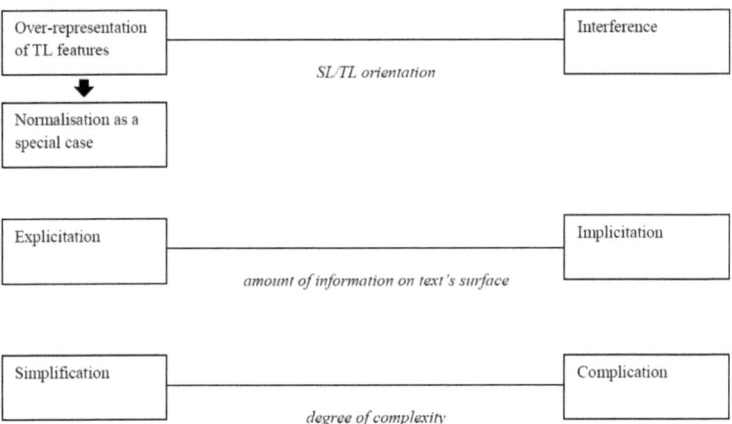

Figure 1. Map of translation universals arranged along several clines

kind of dialectics has already been engaged in and operationalised, such as Teich's (2003) multi-dimensional analysis of features tending towards interference or normalisation in German-English, English-German translation. It might be argued that the first axis all but justifies itself, as the target language configuration and the source text profile pull in different directions. Interference includes the negative type conveyed by the unique items hypothesis. At the other end of the cline, terminological issues could be resolved in more than one way. The one suggested in the diagram could be adhered to or, alternatively, normalisation could be used to designate the general case while some other term, such as flattening, might be apt to refer to the more particular case in which creative elements in the source text are neutralised or standardised. Degree of linkage or overlap between related concepts across languages in the bilingual's mental representations should be factored into the analysis of the relative gravitational pull exerted by structures at either end of the continuum.

On the other two clines, an antonym has been introduced for each of the standard terms explicitation and simplification. Implicitation enjoys wide currency as the opposite of explicitation, e.g. in Klaudy's asymmetry hypothesis and in Becher's revised version of it. In this respect, it is interesting to mention Krüger's (2013) recent, very promising work on explicitation/implicitation. In the framework of cognitive linguistic theory, Krüger sees explicitation and implicitation as cross-linguistic construal operations, i.e. as decisions made by the translator which can be related to the basic construal operations identified, for instance, by Langacker (2008). The two most relevant operations at work as regards explicitation/implicitation are *specificity* (the amount of detail or precision with which a situation is described) and *perspective* (where the speaker is situated in a given context). Perspective (also called *epistemic* perspective) is related to the notion of *common ground*, defined as the sum of knowledge, beliefs and suppositions shared by two speakers (Clark 1996: 93). It is precisely common ground, then, that will condition the degree of specificity in any communicative event, translated or otherwise. Krüger goes to great pains to distinguish between explicitation and addition, on the one hand, and between implicitation and omission, on the other, but we cannot do justice here to the complexity of his discussion for reasons of space. Suffice it to say that this discussion is very valuable in terms of conceptual clarification, along the lines laid by Becher, as it provides a cognitive linguistic framework for the (relatively) objective identification of instances of explicitation/addition or implicitation/omission. Whether we should go on using the term explicitation, like Krüger, or adopt the asymmetry hypothesis, as suggested by Becher, is a matter of opinion and does not alter the terms in which the opposition is couched. As to simplification, the opposite term *complication* has been introduced for the sake of parallelism. Both for the explicitation – implicitation and the simplification – complication axes, again the issue of degree of overlap or linkage between related concepts across languages will have to be taken into account when it comes to testing the general hypotheses on particular items or structures chosen as indicators.

Implicit in the arrangement displayed by Figure 1 is the fact that, rather than an open-ended list of would-be universals, what we need is a (more limited) set of variables underlying the give-and-take of opposing tendencies. The variables at work in that particular arrangement are source language/target language orientation, amount of information on the surface of the text and degree of complexity. However, two caveats are here in place. Firstly, the key terms in those variables (e.g. *orientation, information, complexity*) are vague and will have to be carefully defined in particular research projects, as a way of operationalising hypotheses. And secondly, there is no reason why the number of variables cannot be expanded. What I have attempted to do here is not to provide a closed list of universals, or of variables underlying universals, but to think of more dynamic, integrated ways of investigating them.

5. References

Baker, Mona. 1993. Corpus Linguistics and Translation Studies – Implications and Applications. @ M. Baker, G. Francis & E. Tognini-Bonelli, eds. *Text and Technology. In Honour of John Sinclair*. Amsterdam & Philadelphia: John Benjamins. ISBN 9789027221384, pp. 233-250.

Baker, Mona. 1995. Corpora in Translation Studies: An Overview and Some Suggestions for Future Research. *Target* 7/2: 223-243.

Baker, Mona. 1996. Corpus-based Translation Studies: The Challenges that Lie Ahead. @ H. Somers, ed. *Terminology, LSP and Translation: Studies in Language Engineering, in Honour of Juan C. Sager*. Amsterdam & Philadelphia: John Benjamins. ISBN 9789027216199, pp. 175-186.

Becher, Viktor. 2010. Abandoning the notion of 'translation-inherent' explicitation: against a dogma of translation studies. *Across Languages and Cultures*, 11/1:1-28.

Bernardini, Silvia. 2005. Reviving old ideas: parallel and comparable analysis in translation studies - with an example from translation stylistics. @ K. Aijmer & C. Alvstad, eds. *New Tendencies in Translation Studies*, Göteborg: University of Göteborg, ISBN 9789173465366, pp. 5-18.

Blum-Kulka, Shoshana. 1986. Shifts of Cohesion and Coherence in Translation. @ House, Juliane and Shoshana Blum-Kulka, eds. *Interlingual and Intercultural Communication. Discourse and Cognition in Translation and Second Language Acquisition Studies*. Tübingen: Gunter Narr. ISBN 9783878082729, pp. 17-35.

Chesterman, Andrew. 1997. *Memes of Translation. The Spread of Ideas in Translation Theory*. Amsterdam & Philadelphia: John Benjamins. ISBN 9789027283092.

Clark, Herbert H.. 1996. *Using Language*. Cambridge: Cambridge University Press. ISBN 9780521567459.

Corpas Pastor, Gloria. 2008. *Investigar con corpus en traducción: los retos de un nuevo paradigma*. Frankfurt: Peter Lang. ISBN 9783631584057.

Eskola, Sari. 2004. Untypical frequencies in translated language: A corpus-based study on a literary corpus of translated and non-translated Finnish. @ Mauranen, Anna & Pekka

Kujamäki, eds. *Translation Universals: Do they Exist?* Amsterdam & Philadelphia: John Benjamins. ISBN 9789027216540, pp. 83-99.

Frawley, William. 1984. Prolegomenon to a Theory of Translation. @ Frawley, William, ed. *Translation: Literary, Linguistic and Philosophical Perspectives*, Newark: University of Delaware Press. ISBN 978-0874132267, pp. 159-175.

Halverson, Sandra. 2003. The cognitive basis of translation universals. *Target* 15/2:. 197-241.

Halverson, Sandra. 2009. Elements of Doctoral Training: The Logic of the Research Process, Research Design, and the Evaluation of Research Quality. *The Interpreter and Translator Trainer* 3/1: 79-106.

Halverson, Sandra. 2010. Cognitive translation studies: developments in theory and method. @ G. M. Shreve & E.Angelone, eds. *Translation and Cognition*. Amsterdam & Philadelphia: John Benjamins. ISBN 9789027231918, pp. 349-369.

Hareide, Lidun. 2013. *Testing the Gravitational Pull Hypothesis in translation. A corpus-based study of the gerund in translated Spanish*. Bergen: University of Bergen (PhD dissertation presented in May 2014).

House, Juliane. 2008. Beyond Intervention: Universals in Translation? *Trans-kom* 1, 6-19. Available at <http://www.trans-kom.eu/bd01nr01/transkom_01_01_02_House_Beyond_Intervention.20080707.pdf>. Accessed 13 September, 2009.

Kenny, Dorothy. 2001. *Lexis and Creativity in Translation. A Corpus-based Approach*. Manchester: St. Jerome. ISBN 9781900650397.

Klaudy, Kinga. 2009. The Asymmetry Hypothesis in Translation Research. @ R. Dimitriu & M. Shlesinger, eds. *Translators and Their Readers. In Homage to Eugene A. Nida*. Brussels: Les Editions du Hazard.ISBN 9782930154237, pp. 283–303.

Klaudy, Kinga & Krisztina Károly. 2005. Implicitation in Translation: Empirical Evidence for Operational Asymmetry in Translation. *Across Languages and Cultures* 6/1: 13-28.

Klaudy, Kinga. 2008. Explicitation. @ M. Baker & G. Saldanha, eds. *Routledge Encyclopedia of Translation Studies*. London: Routledge. ISBN 9780415609845, pp. 80–85.

Krüger, Ralph. 2013. A Cognitive Linguistic Perspective on Explicitation and Implicitation in Scientific and Technical Translation. *Trans-kom* 6/2: 285-314. Available at <http://www.trans-kom.eu/bd06nr02/trans-kom_06_02_02_Krueger_Explicitation.20131212.pdf>. Accessed 14 July, 2014.

Langacker, Ronald W.. 2008. *Cognitive Grammar. A Basic Introduction*. Oxford/New York/Auckland: Oxford University Press. ISBN 978-0195331967.

Laviosa, Sara. 2002. *Corpus-based Translation Studies: Theory, Findings, Applications*. Amsterdam & Atlanta: Rodopi. ISBN 9789042014879.

Lefevere, André. 1992. *Translation, Rewriting and the Manipulation of Literary Fame*. London: Routledge. IBSN 9780415077002.

Malmkjær, Kirsten. 2008. Norms and nature in translation studies. @ Anderman, Gunilla & Margaret Rogers, eds. *Incorporating Corpora. The Linguist and the Translator*. Clevedon: Multilingual Matters. ISBN 1853599859, pp. 49-59.

Olohan, Maeve. 2004. *Introducing Corpora in Translation Studies.* London & New York: Routledge. ISBN 0415268850.

Pym, Anthony. 2005. Explaining Explicitation. @ Karoly, K. & A. Fóris, eds. *New Trends in Translation Studies. In Honour of Kinga Klaudy.* Budapest: Akadémiai Kiadó. ISBN 9789630582575, pp. 29–34.

Pym, Anthony. 2008. On Toury's laws of how to translate. @ Anthony Pym, Miriam Shlesinger & Daniel Simeoni, eds. *Beyond Descriptive Translation Studies: Investigations in Homage to Gideon Toury.* Amsterdam & Philadelphia: John Benjamins. ISBN 9789027216847, pp. 311–28.

Teich, Elke. 2003. *Cross-Linguistic Variation in System and Text.* Berlin & New York: Mouton de Gruyter. ISBN 9783111876245.

Tirkkonen-Condit, Sonja. 2002. Translationese – a Myth or an Empirical Fact? *Target* 14/2: 207-220.

Tirkkonen-Condit, Sonja. 2004. Unique items – over- or under-represented in translated language? @ Mauranen, Anna & Pekka Kujamäki, eds. *Translation Universals: Do they Exist?* Amsterdam & Philadelphia: John Benjamins. ISBN 9789027216540, pp. 177-184.

Toury, Gideon. 1977. *Translational Norms and Literary Translation into Hebrew, 1930-1945.* Tel Aviv: The Porter Institute for Poetics and Semiotics, Tel Aviv University.

Toury, Gideon. 1995. *Descriptive Translation Studies and Beyond.* Amsterdam & Philadelphia: John Benjamins. ISBN 9789027224484.

Toury, Gideon. 2004. Probabilistic explanations in translation studies: Welcome as they are, would they qualify as universals? @ Mauranen, Anna & Pekka Kujamäki, eds. *Translation Universals: Do they Exist?* Amsterdam & Philadelphia: John Benjamins. ISBN 9789027216540, pp. 15-32.

Tymoczko, Maria. 1998. Computerized corpora and the future of translation studies. *Meta* 43/4: 652-659.

Zanettin, Federico. 2012. *Translation-Driven Corpora. Corpus Resources for Descriptive and Applied Translation Studies.* Manchester: St. Jerome. ISBN 9781905763290.

A methodological approach to the analysis of natural interpreting: bilingual acquisition data and the CHAT/CLAN tool[1]

[Un enfoque metodológico para el análisis de la interpretación natural: los datos de adquisición bilingüe y la herramienta CHAT/CLAN]

ESTHER ÁLVAREZ DE LA FUENTE y RAQUEL FERNÁNDEZ FUERTES
University of Valladolid, Language Acquisition Lab (UVALAL) (Spain)
alvareze@fyl.uva.es, raquelff@lia.uva.es

Abstract: Previous works on Interpreting Studies, and more specifically on Corpus-based Interpreting Studies (CIS), have pointed out the important role that data analysis plays in outlining the interpreting process internal to any bilingual (e.g. Tirkkonen-Condit and Jääskeläinen 2000; Schlesinger 2008; Bendazzoli and Sandrelli 2009). The present study is meant as a contribution to the CIS research field as it presents a tool available for the computerized analysis of interpretation that has not been previously considered, i.e. the CHAT/CLAN methodology freely available through the CHILDES project (MacWhinney 2000). By applying this methodology, we analyze data from a set of English/Spanish bilingual twins from the FerFuLice corpus (Fernández Fuertes and Liceras 2009) in CHILDES and we show how the CHAT transcription and codification system as well as the CLAN program can be successfully used in the linguistic analysis of the interpretation process. In particular, the quantitative and qualitative analyses made possible through CHAT/CLAN shed light on how interpreting competence emerges and develops and provide new insights into the interpreting process as discussed in CIS.

Key words: Interpreting studies; bilingual acquisition data; CHILDES project; interpreting competence development; computerized analysis

1. Introduction

Corpus-based Interpreting Studies (CIS) comprise an independent research domain within Translation Studies (TS) in which both the use of corpora and the oral dimension of the data discussed constitute the backbone of research (Tirkkonen-Condit and Jääskeläinen 2000; Cencini 2002; Monti et al. 2005; Bendaz-

---

[1] This research was funded by the Castile and Leon Regional Government, Department of Education [VA046A06; UV 30/02], the Spanish Ministry of Science and Technology and FEDER [BFF2002-00442] and the Spanish Ministry of Education and Science [HUM2007-62213/FILO].

zoli and Sandrelli 2005, 2009; Shlesinger 2008; Meyer 2008; Göpferich and Jääskeläinen 2009; Setton 2011; Bendazzoli, Sandrelli and Russo 2011; Straniero Sergio and Falbo 2012, among others)[2].

Depending on the area of interest, previous CIS research involves the analysis of different data sets regarding different variables such as the degree of the translation competence or the translators' different levels of expertise (professionals *versus* bilingual or student trainees), the genres of the texts to be translated (general, such as CREA, BCN, etc., *versus* specialized contexts, such as EPIC), the languages involved in the translation (e.g. Germanic *versus* Romance languages), the type of interpreting (simultaneous *versus* consecutive), the purpose of the corpora (scientific or social research *versus* pedagogical applications), etc. These variables have been qualitatively and/or quantitatively analyzed using coherent and scientific methods which are already well-known in the domain of both TS and CIS (e.g. WordSmith tools, Paraconc, Multiconc, Workbench, etc.). These have offered interesting research possibilities for those translation scholars studying issues related to the linguistic analysis of translations, the development of translation competence, translation norms, or translation universals (Baker 1993, 1995; Toury 1995; Laviosa 1998, 2002, 2008, 2011; Wools 2000; Olohan 2004; Anderman and Rogers 2008; Granger, Lerot and Petch-Tyson 2008; Kruger, Wallmach and Munday 2011, among others).

The present work is framed in the CIS research field and aims at contributing to previous works in presenting the CHAT/CLAN methodology freely available in the CHILDES project (MacWhinney 2000) and how it can be used to analyze Natural Interpreting (NI). In particular, we present a linguistic analysis of the interpretation performed by two English/Spanish bilingual children in the FerFuLice corpus (Fernández Fuertes and Liceras 2009) in CHILDES and we propose how the CHAT/CLAN methodology can be used to offer both a quantitative and a qualitative analysis of the emergence and development of interpreting in bilingual children. Our study, thus, offers new insights into the so-called NI process (Harris 1980a, 1980b, 2003) and explores a tool available for the com-

---

[2] As a general practice in both TS and CIS research, in this article we use the terms *translation, translator* and *translate* as umbrella terms to refer to both the oral and the written mode of translating. When the oral dimension of the translation process is focalized, the terms *interpretation* or *interpreting* are used.

puterized analysis of interpretation that has not been previously used in CIS research.

Our work is divided into the following four main sections. Sections 2 and 3 constitute the background for our work and outline the basic properties of CIS research and NI research respectively. In section 4 we present our study based on the CHAT/CLAN methodology: we first offer a description of our participants, the corpus analyzed and the linguistic variables proposed; and we then present a NI codification procedure that we have designed and that will enable the use of the CLAN program for the analysis of NI. Section 5 offers the conclusions obtained and derived from the use of this methodology.

2. Corpus-based Interpreting Studies (CIS)

Corpus-based Interpreting Studies (CIS) emerged to identify the patterns typical of oral discourse (in contrast to those of written translation) (Shlesinger 1998; Tirkkonen-Condit and Jääskeläinen 2000; Monti et al. 2005; Tommola and Gambier 2006; Pöchhacker, Jakobsen and Mees 2007, among others).

Although the methodology used in CIS depends on the research aim, the data in these studies are mainly elicited by reporting the verbalization of translation processes during task performance, a method known as TAP (Think-Aloud Protocol). Data are often collected using video recordings, reports, interviews, notes or questionnaires (e.g. Jääskeläinen and Tirkkonen-Condit 1991; Lörscher 1992; Danks et al. 1997; Göpferich and Jääsleñäinen 2009).

Many of these methods are devoted to obtain sources of information that can help scholars to determine what translation competence is and how it is acquired. This is one of the reasons why the participants in CIS research are adult interpreters who differ in their translation competence: professional translators, students of translation, and/or untrained bilinguals (e.g. Gerloff 1988; Tirkkonen-Condit 1990; Christoffels, de Groot and Kroll 2006; Gómez Hurtado 2007; Yudes, Macizo and Bajo 2011). They are usually assessed on their performance as interpreters in experimental tests or in real-life events when they verbalize their responses or accounts in professional settings such as simultaneous or consecutive interpreting in court trials, conferences in the European Parliament, etc. (e.g. Monti et al. 2005; Meyer 2008; Bendazzoli and Sandrelli 2009; Setton 2011; Straniero Sergio and Falbo 2012).

Although in the last two decades, research on interpreting performance through corpus-based studies has become an emergent area in empirical TS, «(t)he relative dormancy of CIS through this period also reflect[s] the continuing difficulty of obtaining and analysing substantial authentic data» (Setton 2011: 38). In this respect and given some of the main paradigms of the basic methodology followed by CIS, some methodological questions remain to be tackled in this area of research. In particular, we would like to emphasize three of them: the type of oral data discussed, the profile of the speakers studied and the specific methodology used in the analysis. The consideration of these three issues is, in fact, of interest to CIS since it would certainly expand and enhance prospects in interpreting research. We refer to these questions below.

Given that CIS research is concerned with the patterns that characterize the interpreting process, the type of oral data considered should also involve developmental oral data. This longitudinal dimension has not been explored in CIS (with few exceptions as in Straniero Sergio 2012) and it could, in fact, identify patterns that an interpreter uses repeatedly in his/her speech. These patterns could evolve or not and new ones can emerge through time but that would only be revealed if longitudinal-developmental data are gathered instead of collecting data in a one-time elicitation shot.

With respect to the second issue, all the studies that have been referred to so far deal with the performance of bilingual adult interpreters in either professional or educational settings. However, if the aim is to show how translation competence emerges, the consideration of a different type of participant is called for: simultaneous bilinguals, either children or adults, who have not received any formal instruction in translation but who translate on a regular basis in everyday situations. This profile of participants has seldom received any interest from translation or interpreting studies although Harris (1977) already referred to them as *natural translators*. In fact, only a small portion of studies has taken this type of interpreters as the focus of attention (Harris and Sherwood 1978; Harris 1980a, 1980b; Beckmannova 2004; Álvarez de la Fuente 2008; Cossato 2008; Álvarez de la Fuente and Fernández Fuertes 2012a, 2012b). This ties with Setton's (2011) previous quote in two respects: the data from simultaneous bilinguals on how they translate/interpret daily constitute, in fact, authentic material and it also makes possible the study of the emergence and development of the interpreting activity. Section 3 below discusses these types of studies with more detail. As for the third issue, the methodology used in previous research involves the use of mostly unavailable data. In fact, there are still few corpus-based studies focused on interpreting and, for the most part, they are either not easily available for outside use or they only give access to some selected transcripts or samples in the form of appendixes to doctoral dissertations[3]. Even if some transcriptions are accessible, they do not usually give a detailed representation of the event, which can make them useless for research if the original recording of that event cannot be accessed (Edwards 1995; Cencini 2002). This makes these works not only un-available for comparative purposes but also highly un-replicable.

The present study addresses these three issues and puts forward a proposal to fill out the existing gap in CIS research by analyzing available and accessible longitudinal acquisition data from a set of bilingual twins as natural interpreters, as section 4 will show. The profile of bilingual children as natural interpreters, as well as the use of these types of data in CIS research, is dealt with in the next section.

3. Natural Interpreting (NI): A new concept of corpora use

Although more recently termed as *natural interpretation* (NI) (Harris 2003), Harris (1977: 6) coined the phrase *natural translation* to refer to the translation «done by bilinguals in everyday circumstances without special training for it». An example of NI is shown in 1.

(1)
Investigator$_{\text{Anglophone}}$: Ask her if she wants to go to the store today.
Michael: Tu veux aller au magasin?
[Do you want to go to the store?] French
Investigator$_{\text{Francophone}}$: Oui. Est-ce que Merrill veut y aller aussi?
[Yes. Does Merrill want to go there, too?] French
[3;06-3;07]
(Swain 1972, from Harris 1980a)

Example 1 is part of Swain's (1972) longitudinal data (taken up later by Harris 1980a) and it shows how Michael, an English/French bilingual child, can interpret naturally from English to French when he is about three and a half years old. In this experimental interpreting context, he has to act as a communicative

---

[3] See Setton (2011) for a compilation of studies on interpreting based on authentic corpora.

link between two monolingual investigators so that they can understand each other.

Harris' proposal regarding NI goes beyond a mere terminological issue. He asserts that, if we analyze this natural ability of interpreting in bilingual children, we will be able to understand how translation competence develops and how it interacts with bilingual competence, accounting in this way for the basis of the scientific study of translation (Harris 1977, 1980b). In this respect, the consideration of a new profile of participants as well as that of a corpus-based study in the compilation of NI cases are the two main outcomes of his work.

To begin with, Harris' work meant not only a widening of the scope of translation as an innate skill that develops parallel to bilingualism (Harris and Sherwood 1978; Malakoff and Hakuta 1991; Lörscher 1992; Álvarez de la Fuente 2008; Álvarez de la Fuente and Fernández Fuertes 2012b), but also a consideration of NI as a communicative act that has a particular function in familiar and social contexts (Knapp-Potthoff and Knapp 1987; Tse 1996; Walichowski 2001; Hall 2004; Angelelli 2011; Valero Garcés 2012). The concept of NI, therefore, implies the incorporation of other variables subject to analysis concerning not professional or institutional contexts but daily situations where interpreting is performed by a different type of participants: bilingual children or adults with no formation in translation (Harris and Sherwood 1978: Lozes-Lawani 1994; Bullock and Harris 1997; Sherwood 2000; Beckmannova 2004; Lising 2008; Cossato 2008; Harris 2013).

Finally, Harris' proposal brings about a different concept of corpus methodology that can shed light on how translation competence emerges and develops in bilinguals. To that end, a longitudinal corpus-based study on NI would provide a compilation of translation cases performed by bilingual speakers as interpreters in everyday situations and over a period of time. In other words, this type of study would open a promising research venue in CIS methodology incorporating longitudinal corpora that could be used to investigate, on the one hand, linguistic phenomena that are inherent to the process of interpreting itself and so, to the very emergence and development of translation competence; and, on the other hand, linguistic phenomena that provide evidence of regular tendencies in trans-

lation behaviours or strategies used by bilingual children that can be used to design translation programs and that can be part of the curriculum of trainees[4].
In this respect, several works have followed the lid started by Harris and have analyzed data from bilingual children offering a compilation of NI cases. However, as mentioned in section 2 above, since the study of interpreting through the analysis of corpora has become a new discipline, little progress has been made, in particular, towards developing basic standards in the data collection methodology (Cencini 2002; Bendazzoli and Sandrelli 2009).
This is particularly evident in previous NI studies based on corpora, such as the ones done by Harris (1980a, 1980b) and Harris and Sherwood (1978) who, although pioneers in the compilation of NI cases, only provide samples of isolated examples or notes from other authors' compilations (Ronjat 1913; Leopold 1939-1949; Von Raffler Engel 1970; Swain 1972). These NI cases from bilingual children's longitudinal data were compiled for purposes other than the analysis of NI and they come with no context in most of the cases, as examples 2 and 3 show.

(2)
Father: Non, ne reste pas ici, il fait trop froid, va voir Deda [a German housemaid].
[Don't stay here, it is very cold, go and see Deda] French
Louis: Papas Zimmer ist zu kalt.
[Daddy's room is very cold] German
[2;06]
(Ronjat 1913, from Harris and Sherwoood 1978)

(3)
Michael: Do you see the glasses?
Investigator_Francophone: Pardon?
[Excuse me?] French
Michael: Tu vois ti les lunettes?
[Do you see the glasses?] French
[3;06]
(Swain 1972, from Harris 1980a)

As valuable as these works are, the methodology used in the analysis makes it impossible to actually consider the entire dialogue or the context, to determine, for instance, if we are dealing with an experimental situation in 2 as opposed to

---

[4] Some empirical investigations within TS have already included the longitudinal factor in their analysis, although they are actually focused on the development of the translations performed by translation students (and not by untrained bilinguals) and on their written (and not oral) translation competence (Azbel Schmidt 2005; Göpferich 2010).

3. That is, a re-analysis of the data under other linguistic variables is not possible.

Other type of corpora dealing with NI that also deserves attention is the one of Cossato's (2008) who recorded for seven hours the production of fourteen child and adolescent interpreters differing in age, languages and language proficiency. She provides an appended compilation of the occurrence of specific translational behaviours, like the one in 4, although no systematic linguistic analysis of the cases is provided and the developmental factor is not included, as opposed to Harris' works.

(4)
Elizabeth: this monster has got feet a bit like you cos you have ten toes as well except I think your feet are nicer.
Simon: vad säg vad sager Elizabeth?
[What does what does Elizabeth say?] Swedish
Brigitta: hon sa mina fötter var finare.
[She said my feet were nicer] Swedish

[4;10]
(Cossato 2008)

Given the current situation of NI research within CIS, we can argue that there still exists a need for longitudinal studies on NI that can provide new data about how translation competence emerges and develops in bilingual children.

At the same time, a longitudinal study of NI based on a computerized corpus that is ready available and accessible could be used not only to address the main concerns of CIS research but also to make it possible to conduct systematic analyses of linguistic aspects that could be replicated by other authors interested in focusing on the same or other linguistic variables.

In order to address these two main shortcomings in the study of NI and CIS, we have conducted an analysis of the data from two English/Spanish bilinguals, which we present in the next section. Both the data as well as the programs for transcription and analysis could be accessed freely through the CHILDES project (MacWhinney 2000).

4. A longitudinal bilingual corpus-based study on NI using CHAT/CLAN

Our study presented below includes information relative to the participants (the bilingual children Simon and Leo), the corpus (the FerFuLice corpus available through the CHILDES project), the linguistic variables we set to study (both the purely linguistic ones as well as those involving contextual factors) and the methodological proposal for the analysis of these data (the codification of NI by means of the CHAT/CLAN software (MacWhinney 2000)).

Therefore, the focus of our analysis will be those occurrences where Simon and Leo interpret naturally from English into Spanish (or vice versa) when the situation requires it. A case in point would be the one in 5, where Simon, at the age of 3 years and 9 months, gives some information in English, «I want my lollipop», to his mother, Melanie, and then he translates the same message into Spanish, «yo quiero mi chupa chups», because this is the language the children use to address his father, Ivo.

(5)
[Context: Simon and Leo are playing with their parents at home]
*SIM: mommy I wan(t) my lollipop I want to suck my lollipop .
*MEL: after breakfast .
*LEO: my lollipop +...
%com: the boys go off camera with their father
*IVO: nunca desayunan bien y los sábados no desayunan porque desayunan muy tarde.
*SIM: yo quiero mi chupa chuns [: chups] [% to Ivo] .
                                                                    [3;09]
                                                          (FerFuLice corpus)

4.1. The participants

Our study analyzes the linguistic production of two English/Spanish bilingual identical twins, Simon and Leo, who were born in Salamanca, Spain. The linguistic context where they were raised was based on the so-called *one parent-one language* strategy, that is, since the moment they were born, the father, a native speaker of Peninsular Spanish, has always addressed the children in Spanish, and the mother, a native speaker of American English, speaks to them only in English. The parents generally communicate in Spanish with each other, except when a monolingual English speaker is present. Therefore, we can tell these children have acquired English and Spanish as their first languages in a monolingual-Spanish social context, a type of bilingualism that is referred to in the literature as individual bilingualism (Bhatia and Ritchie 2004).

During the first two years, the children received English input mostly from their mother. When they were two years old, the children started going to day care for three hours a day on weekdays, where the language of the staff and other children was Spanish. They also had contact with English speakers during two-month visits to the United States every summer[5].

4.2. The corpus and the type of data

The data from Simon and Leo are compiled in the FerFuLice corpus (Fernández Fuertes and Liceras 2009) in CHILDES (MacWhinney 2000). Two types of data comprise the FerFuLice corpus: spontaneous longitudinal data and experimental NI data.

As for the procedure followed in this longitudinal corpus, the data collected cover the age range of 1;01 to 6;11. The total of about 83 hours of recordings on videotape and DVD include 178 sessions, of which 117 are in an English context (i.e. with an English interlocutor such as the researcher or their mother) and 61 in a Spanish context (i.e. with a Spanish interlocutor such as the researcher or their father). The English sessions outnumber the Spanish ones because they were shorter and recorded on consecutive days. The recordings were made at intervals of 2-3 weeks until age 3;00 (with some interruptions during the summer holidays), and then once a month. The children were recorded in naturalistic settings, usually at home, and they were mostly engaged in normal playing activities with the interlocutor(s) and/or their parents.

The FerFuLice corpus also includes experimental data in order to balance out the intrinsic limitations of spontaneous data and in order to further explore NI. A total of three experimental tests on NI were designed to elicit oral experimental data. In these tests the children were asked to mediate between two monolingual speakers so that, in order for all to take part in the playing activity, Simon and Leo needed to perform NI[6]. Simon and Leo were tested in three consecutive years and at different ages (4;10, 5;05 and 6;03). The experimental sessions were video recorded and they lasted for almost two hours in total (34, 28 and 42 minutes, respectively).

---

[5] More information on the participants in the FerFuLice corpus can be obtained in the manual section in the CHILDES project (<http://childes.psy.cmu.edu/manuals/04biling.pdf>) as well as in Fernández Fuertes and Liceras (2010).

[6] Swain (1972) had already used the same procedure in the longitudinal data of an English/French bilingual child, Michael (3;01-3;09), although the aim of her research was not the analysis of his translations but mainly the language interference in interrogative constructions.

4.3. The linguistic variables

In order to provide a linguistic analysis of the NI cases produced by Simon and Leo, we establish a total of six linguistic variables. These have to do with the type of NI activity taking place (table 1) or with the linguistic context where the NI activity takes place (table 2). With respect to the NI activity, variable 1 considers whether the activity has been performed completely, that is, the source text (ST) has a corresponding target text (TT) (i.e. complete NI), or only partially because items from the ST have not been set in the target language (i.e. incomplete NI), or rather only a ST exists with no corresponding TT (i.e. null NI). Variable 2 deals with the directionality of the NI activity, that is, out of the two languages involved (i.e. English and Spanish) which one is the source language and which one is the target language. Variable 3 captures the grammatical and interpretative mapping between the ST and the TT in terms of whether there is a total correspondence between the two (i.e. lexical pairings, resulting or not from a communicative need) or the TT includes more information than the ST (i.e. expansive NI) or is rather less informative (i.e. economic NI).

1	2	3
ACTIVITY	DIRECTIONALITY	GRAMMAR-INTERPRETATION MAPPING
- complete	- SP into EN	- lexical pairings
- incomplete	- EN into SP	- expansive
- null		- economic

Table 1. Linguistic variables for the analysis of NI cases

As in table 2, the context of the NI activity was also classified in terms of the type of stimulus the children receive to perform the NI activity (variable 4), the origin of the ST (variable 5) and the type of context in which it was produced (variable 6).

4	5	6
STIMULUS	ST ORIGIN	DATA TYPE
- induced	- auto-translation	- spontaneous
- own initiative	- others	- experimental
	- situational	

Table 2. Contextual linguistic variables for the analysis of NI cases

NI data were analyzed in terms of these variables for the total of 307 files that comprise the FerFuLice corpus and using the CHILDES software tools presented in the following section.

4.4. Methodology and procedure: CHILDES software tools

CHILDES (Child Language Data Exchange System) offers a free and open sharing and exchange of face-to-face oral conversational interactions, both monolingual and bilingual. Most importantly it involves the computerization of these interactions in transcripts in CHAT format in which the CLAN program can be run to perform different automatic analyses. An overview of CHAT and CLAN follows with specific reference to how the CHAT transcription and codification format and the CLAN analyses are used for the study of NI[7].

4.4.1. The CHAT system

CHAT (Codes for the Human Analysis of Transcripts) is the standard transcription and coding system for CHILDES. In a CHAT file, the conversations appear in the so-called main lines which start with an asterisk. Dependent tiers are lines typed below the main line that contain codes, comments, events, and descriptions of interest to the researcher and which start with a percentage symbol. Both the * symbol and the % symbol are followed by a three-letter code which respectively indicates the participant that is speaking and the type of information added regarding what was said. An example of a main line with its dependent tier appears in 6[8].

> (6)
> *MEL: what are you doing L ?
> %com: Camera pans over to Leo, giggling, attempting to climb onto the couch .
> *MEL: my goodness you don't seem like you want to do this puzzle .
> *LEO: I xxx roto@s .
> *$LEO: it fell .
> *MEL: well, you know, that's not breaking it, it's only kind of pulling it apart I'm glad to say .

---

[7] The CHILDES project includes two manuals: one for the transcription and codification of data in the CHAT format and another one for the analysis of these data using the CLAN program. These are freely available in the database manuals section (<http://childes.psy.cmu.edu/ manuals/chat.pdf> and <http://childes.psy.cmu.edu/manuals/ clan.pdf>).

[8] In the main lines non-letter characters such as the sign @ can be used within words to express special meanings. The @s marker that appears in 6 and 7 indicates that, in an English conversation, the word marked with @s comes from Spanish. The @i marker that appears in 9 signals the word as an interjection. For more information on these and other markers see the CHAT manual (<http://childes.psy.cmu.edu/manuals/chat.pdf>).

The different NI cases found in the FerFuLice corpus were codified in a dependent tier called %nic (natural interpreting cases) especially incorporated for the present study. In order to provide the specific codes linked to the variables described in section 4.3. above, a codes-nic.cut file has been created. The 369 lines in the codes-nic.cut file allow us to set the coder mode and classify each of the NI cases found in the data. An example of two main lines containing a NI instance produced by Leo appears in 7.

(7)

*MEL:	how do you say ahora@s yo@s in English ?
*LEO:	ahora@s yo@s, my turn .
%nic:	$NIC:SE:LexNC:Ind:Oth:Spo

The dependent tier %nic codifies the different NI cases found in the oral production, both spontaneous and experimental, of Simon and Leo. As in the %nic line in 7 above, all instances are codified using the six variables in tables 1 and 2 as follows: first the activity is indicated (complete NI in this case: NIC), then the directionality (from Spanish into English in this example: SE), the type of mapping (lexical pairing with no communicative need: LexNC), the stimulus (as an induced NI instance here: Ind), the origin of the ST (others, the mother in this case: Oth) and finally the data type (spontaneous: Spo).

The CHAT format allows us, therefore, not only to use a transcription language common to all other corpora in CHILDES but also to provide a codification of these data in an automatic way by means of the codes-XXX.cut file. This same procedure can be applied to the 28 bilingual corpora available in CHILDES as of today[9].

Data in CHAT format and codified with the %nic dependent tier can now be used as input to run CLAN.

---

[9] New data are frequently being incorporated in CHILDES and constant updates appear in The child language bulletin available online at <http://www.iascl.org/clb.html>. Besides, CHILDES is in fact one of the focus areas of a more comprehensive project, TalkBank (a system for sharing and studying conversational interactions), available at <http://talkbank.org>. TalkBank includes, among others, CHILDES (the child component of TalkBank concerned with first language acquisition), and the BilingBank and the SLABank (concerned with second language acquisition). All the data in TalkBank share the CHAT/CLAN features presented in section 4.4. and could then be analyzed along the terms presented here.

4.4.2. The CLAN program: FREQ, KWAL and MLU

The acronym CLAN stands for Computerized Language ANalysis. It is a program that is designed specifically to analyze data transcribed in CHAT format. CLAN allows you to perform a large number of automatic analyses on transcript data. The analyses include frequency counts, word searches, co-occurrence analyses, MLU counts, interactional analyses, text changes, and morphosyntactic analysis.

One such analysis is FREQ which provides a counting of the data. The examples in 8a and 8b illustrate different outputs corresponding to one of the English files in the FerFuLice corpus (i.e. 24b_03).

(8a)

```
freq +t%nic +s"*Spo" @
*****************************************
From file < 4b_03_.cha>
Speaker: *MEL:
    0 Total number of different item types used
    0 Total number of items (tokens)
Speaker: *LEO:
1 $NIC:SE:CEc:Ind:ATr:Spo
2 $NIC:SE:LexNC:Ind:ATr:Spo
1 $NIC:SE:LexNC:Ind:Oth:Spo
1 $NII:SE:CEx:Ind:ATr:Spo
1 $Null:SE:Zmap:Ind:Atr:Spo
-----------------------------
    5 Total number of different item types used
    6 Total number of items (tokens)
Speaker: *SIM:
    0 Total number of different item types used
    0 Total number of items (tokens)
```

The FREQ output in 8a is the result of using the syntax line "freq +t%nic +s"*Spo" @" where the information given is as follows: the program selected (freq), the tier under analysis (%nic), the sequence under analysis, that is, the variable (all spontaneous NI instances, our variable 6) and finally the file(s) we want to analyze which, once they are selected, make the symbol @ appear in the syntax line. If no specific participant is selected in the syntax line (by adding, for instance +t*LEO), the analysis will take into account all the participants in the file(s). In this case, the three participants appear (Melanie, the mother, and Simon and Leo, the two target children) although only Leo produces spontaneous

NI instances in this specific file: a total of 6 cases (tokens) and of 5 different types, as the specific %nic lines indicate.

The FREQ output in 8b results from searching in the same file as in 8a for the NI cases which are lexical pairings (as in our variable 3) and, specifically, those that do not have a communicative need (LexNC).

(8b)
```
freq +t%nic +s"*LexNC*" @
****************************************
From file <24b_03.cha>
Speaker: *MEL:
  0 Total number of different item types used
  0 Total number of items (tokens)
Speaker: *LEO:
  2 $NIC:SE:LexNC:Ind:ATr:Spo
  1 $NIC:SE:LexNC:Ind:Oth:Spo
-------------------------------
  2 Total number of different item types used
  3 Total number of items (tokens)
Speaker: *SIM:
  0 Total number of different item types used
  0 Total number of items (tokens)
```

As the FREQ output in 8b shows, only one of the target children (i.e. Leo) produces these types of NI instances (3 tokens and 2 different types).

If the specific NI instance together with its context is needed, the KWAL program is run. KWAL searches for a keyword and outputs this keyword in a context. An example of a KWAL output is provided in 9.

(9)
```
kwal +t%nic -w3 +s"*LexNC*" @
kwal is conducting analyses on:
    ALL speaker tiers and those speakers' ONLY dependent tiers matching: %NIC
****************************************
From file <24b_03.cha>
-------------------------------------
line 22. Keyword: $nic:se:lexnc:ind:oth:spo
*LEO:  [^ singing] ooya@i ooya@i .
*SIM:  [^ wakes up crying] waaa@i .
*MEL:  how do you say ahora@s yo@s in English
       [^ speaking from behind camera] ?
*LEO:  ahora@s yo@s, my turn .
%nic:  $NIC:SE:LexNC:Ind:Oth:Spo
-------------------------------------
line 112. Keyword: $nic:se:lexnc:ind:atr:spo
*MEL:  ay@i don't step on the camera no .
*LEO:  lo@s quiero@s sí@s .
*MEL:  can you say that in English ?
*LEO:  lo@s quiero@s hold it that .
%nic:  $NII:SE:CEx:Ind:ATr:Spo $NIC:SE:LexNC:Ind:ATr:Spo
-------------------------------------
```

line 181. Keyword: $nic:se:lexnc:ind:atr:spo
*LEO: ese@s mio@s, tu@s este@s .
*MEL: can you tell me that in English ?
*LEO: yeah .
*LEO: me that you that .
%nic: $NIC:SE:LexNC:Ind:ATr:Spo

The KWAL output in 9 is the result of the syntax line "kwal +t%nic -w3 +s"*LexNC*" @" which is interpreted as follows: the program selected (kwal), the tier under analysis (%nic), how much context you want the program to select (3 utterances before the %nic line), the sequence under analysis (lexical pairings without a communicative need, one of the values of our variable 3) and finally the file(s) we want to analyze (represented by @). As in the FREQ output in 8b, there are 3 instances of this value and so KWAL provides the 3 instances in their contexts.

Since the data in our study (and in all other corpora in CHILDES) are longitudinal, an important value to measure linguistic development in acquisition data is the MLU. The MLU (Mean Length of Utterance) shows how long sentences are on an average and this has been taken as an indicator of language development and has been used to establish different stages in the acquisition process (Brown 1973). The MLU value is derived from two totals: the total number of utterances and the total number of either morphemes (standard MLU) or words (MLUw) for each speaker and in each file/transcript. The MLU could be automatically calculated by running the MLU program. The calculation of standard MLU values involves the incorporation of the dependent line %mor in the CHAT document. This line separates the morphemes that appear in the utterance in the main line so that the number of morphemes produced by the speaker is counted. If no such %mor lines are associated to the different main lines, the MLU program cannot count morphemes and thus has to ignore this line and count words in the main line. Since the FerFuLice corpus does not incorporate the %mor line, only MLUw values can be obtained and an example of an MLU output is shown in 10.

(10)
mlu +t*SIM +t*LEO -t%mor @
mlu is conducting analyses on:
ONLY speaker main tiers matching: *SIM; *LEO;
****
From file <56b_01.cha>

A methodological approach to the analysis of natural interpreting

> Speaker: *LEO:
> Number of: utterances = 55, words = 131
> Ratio of words over utterances = 2.382
> Standard deviation = 2.244
> Speaker: *SIM:
> Number of: utterances = 188, words = 820
> Ratio of words over utterances = 4.362
> Standard deviation = 5.257

The MLU output in example 10 is the result of using the syntax line "mlu +t*SIM +t*LEO -t%mor @" where the information given is interpreted as follows: the program selected (MLU), the tiers under analysis (i.e. the utterances produced by Simon and Leo, the target children), the indication for the program to ignore the tier %mor and finally the file(s) we want to analyze (in this case file 56b). The resulting MLU values, highlighted in grey, show that on an average Leo's utterances are 2 words long (MLU=2.3) while Simon's are longer, 4 words long (MLU=4.3). Information regarding the number of utterances as well as words per child is also provided in the MLU output.

Using the MLU program, we can calculate the different MLU values of the two target children in the entire FerFuLice corpus. This is what graphs 1 and 2 show: the increase in the MLU values of both children and in the two languages represents their linguistic development and, in particular, how this development is reflected in the increasing length of their utterances. In graphs 1 and 2 the different MLU values have been plotted and these correspond to spontaneous data (marked with blue stars for English and with red squares for Spanish) and to experimental data (the 3 NI experimental tests represented using green circles).

FREQ, KWAL and MLU are three of the 29 calculations that CLAN allows you to use, depending on the type of analysis you want to perform (e.g. KEYMAP lists the frequencies of codes that follow a target code; RELY measures reliability across two transcriptions). These automatic analyses render the classification of the NI instances produced by Simon and Leo in the FerFuLice corpus that will be discussed in the next section.

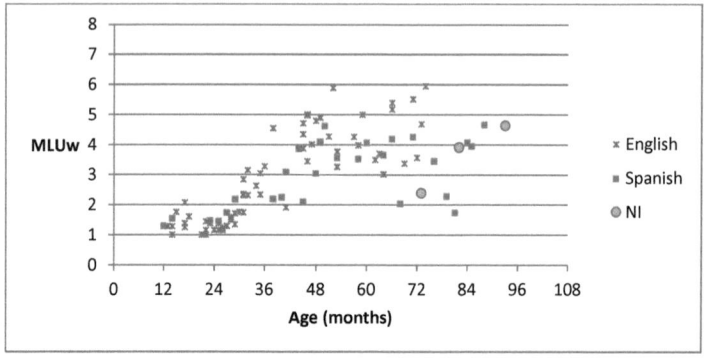

Graph 1. Developmental data: Leo´s MLU

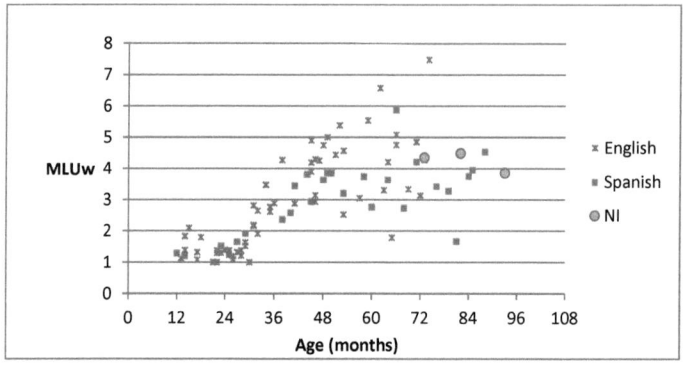

Graph 2. Developmental data: Simon´s MLU

4.5. NI data analysis sample based on CHAT/CLAN outputs

Using the CLAN program as shown above, all the NI cases that appear in the FerFuLice corpus have been extracted. The classifications that follow focus on the analysis of variables 1 and 3 which point to how successful the NI is in the case of these children and what type of grammar-interpretation mapping is established between the two languages involved in the interpreting process[10].

---

[10] See Álvarez de la Fuente and Fernández Fuertes (2012a) for a detailed description and discussion of the results derived from the rest of the linguistic and non-linguistic variables as well as for a developmental account based on MLU calculations.

Simon and Leo have produced a total of 247 occurrences (139 produced by Simon and 108 by Leo). Table 3 shows a classification of these occurrences in terms of our variable 1 (as in table 1 above).

	COMPLETE	INCOMPLETE	NULL
SIMON	**103** (74%)	7 (5%)	29 (21%)
LEO	**73** (67%)	4 (4%)	31 (29%)

Table 3. NI production: the type of activity

The children produce significantly more complete NI cases (all p-values<0,05) which shows that these children are able to interpret efficiently[11].

The complete NI cases in table 3 have been classified in table 4 in terms of the grammar-interpretation mapping that is produced. Most of the 176 complete NI cases correspond to lexical pairings not due to a communicative need (all p-values<0.05), although, in the case of Simon, the proportion of lexical pairings and economic translations is rather similar (p-value=0.121).

	PAIRING (NO CN)	PAIRING (CN)	ECONOMIC	EXPANSIVE
SIMON	**40** (39%)	13 (12%)	**32** (31%)	18 (17%)
LEO	**37** (50%)	12 (16%)	15 (20%)	9 (12%)

Table 4. COMPLETE NI production: grammar-interpretation mapping

This distribution of complete NI instances reflects that the interpreting activity is in a way inherent to the bilingual acquisition process; that is, that interpreting is part of the linguistic ability bilingual children have and it is not a product of an experimental context or exclusively triggered by specific contextual factors.

A developmental representation of both the spontaneous and experimental NI cases appears in graph 3.

---

[11] We have carried out statistical analyses (i.e. contrasts of proportions) in order to determine whether differences between values were significant or not.

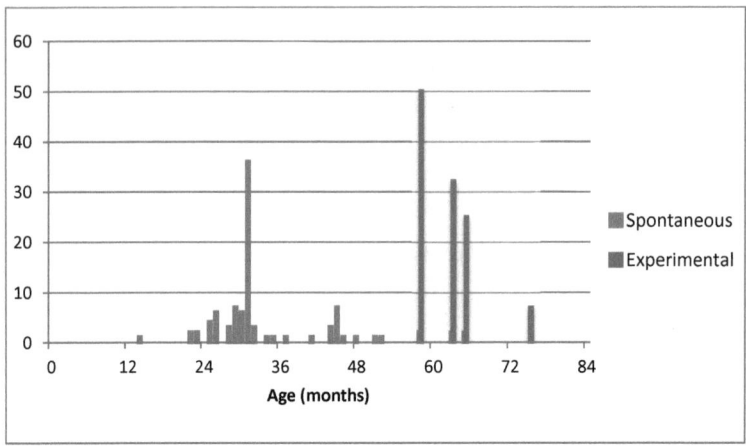

Graph 3. Developmental production of complete NIs

The information provided in graph 3 shows how these children's NI ability is maintained and developed through time so that NI is not a one-time activity but it is rather an intrinsic ability of their bilingual development.

5. Conclusions

This study is framed under the CIS research field and has been concerned with the linguistic analysis of NI cases using the CHAT/CLAN methodology designed for the CHILDES project (MacWhinney 2000). We have selected the English/Spanish FerFuLice corpus in CHILDES that involves the longitudinal oral production data from two English/Spanish bilingual children over a period of almost 6 years. By analyzing these data we have shown how the use of CHAT/CLAN constitutes a valuable e-tool that could be successfully incorporated in the CIS research field in general and for the study of NI cases in particular.

Our study points to an interdisciplinary area of research where the interaction between bilingual competence and interpreting competence offers a new perspective in the interpreting process analysis through the empirical research of NI based on longitudinal bilingual acquisition data. This perspective leads to the recognition and inclusion of other types of studies under CIS research, not as low-status or sub-corpora (Halverson 1998) but as legitimate objects of investigation and, therefore, studies of relevance and significance like those concerning the nature of translation.

The full exploitation of this new perspective requires the development of a new methodology based on a standardized system for data transcription and analysis, being a case in point the CHILDES project presented here. This project provides a unified transcription and codification system as a language common to all corpora (i.e. the CHAT transcription system, which involves written transcripts of oral data and, in some cases, pairing of transcripts and their corresponding audio or video files), as well as an e-tool that performs automatic analyses (i.e. the CLAN program). At the same time, this data bank provides a rich source of detailed transcripts of the linguistic production of simultaneous bilingual children with different language pairs, whose access is free and user-friendly for any researcher who is interested in examining real child data.

The analysis of longitudinal oral data based on a methodological tool - very well known in acquisition work but not so much in CIS research -has shown that the use of CHAT/CLAN can contribute to fill a research gap in the following three respects: the analysis of the interpreting process from a longitudinal perspective, the consideration of data from untrained interpreters and the use of a methodology and a computerized tool that both speeds up the process of quantitative and qualitative data analysis and leaves room for re-analysis of data under other or similar linguistic variables.

6. References

Álvarez de la Fuente, Esther & Raquel Fernández Fuertes. 2012a. How two English/Spanish bilingual children translate: in search for bilingual competence through natural interpretation. @ M.A. Jiménez Ivars & M.J. Blasco Mayor, eds. *Interpreting Brian Harris. Recent developments in translatology*. Viena: Peter Lang. ISBN 9783034305891, pp. 95-115.

Álvarez de la Fuente, Esther & Raquel Fernández Fuertes. 2012b. In search of the initial translator in translation and bilingualism studies. @ M.A. Jiménez Ivars & M.J. Blasco Mayor, eds. *Interpreting Brian Harris. Recent developments in translatology*. Viena: Peter Lang. ISBN 9783034305891, pp. 11-49.

Álvarez de la Fuente, Esther. 2008. *Análisis lingüístico de la traducción natural: datos de producción de dos niños gemelos bilingües inglés/español*. Doctoral dissertation, University of Valladolid. Madrid: ProQuest Information and Learning España. Available online at: <http://uvadoc.uva.es/handle/10324/71>. Accessed 23 February 2014.

Anderman, Gunilla & Margaret Rogers, eds, 2008. *Incorporating corpora. The linguist and the translator*. Clevedon: Multilingual Matters. ISBN 1853599859.

Angelelli, Claudia V. 2011. Expanding the abilities of bilingual youngsters: can translation and interpreting help? @ M.J. Blasco Mayor & M.A. Jiménez Ivars, eds. *Interpreting naturally. A tribute to Brian Harris*. Berne: Peter Lang. ISBN 9783034305884, pp. 103-120.

Azbel Schmidt, Morena. 2005. How do you do it anyway? A longitudinal study of three translator students translating from Russian into Swedish. @ *Stockholm Slavic Studies* 30. Stockholm: Stockholm University, ISSN 0585-3575. Available online at: <http://su.diva-portal.org/smash/get/diva2:197703/FULLTEXT01.pdf>. Accessed 23 February 2014.

Baker, Mona. 1993. Corpus linguistics and translation studies: Implications and applications. @ M. Baker, G. Francis & E. Tognini-Bonelli, eds. *Text and technology: In honour of John Sinclair*. Amsterdam: John Benjamins. ISBN 9789027221384, pp. 17-45.

Baker, Mona. 1995. Corpora in translation studies: An overview and some suggestions for future research. *Target* 7: 223-243, ISSN 1569-9986.

Bathia, Tej K. & William C. Richie, eds, 2004. *The handbook of bilingualism*. Oxford: Blackwell. ISBN 0631227342.

Beckmannova, Petra. 2004. Dolmetschen als angeborene Fähigkeit: das Phänomen des natürlichen Dolmetschens bei einem Bilingualen Kind im Alter von drei bis fünf Jahren – ein Tagebuch. Doctoral dissertation, University of Wien.

Bendazzoli, Claudio & Annalisa Sandrelli. 2009. An approach to corpus-based interpreting studies: Developing EPIC (European Parliament Interpreting Corpus). @ *MuTra-Challenges of multidimensional translation: Conference proceedings*. Available online at: <http://www.euroconferences.info/proceedings/2005_Proceedings/2005_Bendazzoli_Sandrelli.pdf>. Accessed 23 February 2014.

Bendazzoli, Claudio & Annalisa Sandrelli. 2009. Corpus-based interpreting studies: early work and future prospects. @ *Traudumatica 7. L'aplicció dels corpus linguistics a la traducció*, ISSN: 1578-7559. Available online at: <http:webs2002.uab.es/tradumatica/revista/num7/articles/08/08art.htm>. Accessed 23 February 2014.

Bendazzoli, Claudio, Annalisa Sandrelli & Mariachiara Russo. 2011. Disfluencies in simultaneous interpreting: a corpus-based analysis. @ A. Kruger, K. Wallmach & J. Munday, eds. *Corpus-based translation studies: Research and applications*. London: Continuum. ISBN 9781441115812, pp. 282-306.

Brown, Roger. 1973. *A first language: The early stages*. London: George Allen & Unwin. ISBN 9780674303263.

Bullock, Carolyn & Brian Harris. 1997. Schoolchildren as community interpreters. @ S.E Carr & R. Roberts, eds. *The critical link: interpreters in the community*. Amsterdam: John Benjamins. ISBN 9789027216205, pp. 227-235.

Cencini, Marco. 2002. On the importance of an encoding standard for corpus-based interpreting studies. @ *inTRAlinea. Online translation journal, Special issue*: CULT2K. ISSN 18-27-000X. Available online at: <http://www.intralinea.org/specials/article/On_the_importance_of_an_encoding_standard_for_corpus-based_interpreting_stu>. Accessed 23 February 2014.

Christoffels, Ingrid K., Annette M.B. de Groot & Judith F. Kroll. 2006. Memory and language skills in simultaneous interpreters: The role of expertise and language proficiency. @ *Journal of memory and language* 54: 324-345, DOI: 10.1016/j.jml.2005.12.004.

Cossato, Diana. 2008. La mediazione linguistica in contesti bilingui: la parola ai bambini. MA dissertation, University of Trieste.

Danks, Joseph H., Gregory M. Shreve, Stephen B. Fountain & Michael K. McBeath, eds, 1997. *Cognitive processes in translation and interpreting*. London: Sage. ISBN 9780761900542.

De Houwer, Annick. 1990. *The acquisition of two languages from birth*. Cambridge: MIT Press. ISBN 9780521024358.

Edwards, Jane A. 1995. Principles and alternative systems in the transcription, coding and mark-up of spoken discourse. @ Geoffrey N. Leech, Greg Myers & Jenny Thomas, eds. *Spoken English on computer: transcription, mark-up and application*. London: Longman. ISBN 9780582250215, pp. 19-34.

Fernández Fuertes, Raquel, Esther Álvarez de la Fuente & Juana M. Liceras. 2007. Los datos de adquisición bilingüe inglés/español: separación y mezcla de códigos. @ Ricardo Mairal, ed. *Aprendizaje de lenguas, uso del lenguaje y modelación cognitiva: perspectivas aplicadas entre disciplinas*. Madrid: UNED. ISBN 9788461168972, pp. 247-261.

Férnandez Fuertes, Raquel & Juana M. Liceras, coords, 2009. English/Spanish bilingual data. @ *The CHILDES database*. Available online at: <http://childes.psy.cmu.edu/data/Biling/FerFuLice.zip>. Accessed 23 February 2014.

Fernández Fuertes, Raquel & Juana M. Liceras. 2010. Copula omission in the English developing grammar of English/Spanish bilingual children. @ *International journal of bilingual education and bilingualism* 13/5: 525-551.

Genesee, Fred. 2003. Rethinking bilingual acquisition. @ J-M. Dewaele, A. Housen & L. Wei, eds. *Bilingualism: beyond basic principles. Festschrift in honour of Hugo Baetens Beardsmore*. Clevedon: Multilingual Matters. ISBN 9781853596254, pp. 204-228.

Genesee, Fred, Elena Nicoladis & Joanne Paradis. 1995. Language differentiation in early bilingual development. @ *Journal of child language* 22/3: 611-631.

Gerloff, Pamela. 1988. From French to English: A look at the translation process in students, bilinguals and professional translators. Doctoral dissertation, Harvard University.

Gómez Hurtado, Mª Isabel. 2007. Traducir: ¿capacidad innata o destreza adquirida? @ *Quaderns. Revista de traducció* 14: 139-163, ISSN 1138-5790. Available online at: <http://www.raco.cat/index.php/quadernstraduccio/article/viewFile/70321/80556>. Accessed 23 February 2014.

Göpferich, Susanne. 2010. Data documentation and data accessibility in translation process research. @ *The translator* 16/1: 93-124.

Göpferich, Susanne & Riitta Jääskeläinen. 2009. Process research into the development of translation competence: where are we, and where do we need to go? @ *Across languages and cultures* 10/2: 169-191.

Granger, Sylviane, Jaques Lerot & Stephanie Petch-Tyson, eds, 2008. *Corpus-based approaches to contrastive linguistics and translation studies*. Amsterdam: Rodopi. ISBN 9789042010468.

Hall, Nigel. 2004. The child in the middle: agency and diplomacy in language brokering events. @ G. Hansen, K. Malmkjaer & D. Gile, eds. *Claims, changes and challenges in translation studies*. Amsterdam: John Benjamins. ISBN 9789027216564, pp. 285-297.

Halverson, Sandra. 1998. Translation studies and representative corpora: Establishing links between translation corpora, theoretical/descriptive categories and a conception of the object of study. @ *Meta* 43: 494-514.

Harris, Brian. 1977. The importance of natural translation. @ *Working on papers in bilingualism* 12: 96-114.

Harris, Brian. 1980a. How a three-year-old translates. @ *Patterns of bilingualism*. Singapore: National University of Singapore Press. ISBN 9789971740009, pp. 370-393.

Harris, Brian. 1980b. Elicited translation by a three-year old English/French bilingual. @ D. Ingram, F.C.C. Peng & P. Dale, eds. *Proceedings of the first international congress for the study of child language*. Association for the study of child language: University Press of America. ISBN 9780819110848, pp. 610-631.

Harris, Brian. 2003. Aspects of interpretation. @ *Curso superior de traducción*. Valladolid: University of Valladolid.

Harris, Brian. 2013. An annotated chronological bibliography of natural translation studies with native translation and language brokering 1913-2012. @ *Academia. edu*. Available online at: <https://www.academia.edu/5855596/Bibliography_of_natural_translation>. Accessed 23 February 2014.

Harris, Brian & Bianca Sherwood. 1978. Translating as an innate skill. @ D. Gerver & W.H. Sinaiko, eds. *Language interpretation and communication*. New York: Plenum. ISBN 9780306400513, pp. 155-170.

Jääskeläinen, Riitta & Sonja Tirkkonen-Condit. 1991. Automatised processes in professional vs. non-professional translation: a think-aloud protocol study. @ S. Tirkkonen-Condit, ed. *Empirical research in translation and intercultural studies*. Tübingen: Gunter Narr Verlag. ISBN 9783823340751, pp. 89-110.

Knapp-Potthoff, Annelie & Karlfried Knapp. 1987. The man (or woman) in the middle: discoursal aspects of non-professional interpreting. @ K. Karlfried, W. Enninger & A. Knapp-Potthoff, eds. *Analyzing intercultural communication*. Berlin: Mouton. ISBN 0899253334, pp. 181-211.

Köppe, Regina & Jürgen Meisel. 1995. Code-switching in bilingual first language acquisition. @ L. Milroy & P. Muysken, eds. *One speaker, two languages: cross-disciplinary perspectives on code-switching*. Cambridge: Cambridge University Press. ISBN 9780521479127, pp. 276-301.

Kruger, Alet, Kim Wallmach & Jeremy Munday, eds, 2011. *Corpus-based translation studies. Research and applications*. London: Continuum. ISBN 9781441115812.

Laviosa, Sara. 1998. The corpus-based approach: A new paradigm in translation studies. @ *Meta* 43/4: 474-479.

Laviosa, Sara. 2002. *Corpus-based translation studies: Theory, findings, applications.* Amsterdam: Rodopi. ISBN 9789042014879.

Laviosa, Sara. 2008. Corpora & Translation Studies. @ S. Granger, J. Lerot & S. Petch-Tyson, eds. *Corpus-based approaches to contrastive linguistics and translation studies.* Amsterdam: Rodopi. ISBN 9789042010468, pp. 45-54.

Laviosa, Sara. 2011. Corpus-based translation studies: Where does it come from? Where is it going? @ A. Kruger, K. Wallmach & J. Munday, eds. *Corpus-based translation studies: Research and applications.* London: Continuum. ISBN 9781441115812, pp. 13-32.

Leopold, Werner F. 1939-1949. *Speech development of a bilingual child. A linguist's record.* Evanston, IL: Nortwestern University Press. ISBN 9780404507060.

Lising, Loy. 2008. Translation: A bilingual metalinguistic skill that facilitates better comprehension. @ A. Nikolaev & J. Niemi, eds. *Two or more languages: Proceedings from the 9th Nordic Conference on Bilingualism.* Joensuu, Finland: University of Joensuu. ISBN 9789522191007, pp. 134-146.

Lörscher, Wolfgang. 1992. Process-oriented research into translation and implications for translation teaching. @ *Interface* 6/2: 105-117.

Lozes-Lawani, Christiane. 1994. *La traduction naturelle chez les enfants fon de la Republique de Benin.* Doctoral dissertation, University of Ottawa.

MacWhinney, Brian. 2000. *The CHILDES project: tools for analyzing talk.* Mahwah, NJ: Lawrence Erlbaum Associates. ISBN 9780805829952. Available online at: <http://childes.psy.cmu.edu>. Accessed 23 February 2014.

Malakoff, Marguerite & Kenji Hakuta. 1991. Translation skills and metalinguistic awareness in bilinguals. @ E. Bialystok, ed. *Language processing in bilingual children.* Cambridge: Cambridge University Press. ISBN 9780521379182, pp. 141-166.

Meyer, Bernd. 2008. Interpreting proper names: Different interventions in simultaneous and consecutive interpreting. @ *trans-kom* 1/1: 105-122. ISSN 1867-4844. Available online at: <http://www.trans-kom.eu/bd01nr01/trans-kom_01_01_08_Meyer_Interpreting_Proper_Names.20080707.pdf>. Accessed 23 February 2014.

Monti, Cristina, Claudio Bendazzoli, Annalisa Sandrelli & Mariachiara Russo. 2005. Studying directionality in simultaneous interpreting through an electronic corpus. @ *Meta* 50/4. 1079-1147. ISSN 0026-0452. Available online at: <http://id.erudit.org/iderudit/019850ar>. Accessed 23 February 2014.

Moropa, Koliswa. 2011. A link between simplification and explicitation in English-Xhosa parallel texts: Do the morphological complexities of Xhosa have an influence? @ A. Kruger, K. Wallmach & J. Munday, eds. *Corpus-based translation studies. Research and applications.* London: Continuum. ISBN 9781441115812, pp. 259-281.

Olohan, Maeve. 2004. *Introducing corpora in translation studies.* London: Routledge. ISBN 9780415268844.

Pöchhacker, Franz, Arnt L. Jakobsen & Inger Mees, eds, 2007. *Interpreting studies and beyond: A tribute to Miriam Shlesinger.* Copenhagen: Samfundslitteratur. ISBN 9788759313497.

Ronjat, Jules. 1913. *Le developpement du langage observe chez un enfant bilingue.* Paris: Librairie Ancienne H. Champion.

Setton, Robin. 2011. Corpus-based interpreting studies (CIS): Overview and prospects. @ A. Kruger, K. Wallmach & J. Munday, eds. *Corpus-based translation studies. Research and applications.* London: Continuum. ISBN 9781441115812, pp. 33-75.

Sherwood, Bianca. 2000. *Features of NT in a language testing environment.* Doctoral dissertation, University of Ottawa.

Shlesinger, Miriam. 1998. Corpus-based interpreting studies as an offshoot of corpus-based translation studies. @ *Meta* 43/4: 486-493.

Shlesinger, Miriam. 2008. Towards a definition of interpretese. An intermodal, corpus-based study. @ H. Gyde, A. Chesterman & H. Gerzymisch-Arbogast, eds. *Efforts and models in interpreting and translation research. A tribute to Daniel Gile.* Amsterdam: John Benjamins. ISBN 9789027291080, pp. 237-253.

Straniero Sergio, Francesco. 2012. Using corpus evidence to discover style in interpreters' performances. @ F. Straniero Sergio & C. Falbo, eds. *Breaking ground in corpus-based interpreting studies.* Viena: Peter Lang. ISBN 9783034310710, pp. 211-230.

Straniero Sergio, Francesco & Caterina Falbo. 2012. *Breaking ground in corpus-based interpreting studies.* Viena: Peter Lang. ISBN 9783034310710.

Swain, Merrill K. 1972. *Bilingualism as a first language.* Doctoral dissertation, University of California, Irvine.

Tirkkonen-Condit, Sonja. 1990. Professional vs. non-professional translation: a think-aloud protocol study. @ M.A.K Halliday, J. Gibbons & H. Nicholas, eds. *Learning, keeping and using language.* Amsterdam: John Benjamins. ISBN 9789027220745, pp. 381-394.

Tirkonnen-Condit, Sonja, ed, 1991. *Empirical research in translation and intercultural studies.* Tübingen: Gunter Narr Verlag. ISBN 9783823340751.

Tirkkonen-Condit, Sonja & Riitta Jääskeläinen, eds, 2000. *Tapping and mapping the processes of translation and interpreting.* Amsterdam: John Benjamins. ISBN 9789027216427.

Tommola, Jorma & Yves Gambier, eds, 2006. *Translation and interpretating: Training and research.* Turku: University of Turku. ISBN 9789512930456.

Toury, Gideon. 1995. *Descriptive translation studies and beyond.* Amsterdam: John Benjamins. ISBN 9789027224484.

Tse, Lucy. 1996. Language brokering in linguistic minority communities: the case of Chinese-and Vietnamese-American students. @ *The bilingual research journal* 20/3-4: 485-498.

Valero Garcés, Carmen. 2012. FITISPos[TM]: Research - Action in public service interpreting and translation. @ M.A. Jiménez Ivars & M.J. Blasco Mayor, eds. *Interpreting Brian Har-*

ris. Recent developments in translatology. Viena: Peter Lang. ISBN 9783034305891, pp. 203-225.

Von Raffler-Engel, Walburga. 1970. The concept of sets in a bilingual child. *@ Actes du X congres international des linguistes.* Romania: Editions de l'Academie de la Republique Socialiste de Roumanie.

Walichowski, Miranda. 2001. Language brokering: laying the foundation for success and bilingualism. *Research in bilingual education. Symposium conducted at the annual educational research exchange.* College Station, Texas.

Woolls, David. 2000. From purity to pragmatism: user-driven development of a multilingual parallel concordancer. S.P. Botley, A.M. McEnery & A. Wilson, eds. *Multilingual corpora in teaching and research.* Amsterdam: Rodopi. ISBN 9789042005518, pp. 116-133.

Yudes, Carolina, Pedro Macizo & Teresa Bajo. 2011. The influence of expertise in simultaneous interpreting on non-verbal executive processes. *Front psychol* 2: 309. DOI: 10.3389/fpsyg.2011.00309. Available online at: <http://www.ncbi.nlm.nih.gov/pmc/articles/PMC3203554/>. Accessed 23 February 2014.

ELF pragmatics and interpreting

[Pragmática del inglés como lengua franca e interpretación]

CLARA PIGNATARO
IULM University (Italy)
clara.pignataro@iulm.it

Abstract: English as a lingua franca (ELF) has become a worldwide phenomenon (Kellet Bidoli 2012), posing challenges to interpreters (Kurz 2008) and to interpreter trainers that have not been studied in depth (Albl-Mikasa 2010). With globalization most communication is taking place between second language users and the fact that English has become a worldwide lingua franca has significant linguistic (Cogo and Dewey 2012) and pedagogic implications. Against this background, a corpus-driven analysis is being carried out on video recorded face-to-face interactions (Cogo 2009, Straniero Sergio 2012) interpreted in consecutive mode, from English into Italian, by Italian conference interpreters during Literature Festivals with the aim to raise interpreting students' awareness about the impact that ELF pragmatics has on the interpreter's comprehension and production process and encourage them to develop their own ELF pragmatics (Keckses 2014, Murray 2013).
Keywords: English as a Lingua Franca (ELF); corpus-driven studies; conversation analysis; face to face interactions

1. Introduction

Interest in English as a lingua franca (henceforth ELF) has generated a growing amount of empirical research in the attempt to describe the nature of ELF interactions (Murray 2012) but it is only recently that the attention of researchers has focused on the implications for interpreters: "English is silently pervading interpreting settings in its many varieties and guises so that interpreters are increasingly confronted with a wide range of *Englishes* of different linguistic origins, more often than not with far from standard phonology, lexis and syntax" (Kellet Bidoli 2012: 14). ELF speakers use pragmatic and interactional strategies to promote communication, and create a positive communicative experience (Cogo and Dewey 2012: 139) to "prevent, avert or pre-empt problems of misunderstanding" (Mauranen 2006). The general point is that interpreting from ELF speakers is more demanding and requires the use of proactive strategies (Murray 2012: 321) such as repetition, paraphrase and self-repair to make the target text

(TT) more coherent, with an extra cognitive effort and involvement for the interpreter and pragmatic competence.

More specifically, my intent is to observe how language is used in ELF interpreter-mediated face-to-face interactions and how ELF pragmatics impact on the interpreter's work where he/she acts as an active participant in the co-construction of meaning. Drawing upon Cogo and Dewey (2012), the overall aim my work is to conduct a corpus-driven analysis of pragmatic strategies used in ELF face-to-face mediated interactions (Cogo 2010: 297) with a focus on the cooperative work of participants and on the interpreter's pragmatic competence (Kecskes 2014). More precisely, in this paper, I will focus on the participants' use of *interactional features* such as, *additions* and *paraphrase* to ensure "smooth delivery and efficiency of the exchange" (Cogo 2010: 302). Drawing on a larger ethnographic project on ELF pragmatics, this study focuses on a sub-corpus of recorded and transcribed interpreter-mediated ELF interactions which occurred in the context of Literature Festivals to which I apply a combination of corpus techniques and techniques of Conversation Analysis within a pragmatic framework in order to spot "patterned interactional behaviours" (Firth 2009: 164) focusing on the way interpreters participate in the interaction by accommodating and manipulating their target text to convey coherence (Beaugrande & Dressler 1981). The analysis is conducted using *Transana*, a software for qualitative analysis. The final aim of my corpus-driven investigation is to bring authentic data to the classroom of trainee interpreters, to show with authentic data how ELF language is used and manipulated through specific pragmatic strategies. My intention is not to outline general interactional norms to be applied to each and every ELF interaction context, but to identify the most recurring ones used by the interpreter to overcome hesitation moments in order to convey coherence to the TT. First, I will explore the peculiarities of ELF language and its research field, then I will focus on the context where the interactions take place, that is to say, Literature Festivals in Italy. The interpreter-mediated encounters involve non-native speakers (NNSs) using ELF as a language for communication. Then, drawing on my corpus, I will focus on the pragmatic strategies used by the interpreter to manipulate the target text to negotiate meaning (Firth 2009: 163).

2. ELF research field

English as a Lingua Franca (ELF) is a "thriving research field which has found its place in applied linguistics in the last decade"[1] and the body of ELF data available for analysis is substantial (Cogo and Dewey 2012). The first ELF corpus was launched in 2001, the Vienna Oxford International Corpus of English (VOICE[2]). In 2003 Mauranen announced another important corpus, the corpus of English as a Lingua Franca in Academic Settings (ELFA[3]). What's more important is that the research continues to grow: "what we have now is a thriving, vibrant and dynamic field of enquiry devoted entirely to the study of this type of English use" (Cogo and Dewey 2012: 4). ELF is a young discipline, even younger than Interpreting Studies; they both belong to the field of Applied Linguistics but "it is only recently that the two fields have begun to consider the mutual relevance of each other" (Albl-Mikasa 2013: 192) and it is only in the last decade that scholars have focused their attention on ELF impact on interpreting (Albl-Mikasa 2010, 2012, 2013; Reithofer 2010).

ELF interactions among non-native speakers work, and they do so "in intriguingly creative ways" (Albl-Mikasa 2012:101): meaning negotiation and mutual intelligibility are secured on the basis of "pragmatic intercultural and collaborative skills, accommodation and negotiation strategies, and creative appropriation of linguistic resources (Albl-Mikasa 2013: 102). As argued by Seidlhofer (2011) "ELF users find ways of meeting their functional requirements by exploiting the resource of the virtual language, and this involves breaking free from the constraints of established norms" (Seidlhofer 2011: 143). In particular, in multilingual and multicultural environment "the language is not considered fixed but negotiated online and determined by particular situational contexts" (Hülmbauer 2008: 29) and the language may vary during a meeting, depending on tasks and practical purposes (Hülmbauer 2008: 29). As Firth states "seen in terms of the participants' orientations to their own concerted activities, the dominant impression is that lingua franca talk is not only meaningful, it is also *'nor- mal'* and, indeed, *'ordinary'*. The crucial point, though, is that the talk is *made* 'nor- mal' and 'ordinary' by the participants themselves, in their local discursive practices"

---

[1] < http://www.english-lingua-franca.org/about/elf-ren >
[2] < https://www.univie.ac.at/voice/ >
[3] < http://www.helsinki.fi/englanti/elfa/elfacorpus#citation >

(Firth 1996: 242). It is this *normality* that the interpreter has to come to terms with, in order to overcome hesitations and become an active participant and co-constructor of meaning in the interactions. According to Firth, normality in ELF talk is achieved by the participants through a "situated application of a range of conversational mechanisms [...] and resources giving rise to different kinds of interactional work" (Firth 1996: 240). Norms and strategies are not to be applied or used in absolute terms: the context determines the most appropriate interactional strategies to be adopted.

> The mobilization of conversational mechanisms and resources *can be* done differently in some circumstances, thereby giving rise to different kinds of 'interactional work' than has been accounted for previously in monolingual studies. Such 'interactional work' has two major aims: first, to pursue, through talk, substantive institutional goals (e.g. to agree upon conditions of economic exchange); second, to furnish the talk with a 'normal' and 'ordinary' appearance in the face of sometimes 'abnormal' and 'extra- ordinary' linguistic behaviour. (Firth 1996: 242)

and

> ELF interactants are highly pragmatic, opting for a kind of communication that enables them to get business done without forcing them to adopt pragmatic behaviours with which they may be uncomfortable. It is that virtual willingness to compromise that makes ELF talk so apparently robust and consensus oriented, and, in part it works because participants are effectively agreeing to adopt an intersociety persona that does not threaten the individual (Murray 2012: 322).

Learning to behave as an *intersociety persona* is of vital importance for interpreters in ELF settings. And it is through the observation and analysis of professional interpreters working in real contexts that trainees can become aware of appropriate pragmatic behaviours.

2.1. The context: Consecutive interpreting for literary festivals

Consecutive Interpreting is the preferred translation methodology at Literature Festivals, but not a classical consecutive, a more flexible; notes are taken and not always read due to time constraints therefore the interpreter must memorize to convey the gist of the source text. Indeed, Consecutive Interpreting (CI) used during Literature Festivals is a *sui generis* consecutive interpreting: the dialogic context with rapid answer-question turns imposes time constraints that modify the way interpreters are used to applying their consecutive technique. First of all, the interpreter is forced to resort to what Mead describes a "non-linear approach with a view to maximizing impact" (2012:172). In most cases the event is "an interview, reading or presentation involving one or more authors [...] the writers involved are mostly Italian-speaking; for those who are not, interpretation is provided in order to ensure that they can be followed by a largely Italian-speaking audience" (Mead 2012: 174). The classic interpreting format for these events is a one-to-one interview with an author, lasting about one hour and a half with the interpreter sitting next to the author/s. During the interview a whispered interpretation is provided to the author when Italian speakers ask questions and when the authors answer the interpreter uses a microphone to interpret consecutively the speaker's answers for the target audience. The authors' comments do not have a fixed duration, but they are kept short to enable the interpreter to transfer the content to the audience and to ensure fluidity of speech. Generally speaking, the "content of the interviews is not all the times literary" (Mead 2012: 175) and even "when the discussion is focused on writing and books the writer's perspective and register are often not strictly literary" (Mead 2012: 176); speakers attempt to communicate and "establish a rapport with the audience" and authors tend to use "humour as an ice-breaker" (Mead 2012: 175) to involve the audience. The interpreter's task here is thus to "convey information and a certain degree of explanation/argumentation" (Mead 2012: 176).

2.2. ELF and interpreting

Albl-Mikasa (2010) conducted an interesting study based on interviews and personal observations on how interpreters perceive ELF speakers. In her questionnaire survey among 32 professional interpreters it stands out that 69% of interpreters prefer source-text production by Native Speakers, because of their "reliable structures, accurate expressions, conscious choice of words, more pleasant idiomaticity, fewer mistakes/false friends, smoother word flow, fluency" (Albl-Mikasa 2010: 135) and only 6% prefer source text by NNSs. The interpreters complained that their work was increasingly challenging and tiring due to the additional cognitive load they had to expend in the comprehension phase to "grasp foreign accents and recover unfamiliar expressions, to resolve unorthodox syntactic structures and compensate for the lack of pragmatic fluency on the part of the non-native speaker" (Albl-Mikasa 2013: 192). More specifically, interpreters point to "capacity-related operational consequences" (Albl-Mikasa 2010: 135-136) when interpreting from non-native speakers, thus requiring "a higher level of concentration, additional listening effort, [...] additional effort for the correction of the source text prior to interpreting, additional processes aimed at disambiguation, [...] at unraveling unusual word combinations" (Albl-Mikasa 2010: 136). Native speakers are not necessarily easier, but more pleasant to interpret "as their speech flow, speech structure and precision in expression are conducive to the interpreters' task" (Albl-Mikasa 2010: 136). Moreover, it was also reported that their major hurdle was the restricted power of expression of ELF speakers. Non-native speakers have more difficulty in expressing the point they want to make, thus putting an extra effort on the interpreter's cognitive load. This extra cognitive load imposed on the interpreter makes his target text more redundant, with a wide use of additions, repetitions and re-phrasing. In the following section I will briefly describe the work I am carrying out to develop a corpus of English as a lingua franca in interpreting scenarios with the intent to apply it during interpreters' training sessions.

3. Developing the corpus: English as a Lingua Franca in Interpreting Scenarios (ELFIS)

ELFIS is an in-progress, parallel, multimodal corpus or speech corpus, compiled for research and training purposes, with the aim to studying interpreter-mediated interactions in ELF scenarios with a Conversation Analysis and Qualitative Analysis Approach. The media files are aligned with their transcript/s for analysis. The files are being downloaded from the web and they refer to Literature Festivals held in Italy. The data examined in this paper are a part of a larger work in progress of a corpus-driven research; they refer to an interview taking place on the occasion of Pordenone Legge, involving an Israeli writer and a singer, a guitarist and an Italian Interpreter. The first step was data collection and material selection. The process of data collection started in 2011 and the process is still continuing. The data are authentic and consist of 4 videos amounting to a total of 2 hours and 12 minutes involving the same interpreter. The source language is English and the target language is Italian. English is used by the participants as a contact language or lingua franca. The interpreting mode is consecutive (Mead 2012) and the directionality is English (B) into Italian (A). In particular, this interview was selected because it presents the interpreter "with the challenge of conveying emotional intensity" (Mead 2012: 178) which is often rendered by the interpreter through expansions/repetitions and additions to make the text function appropriately in the target culture. As illustrated by the data, repetitions and addition are used by the interpreter to convey coherence to the target text that lacks fluency. As already pointed out by Albl-Mikasa in her studies, non-native speakers present problems of express-ability (2013) and although communication in ELF interactions works the interpreters involved in such interactions perceive heavy "adverse effects [...] on their cognitive processing" (Albl-Mikasa 2013: 101) and this is due to the non-native speakers' "restricted power of expression" (ibid: 101). Therefore, as stressed by Albl-Mikasa (2013 b), an ELF pedagogy in interpreter training is needed, to make students aware (ibid: 11) about the changing working conditions and to work on comprehension and production strategies, "reconsidering their production competence" (ibid: 6). The idea to study ELF interpreter-mediated interactions goes towards the direction outlined by Albl-Mikasa (2013 a, 2013 b) in her preliminary suggestions for an ELF pedagogy in interpreter training[4] and in her ELF-oriented training proposal (Albl-Mikasa 2013 b).

3.1. Transcription

The first step in analysing media-based audio data is to create a transcript. All transcripts are the product of important analytic choices: what information should I transcribe? What information is reflected in the transcript? Transcribing a media file provides vital information about the content of a media file; only the part of the data I need for my particular analysis will be transcribed (partial transcription). Transcription within *Transana* is a manual process, but *Transana* has some interesting tools that make transcription faster and easier. One of *Transana*'s most useful features is its ability to link specific points in a video

---

[4] She outlines her suggestions in an interesting article: "Teaching Globish? The need for an ELF Pedagogy in Interperter Training" (2013) with the aim to spark a debate on such orientations. Her considerations are based on a 90,000-word corpus of in-depth interviews with 10 professional conference interpreters. The implications of ELF on interpreting are worrisome and it is only recently that they have become the object of research activities (Albl-Mikasa 2010, 2012, 2013; Reithofer 2010). On the basis of her studies she has identified adverse effects on ELF usage on interpreters in marketing conditions and as far as the processing and capacity management is concerned (for an in depth analysis see Albl-Mikasa 2013: 102). For the purpose of our study I will take into account the processing and capacity management issues.

with the corresponding points in the transcription; this connection is created manually by the researcher by inserting time codes. Time codes are markers in a transcript that help *Transana* synchronize the transcript and the video. The researcher may decide to use time codes in a variety of ways and place them in correspondence with a pause or at the border of a chunks of speech in order to be better able to compare the source text and the target text and isolate analytically significant segments. Smaller segments of speech can be analyzed more readily, and then linked to the rest of the utterance. When we speak we process speech in chunks of up to five words (Mauranen 2006: 220) and this is something we do naturally; though the delineation of these sequences of elements or chunks is "strictly empirical" (Goffman 1981: 213), for my analysis, I will refer to the notion of "chunking" (Mauranen 2006: 219) and I will try to investigate what happens within and among these chunkings in terms of text production and text manipulation or editing. This is why I decided to place time codes for audio-text synchronization at the end of each chunk, which usually corresponds with a unit of meaning and/or a pause. Though "strict linearity is too rigid a model for the production and reception of speech" (Mauranen 2006: 30) I will refer to the "pause" principle as a "valuable evidence for boundaries" (ibid: 30) and to chunking as a "sequence of elements or segments" to analyse as a basic minimal structure. In principle I will analyse the way the interpreter constructs his/her target text in a real time manner, where "no invisible mending is possible in the spoken form" (Goffman 1981: 211) but "invisible patching" (Goffman 1981: 211) is sometimes possible, for example, through repairs and additions. The link between the transcription and the media file is very useful for trainees: reading what is being said as the media file plays is crucial when searching for and analyzing analytically significant segments in the transcript. Transcripts are automatically saved in .rtf and they can be queried. *Transana* allows users to work with multiple transcripts. For the purpose of my study I decided to work both on source (ST) and target text (TT) and I keep them separated for methodological and practical reasons; the corpus is being used for training purposes and ST is used by students for practice in the classroom and contrasted with the TT and its transcript. Students are also encouraged to transcribe both source and target text for their own analysis. The corpus has not been POS-tagged because this is not the aim of the project; the purpose is to investigate interactions in ELF contexts and the impact of non native source speech on interpreters.

3.2. Research methodology

Lingua Franca interactions are being addressed from a Qualitative and Conversation Analysis (CA) approach to shed light on how ELF impacts on the interpreter's source text comprehension and production, more specifically on the interpreter's the pragmatic competence and his ability to produce a coherent target text through the use of additions and paraphrase as "interactional resources deployed and required in order to conduct meaningful, orderly and indeed ordinary discursive practices" (Firth 1996: 240). My research questions: RQ1: What happens to the target text when we interpret from an ELF speaker and RQ2: How to apply a corpus of ELF communicative events to interpreters' training? These research questions are very much related to one another, in the sense that the interpreter's target text quality is determined by the interpreter's capacity management skills and concentration. We know that the comprehension effort is put under stress and the workload is greater when the source text is from a non-native speaker (Albl-Mikasa 2010) and these difficulties are reflected in the interpreter's output, such as in text redundancy and repetitions, as it will be illustrated by the examples.

3.3. Corpus extraction procedures

Creating a corpus involves a series of challenges: recording the material or looking for the material on the web, selecting the interviews to be included into the collection, converting file formats, importing the video files into *Transana*, transcribing and categorizing video files and creating clips with analytically interesting features to be used in the classroom. Defining parameters for the selection of the communicative event to be included in the corpus was an important step in devising my corpus. Therefore, tracing the profile of the interpretation and identifying the "eligible" ones to be included was the very first step of my research. Following Straniero Sergio and Falbo's considerations (2013) the communicative event involving an interpreter can be described by five superordinate macro-factors and these are "interpreter, situational context, mode, language and directionality, type of interaction" (Straniero Sergio & Falbo 2012: 12). The combination of these macro-factors provides an image of the communicative event and a representation of the real world (Straniero Sergio & Falbo 2012). The selection of my corpus focuses on Literature Festivals and interpreter mediated interviews involving ELF speakers and an Italian interpreter, interpreting in consecutive mode from English into Italian. The videos were downloaded from the web, converted into MPEG1 and placed in *collections*. The video recorded interactions are imported, transcribed and analysed using *Transana*[5], a software for qualitative analysis. *Transana* is a software for qualitative analysis of visual and auditory data. The software lets the researcher to transcribe, visualize, code and analyse auditory data in a wide variety of ways. In *Transana* meaningful portions or analytically significant segments of videos can be identified from larger media files, categorized and searched through using the Search Tool function. These analytically important segments are called clips in *Transana* and they are basic analytic units; clips are placed in collections. The first analytic act a researcher performs is naming clips within a collection. A collection is a place where clips with something in common are placed, a theoretical construct or a container used for holding clips that are somewhat related to each other and a clip contained in that collection is a piece of evidence for that theoretical construct. For example, if I want to study additions I will create a collection named additions and place clips where additions are exhibited in that collection. Collections normally evolve as the understanding of data widens. A collection might start out as a broader construct such as additions; as you proceed and understand that construct better you may want to create sub categories of that broad construct such as paraphrase. Clips will be sorted and placed in these more nuanced subcategories or "nested collections" to elaborate a more nuanced understanding that emerged from the data.

4. An attempt to address RQ 1: what happens to the interpreted target text when we interpret from an ELF speaker?

An issue interpreters are facing in ELF contexts is the quality of English used by NNSs having different levels of proficiency; interpreting from ELF speakers is demanding and I illustrate my argument by looking at the 1) "adverse effects of ELF speaker's output" (Albl-Mikasa 2013: 101) which is reflected on the interpreters hesitations and the ways interpreters manipulate their target text through

---

[5] < www. *transana*.org >

repetitions. The analytical categories I am focusing on are proactive strategies: paraphrase, self-repair, repetitions that characterize ELF talk (Murray 2012, Mauranen and Ranta 2009, Hülmbauer 2008). Redundancy, repetitions and hesitations are typical manifestations of oral language and in consecutive interpreting they are used by the interpreter "to keep discourse smooth and open" (Straniero Sergio 2007: 341). Lichtkoppler (2007) focuses on the role of repetition in ELF highlighting its high frequency and stating that repetitions are used functionally and productively. Heike (1981 reported in Straniero Sergio 2007: 339) distinguishes between prospective repeats and retrospective repeats. The first is used to take time in speech planning and the second is used to establish cohesion with the previous part of the speech or to correct a wrong utterance. The active role of the interpreter is visible in the editing work in the TT. In order to cope with lack of smoothness in the ST the interpreter tends to produce a redundant text through additions, reformulations and repetitions. House suggests that "pragmatic fluency deficiency is responsible for non smoothness of the turn-making machinery and conversational mismanagement (House 2002: 236). The lack of smoothness of the TT makes the interpreter's work even harder as it is shown in the following extract:

4.1. Lack of smoothness in the source text and the use of repetition[6]

1. Speaker 1: when you where reading the passage about Marianne Faithfull (.) and about how mus-your life 2. actually ehm (.) changes your music

3. Interpreter: quando ti sentivo leggere questo passaggio che hai citato (.) Marianne Faithfull (.) è che

4. davvero// *la vita ti cambia* (.) *ti cambia* (.) *cambia la tua musica* (.) *cambia il tuo modo di cantare*

Backtranslation:

When I heard you reading this passage that you quoted about Marianne Faithfull (.) is that (.) life really// changes you (.) it changes you (.) changes your music (.) changes your way of singing

---

[6] Transcription conventions:
 A: Anchorman
 G: Guest
 I : Interpreter
 (.): pause < 3minutes
 :: lengthening of vowel

In segment [1] the non-smoothness of the TT is determined by silent and filled pauses. Topic negotiation and self-rephrasing ("mus-your life ehm changes") are used by ELF speakers to make discourse explicit and clearer to the interlocutor (Cogo 2006: 256) and "it has been found that it is used more often as an adjustment of form, rather than as a change of meaning. These adjustments are aimed at improving clarity and increasing explicitness" (Cogo 2006: 256). Also Hülmbauer, Bohringer, Seidlhofer (2008: 30) point out the potential functions of silent and filled pauses in ELF and state that "apart from serving as a means of gaining time for speech encoding, pauses may also play a role in the interactive creation of meaning or even act as structural markers of the speech event." Due to this pragmatic fluency deficiency, the interpreter displays involvement in the co-construction of meaning and this is evident in his editing work ("really changes// life really// changes (.) it changes you (.) changes your music (.) changes your way of singing") by repeating the verb "to change" the interpreter buys time to think what to say next (micro-planning) and reinforces the meaning of the word. What the interpreter does, after all, is not so different from what any other speaker does when addressing an audience. In fact, in spoken communication – and especially when speaking before an audience, we always try to conceal our difficulties, to avoid appearing too hesitant. For this reason, "it is better to repeat oneself, rather than simply stop speaking while the mind searches for another idea" (Francesco Straniero 2007: 472), avoiding those pauses that in television are perceived as "silent indecision" (Goffman 1981: 215, cited in Straniero Sergio 2007: 472).

> The hesitation or pause can constitute a negative notification, as it were: a blank is left where the speaker otherwise would have drawn attention to his error, the slot filled with what can be heard as silent indecision). The implication is that the speaker is intensely concerned with his predicament and is not in complete control of himself. It is as if he cannot contain his concern for whether or not he will manage himself as he would like; potential disaster seems to be in his mind. [...] and throughout, there is the sense that should the hearers turn on the speaker and remark on his error, he will have begun to show appropriate shame. (Goffman 1981: 215)

We know that "hesitations and doubt put the interpreter in a bad position, because they go against the expectations linked to his role as a professional of the spoken word" (Straniero Sergio 2007: 472).

Every time we outline the main differences between speech and writing the main feature that is mentioned is "its real time nature" (Mauranen 2009: 217) which is an "unavoidable hardship of life" (ibid). Although disfluencies and hesitations are "common features of normal speech" (ibid) we tend to describe these phenomena "in a somehow apologetic manner, as if in need of explanation or justification" (ibid). Boomer and Laver (1968:2 quoted in Goffman 1981: 206) suggest that:

> It is important to recognize that in speech "normal" does not mean perfect. The norm for spontaneous speech is demonstrably imperfect. Conversation is characterized by frequent pauses, hesitation sounds, false starts, misarticulations and corrections... In everyday circumstances we simply do not hear many of our own tongue-slips nor those made by others. They can be discerned in running speech only by adopting a specialized "proofreader" mode of listening. In ordinary conversation it is as though we were bound by a shared, tacit, social agreement, both as listeners and as speakers, to keep the occurrence of tongue-slips out of conscious awareness, to look beyond them, as it were, to the regularized, idealized utterance.

Additions and repetitions are also used to stress a concept and are accompanied by a prosodic mark or rising intonation as the work "change" is reiterated. Repeating or reformulating already expressed concepts contributes to conveying coherence to the interpreted text as "coherence is not a mere feature of texts, but rather the outcome of cognitive processes among text users […] a text does not make sense by itself but the sense is attained by the interaction of the knowledge present in the text with the receiver's stored knowledge of the world" (De Beaugrande and Dressler 1981:6).

4.2. Addition to preserve inter-turn coherence

> 5. A: [...] il titolo (.) di (.) di questa raccolta di (.) di racconti Ruti vuole dormire è (.) che è quella del
> 6. primo racconto (.) in realtà coglie un momento che è **importante per i bambini** (.) quello della sveglia o 7. dell'andare a letto e ehm: David Grossman ha: (.) ha raccontato anche in una: recente intervista fatta con noi
> 8. (.) quanto sia **importante mantenere (.) questo momento** (.) un moment (.) trovare un tempo di lettura pe:r
> 9. per i bambini e: (.) forse nello scrivere ehm (.) ehm (.) nello scrivere i racconti David (.) pensa anche a se stesso
> 10. come lettore di racconti (.) no? **è un momento particolarmente importante questo**
> Backtranslation:

M. [...] the title (.) of this collection of stories of (.) stories Ruti wants to sleep is (.) that is the one of the first story (.) actually revolves around an **important moment for children** (.) waking up time or bed time and ehm: David Grossman has (.) has told in a: recent interview with us about the **importance of keeping (.) this moment** (.) a **moment finding a moment to read to children** and: (.) maybe ehm (.) ehm (.) in writing his stories David (.) also thinks of himself as a reader of stories (.) don't you? **This is a particularly important moment**
11.G: [...] and and when (.) when I write for children I think about these **ten minutes no more than that in** 12. **the evening**
13. I: beh (.) quando appunto scrivo per i bambini cerco da-davvero di pensare a **quei dieci importantissimi** 14. **minuti la sera**
Backtranslation:
I: well (.) when I write for children I try to rea-really think of **those ten extremely important ten minutes in the evening**

In segment [2], the interpreter adds a reinforcer, with the superlative "quei dieci importantissimi minuti la sera" (line 14 "those very important ten minutes in the night"), referring to what the moderator said previously. Indeed, the moderator uses the adjective 'important' three times (in line 6, 8 and 10). The guest indicates his agreement with the moderator's statement, saying *«yes»* at the start of his reply. The interpreter uses the adjective "importantissimi" (line 13-14: "those ten extremely important minutes in the evening") in in order to maintain inter-turn coherence between the moderator's question and the guest's reply.

4.3. Paraphrase

It is sometimes difficult to distinguish additions from paraphrase. Sornicola subdivides paraphrase into "inter-textual and intra-textual" (Surnicola 1999: 30). The former are produced between texts of different speakers, or between different texts by the same speaker, while the latter occur in a single text produced by one or more speakers" (Sornicola 1999:30). In particular, inter-textual paraphrase "can characteristically be produced by a fully developed "paraphrasal competence". This consists of the ability to reformulate, which in addition to requiring a fairly ample stock of vocabulary and lexical structures (a necessary but not sufficient condition), but also a specific skill in transforming the text" (Sornicola 1999: 30). To Sornicola, paraphrase "is the most purely textual among the functions of discourse" (Sornicola 1999:30), with its own pragmatics. These can be divided into narrow-spectrum, or local paraphrases, and broad-spectrum paraphrases. For example, local paraphrases are those in which one glosses a lexeme with another lexeme or in which the structure of a sentence is transformed into another sentence structure, without expansion processes involved in the transformation. Broad spectrum paraphrases instead involve transformations through expansions of various kinds. In this case, we can say that paraphrases of spontaneous speech are often "broad spectrum paraphrases" (1999: 43). Moreover, in narrow spectrum paraphrases "the structures in paraphrastic relation are always adjacent in the linear dimension of the text, or at the most separated by one or two intermediate structures; in this case they could be called discontinuous narrow-spectrum paraphrases" (Sornicola 1999: 43). According to Straniero Sergio (2007), the interpreter makes recourse to synonyms, hyponyms and hypernyms, creating genuine paraphrastic chains and re-elaborating the antecedent lexical element and the ability to paraphrase is closely correlated with linguistic competence (Sornicola 1999) which is considered a useful tool for the identification of potential and reinforcement of linguistic skills.

The paraphrase is a "proactive strategy" (Murray 2012: 321) and it is used as a micro-planning device, as in the case of repetition (Straniero Sergio 2007). Straniero Sergio reports the observations made by Sornicola (1999: 48-49) apropos of the psycholinguistic nature of paraphrase, which, according to the author, apply perfectly to the interpreter:

> The initial informational content is reformulated, with additions that represent small increments or detours from the "initial plan". In this sense one can say that paraphrases of speech, even those that most closely approximate ideal structures, contain shifts within themselves, minimal though they may be. This is entirely natural, if we consider paraphrase phenomena as the other side of the interface between thought and linguistic activity, what we might call "thought in movement" and "linguistic plan in movement". This is a property of real speech rather than of ideal speech.

According to Straniero Sergio (2007), two factors determine the "paraphrasal development" of the source text by the interpreter, and these are 1) the principle of linearity, "which is an important requisite for producing a discourse" (Straniero Sergio 2007: 475) and 2) the speaker's communicative intent.

5. Trying to address RQ2: how to apply an ELF corpus to interpreter training?

Describing and understanding an emergent phenomenon which has become so prominent in our globalized world (Hülmbauer, Bohrlinger, Seidlhofer 2008: 33-34) requires observation of really occurring interactions (Laviosa 2002) and ELF research and corpus-driven interpreting (Straniero Sergio, Caterian Falbo 2012) studies can contribute to explore this world. Observing and analyzing interpreting strategies and norms through a corpus can become an interesting tool to raise students' awareness of intercultural phenomena in communication and pragmatic competence by focusing on the skills and strategies to be adopted in specific settings. As suggested by Murray (2012) these "awareness raising" sessions (Murray 2012: 320) provide trainees with the strategies "to negotiate their own hybrid pragmatics for each interaction and with whichever interlocutor they engage […] so that they create a kind of temporary space where participants negotiate a new pragmatics for current purposes and mutually agree to relinquish any firm allegiance to their L1 pragmatic norms" (Murray 2012: 321). Murray (2012) suggests three complementary strategy types: 1) empirically based strategies, based on what we have learnt from ELF pragmatics studies; 2) inductive strategies to raise trainees' awareness by using an inductive, bottom up approach "whereby the observations of particulars leads to an understanding of general principles" (Murray 2012: 321) and 3) deductive strategies that raise trainees' awareness by using a deductive, top-down approach "through which learners develop an appreciation of those general, universal principles that govern linguistic choices and the way in which we are appropriate with language" (Murray 2012: 321). I adopt both an inductive and deductive approach, by asking students to listen to and observe how the interactions take place and how the interpreted text is being manipulated. The training session is organized a specific ELF module for first year MA interpreting students as a complement to consecutive interpreting workshop. A theoretical framework is provided to students and the thematic focus is on pragmatic features of ELF communication and interpreting norms and strategies. Video files and their transcripts can be used as training/practice materials in the classroom and at home; the session can be guided or the exercise can be carried out at home for self-assessment purposes. It is important to explain to students that their interpreting norms and strategies can be analyzed only after a transcription of both source and target text has been made and *Transana* is a valuable tool that can be easily used by trainers and trainees to analyze and transcribe videos in the classroom and at home for practice. In the classroom, the teacher selects speeches by context and/ or by interactional features to illustrate a real life example of how interpreters act and react in specific ELF contexts and to encourage students to find their own pragmatic solution. The exercise in the classroom is organized as follows: the video is played and the students listen to the source language, then the video is stopped and the students are asked to take note of what they understood and they are asked to make their own consecutive; then the video is played again to listen to the consecutive interpretation performed by the professional interpreter and a discussion will follow. Students are asked to make their own comments on the interactional strategies used by the interpreter and on language-specific structures; the analysis is carried out both by listening and watching the video and by reading the transcript of the interpretation. Analyzing the interpreters' target text through transcription is extremely interesting for students who become easily aware of the pragmatic strategies adopted during interactions. At home, trainees can use *Transana* for assessment exercises and work on video files suggested by trainees or, more interestingly, they are encouraged to look for video files pertaining to the same speech genre, make their own transcription and analyze the interactions.

6. Concluding remarks

The unprecedented global spread of ELF poses challenges to the interpreting profession and interpreters' trainers (Albl-Mikasa 2010, 2013 b). Little research has been carried out on the effects of source text production on the interpreter's comprehension and production phase process in pragmatic terms (ibid).

The interaction discussed and analyzed in the context of Literature Festival has its peculiarities which can not be generalized. Nevertheless, the use of a corpus for the analysis of interpreted mediated interactions involving NNS provides learners with their own tools for analysis and the necessary strategies to negotiate their own "hybrid pragmatics for each interactional and with whichever interlocutor they engage" (Murray 2009: 321) and it can serve as a platform to "that raise learners' awareness by using an inductive, bottom-up approach whereby the observation of particulars leads to an understanding of general principles" (Murray 2009: 321). Transcribing and analysing interactions is a practice that encourages learners "to become their own ethnographers and observe how speech acts are realized" (Murray 2009: 320) while providing them with an opportunity to use authentic data and discover how ELF speakers' input affects their coping strategies (Albl-Mikasa 2013 b). In my approach I have been guided by 3 pedagogical principles. The first is that students can improve their interpreting skills by observing and analysing their own work and other interpreters' work through the transcription of the interpreted text. The second being that encouraging students to analyse interpreters' performances may contribute to sensitize them to the relationship between discourse practices and context. The third principle is a commonplace of interpreting pedagogy: people learn to interpret by interpreting. Students are asked to interpret particular passages to practice in imitation and to create their own interpreted text, helping them to understand that ELF conditions sometimes require. Through the observation of the pragmatic aspects of really occurring interpreted-mediated ELF interactions learners will be gradually encouraged to "induce those broader principles that govern the linguistic choices we make in order to communicate effectively and appropriately" (Murray 2009: 321) in a specific context and the "surprise effect" (Albl-Mikasa 2013 b: 8) and the frustration level produced by non-standard ELF language and pragmatic features would be lowered. This does not mean that new norms for interpreters working in ELF contexts will be proposed, rather, seen more in terms of a process rather than a product, the attempt is to raise the awareness of intercultural phenomena in communication.

7. References

Albl-Mikasa, Michaela. 2010. Global English and English as a Lingua Franca (ELF): Implications for the Interpreting Profession. @ *Trans-kom* 3/2: 126-148. Retrieved May 20, 2014, from < http://www.trans-kom.eu >.

Albl- Mikasa, Michaela. 2012. Interpreting Quality in Times of English as a Lingua Franca (ELF): New Variables and Requirements. @ L. Zybatow, A. Petrova & Michael Ustaszewski, eds. *Translation studies: old and new types of translation in theory and practice. proceedings of the 1st international conference translata, translation & interpreting research: yesterday? today? tomorrow?* Frankfurt am Main: Peter Lang. ISBN: 978-3631635070, pp. 267- 273.

Albl-Mikasa, Michaela. 2013 (a). Express-ability in ELF communication. @ *Journal of English as a Lingua Franca* 2/1: 101-122. DOI 10.1515/jelf-2013-0005.

Albl-Mikasa, Michaela. 2013(b). Teaching Globish? The need for an ELF Pedagogy in interpreter training. @ *International Journal of Interpreter Education*, 5/1: 3-16. ISSN: 2150-5772.

Beaugrande Robert de & Wolfang U. Dressler. 1981. *Introduction to Text Linguistics*. London: Longman. ISBN: 9789027207852.

Cogo, Alessia & Martin Dewey. 2012. *Investigating English as a Lingua Franca. A corpus-driven Investigation*. London/New York: Continuum International Publishing Group. ISBN 9781441137258.

Cogo, Alessia. 2009. Accomodating difference in ELF conversations: a study of pragmatic strategies. @ A. Mauranen & E. Ranta, eds. *English as a Lingua Franca: Studies and Findings*. Newcastle: Cambridge Scholar Press. ISBN 9781443817264, pp 254-273.

ELFA. 2008. *The Corpus of English as a Lingua Franca in Academic Settings*. Director: Anna Mauranen. Available at <http://www.helsinki.fi/elfa/elfacorpus> [Last accesses 20/05/14].

Firth, Alan. 1996. The discursive accomplishment of normality: on lingua franca English and conversation analysis. @ *Journal of Pragmatics* 26/2: 237-59.

Firth, Alan. 2009. The lingua franca factor. @ *Intercultural Pragmatics* 6/2: 147-170.

Goffman, Erving. 1981. *Forms of Talk*. Philadelphia: University of Pennsylvania Press. ISBN 0812277902.

House, Juliane. 2002. Developing Pragmatic Competence in English as a Lingua Franca. @ K. Knapp & C. Meierkord, eds. *Lingua Franca Communication*. Frankfurt am Main: Peter Lang. ISBN 9783631364604, pp. 245-267.

Hülmbauer, Cornelia, Heike Boheringer & Barbara Seidlhofer. 2008. Introducing English as a lingua franca (ELF): precursor and partner in intercultural communication. @ *Synergies* 3: 25-36.

Kecskes, Isvan. 2014. *Intercultural Pragmatics*. New York: Oxford University Press. ISBN 9780199892655.

Kurz, Ingrid. 2008. The impact of non-native English on students' interpreting performance. @ G. Hansen, A. Chesterman & H. Gerzymisch-Arbogast, eds. *Efforts and models in interpreting and translation research*. Amsterdam: John Benjamins. ISBN: 9789027216892, pp. 179–192.

Laviosa, Sara. 2002. *Corpus-based Translation Studies. Theory, Findings, Applications*. Amsterdam/New York: Rodopi. ISBN 9042014873.

Lichtkoppler, Julia. 2007. Male. Male. Male? The sex is male. The role of repetition in English as a lingua franca. @ *Vienna English Working Papers* 16/1: 39-65. Available at <http://anglistik.univie.ac.at/fileadmin/user_upload/dep_anglist/weitere_Uploads/Views/views_0701.PDF> [Last accessed 26/05/ 2014].

Mauranen, Anna & Elina Ranta. 2009. *English as a Lingua Franca: Studies and Findings*. Newcastle: Cambridge Scholars Press. ISBN 978-1-443812962.

Mauranen, Anna. 2006. Signaling and preventing misunderstanding in English as lingua franca communication. @ *International Journal of the Sociology of Language* 177: 123-150.

Mauranen, Anna. 2009. Chunking in ELF: expressions for managing interaction. @ *Journal of Intercultural Pragmatics* 6/2: 217-233.

Murray, Neil. 2013. English as a lingua franca and the development of pragmatic competence. @ *ELT Journal Volume* 66/3: 318-326.

Mead, Peter. 2012. Consecutive interpreting at a literature festival. @ C. J. Kellet Bidoli, ed. *Interpreting across genres: multiple research perspectives*. Trieste: EUT Edizioni Università di Trieste. ISBN: 9788883033650.

Reithofer, Karin. 2010. English as a lingua franca vs. interpreting. Battleground or peaceful co-existence. @ *The Interpreters' Newsletter* 15: 143-157.

Seildhofer, Barbara. *Understanding English as a Lingua Franca*. Oxford, UK: Oxford University Press. ISBN 9780194375009.

Sornicola, Rosanna. 1999. Un contributo allo studio sperimentale delle unità strutturali della parafrasi. @ L. Lumbell & B. Mortara Garavelli, eds. *Parafrasi. Dalla ricerca linguistica alla ricerca psicopedagogica*. Torino: Edizioni dell'Orso. ISBN 8876944206, pp. 29-49.

Straniero, Sergio, Falbo, Caterina. 2012. *Breaking Ground in Corpus-based Interpreting Studies*. Bern: Peter Lang AG. ISBN: 9783034310710.

VOICE. 2013. The Vienna-oxford international corpus of English (version 2.0). Director: Barbara Seidlhofer; Researchers: Angelica Breiteneder, Theresa Klimpfinger, Stefan Majewskj, Ruth Osimk-Teasdale, Marie-Luise Pitzl, Michael Radeka. Retrieved April 20, 2013, from < http:// voice.univie.ac.at>

Determinación de la representatividad cuantitativa de un corpus *ad hoc* bilingüe (inglés-español) de manuales de instrucciones generales de lectores electrónicos

[Establishing the quantitative representativeness of an E-Reader Users' Guide *ad hoc* corpus (English-Spanish)]

MIRIAM SEGHIRI
Universidad de Málaga (España)
seghiri@uma.es

> **Abstract:** According to Francis (1982), a corpus can be described as a "collection of texts assumed to be representative of a given language, dialect, or other subset of a language". However, nowadays the concept of *representativeness* is very imprecise considering its acceptance as a central characteristic that distinguishes a corpus from any other kind of collection (Seghiri, 2006 and 2011). Actually, there is no general agreement as to what the size of a corpus should be and, in practice, "the size of a corpus tends to reflect the ease or difficulty of acquiring the material" (Giouli and Piperidis, 2002). For this reason, in this paper we will attempt to deal with this key question, i.e., we will focus on the complex notion of representativeness, from both the qualitative (to be done *a priori*) and quantitative (*a posteriori*) for ad hoc corpora. Finally, we will describe a computer application named ReCor, based on the N-Cor algorithm, that will be used to verify whether a sample of *E-Reader Users' Guide* compiled might be considered representative.
>
> **Keywords:** representativeness; *ad hoc* corpus; ReCor; e-reader; users' guide

1. Introducción

Las ventajas de utilizar los corpus *ad hoc* en la práctica traductora han sido puestas de manifiesto por multitud de autores (cfr. Pearson, 1998; Bernardini y Zanettin, 2000; Zanettin, 2002; Sánchez-Gijón, 2003; Corpas Pastor, 2004 o Seghiri, 2006 y 2011, entre otros). Un corpus *ad hoc* sería aquel que se crea exclusivamente a partir de recursos electrónicos disponibles en la red Internet bien para la realización puntual de un determinado encargo de traducción, bien para la documentación de un bloque textual (cfr. Corpas Pastor, 2002), cuyo principal objetivo es satisfacer las principales necesidades del traductor de forma *económica* —pues los textos que conformarán el corpus se encuentran disponibles en la red Internet—, *rápida* —dado que los documentos pueden descargarse en segundos— y *fiable* (pues permite observar, entre otros, la macro- y microestructura textual así como la terminología propia del campo de especialidad *in vivo*). Así, en el presente trabajo[1] presentaremos una metodología protocolizada para la compilación de un corpus *ad hoc* de manuales de instrucciones general de lectores electrónicos en la que se garantizará la representatividad cualitativa, a través de un diseño y un protocolo claro de compilación, en cinco pasos, y, por último, lo que es más novedoso, cuantitativa, gracias al programa ReCor diseñado para tal fin[2]. Los intentos de fijar un tamaño mínimo para corpus especializados han sido varios, entre los que destacan los presentados por Heaps (1978), Young-Mi (1995) o Sánchez Pérez y Cantos Gómez (1997). Sin embargo, tales propuestas presentan importantes deficiencias porque bien se basan en la ley de Zipf (cfr. Yang et al, 2000: 21), bien intentan establecer el tamaño mínimo de la muestra *a priori*, esto es, antes de compilar el corpus (cfr. Seghiri, 2011); en nuestro caso, la aplicación informática *ReCor* permite establecer el tamaño mínimo de los corpus *a posteriori*, esto es, una vez el corpus se ha compilado o durante el proceso de compilación; además, se basa en un algoritmo propio, llamado N-Cor, que se encuentra patentado (ref. ES2320511)[3] a través de la Oficina Española de Patentes y Marcas.

---

[1] El presente trabajo se enmarca parcialmente en el seno del proyecto europeo Marie Curie FP7 "EXPERT: EXPloiting Empirical appRoaches to Translation" (2012-2015), así como en los proyectos de I+D nacionales "INTELITERM: Sistema inteligente de gestión terminológica para traductores" (2012-2015), "TERMITUR: Diccionario inteligente TERMInológico para el sector TURístico (alemán-inglés-español)" (2014-2017) y "TRADICOR: sistema de gestión de corpus para la innovación didáctica en traducción e interpretación" (2013-2015).

[2] La aplicación informática *ReCor*, ideada por las doctoras Gloria Corpas Pastor y Miriam Seghiri, de la Universidad de Málaga, supone una solución eficaz para determinar *a posteriori*, por primera vez, de forma objetiva y cuantificable, el tamaño mínimo que debe alcanzar un corpus para que sea considerado representativo en términos estadísticos. Actualmente la aplicación se encuentra patentada (ref. P200695657) a través de la Oficina Española de Patentes y Marcas del Ministerio de Industria, Turismo y Comercio Asimismo, ReCor ha recibido el *Premio de Investigación en Tecnologías de la Traducción* (2007) concedido por el Observatorio de Tecnologías de la Traducción. Para más información sobre el programa, véanse los trabajos de Seghiri (2006 y 2011).

[3] Para más información sobre la patente y su acceso, consúltese la siguiente dirección URL: http://umapatent. uma. es/es/patent/metodo-para-la-determinacion-de-la-representa4b0.

2. Los manuales de instrucciones generales de lectores electrónicos

Antes de abordar el proceso de compilación del corpus, creemos conveniente justificar la elección de la temática —los lectores electrónicos— y del género textual —los manuales de instrucciones generales— elegidos. Por lo que se refiere a la temática, buscamos «lector electrónico» en el Diccionario de la Real Academia Española. Al no estar recogido, decidimos preguntar sobre su denominación y definición a través del formulario[4] de consultas lingüísticas que pone a disposición de los usuarios la Real Academia y recibimos la siguiente respuesta:

> [l]a expresión e-book se emplea en inglés para hacer referencia a los libros en formato digital y al dispositivo electrónico que permite su lectura, para el cual existe también la denominación e-reader (forma abreviada de e-book reader). Las equivalencias más recomendables en español de e-book son, siguiendo las indicaciones del Diccionario panhispánico de dudas, libro electrónico y ciberlibro. [...] La versión electrónica o digital de un libro puede estar colgada en Internet o almacenada en un CD-ROM y leerse a través de la pantalla de diversos aparatos (un PC, un portátil, una PDA o incluso un teléfono móvil), pero en los últimos años han aparecido dispositivos cuya única finalidad es la lectura de libros digitales. A estos dispositivos se les llama en inglés —como ya hemos adelantado—, además de e-book, e-reader, es decir, lector electrónico. Paralelamente, en páginas de Internet escritas en nuestro idioma, se documenta el empleo de las expresiones lector de libros electrónicos, libros digitales o ciberlibros, lector electrónico o incluso lector, en alternancia con libro electrónico (curiosamente, apenas puede documentarse ciberlibro en referencia al dispositivo de lectura).

En esta misma línea, el término en inglés *e-reader* viene descrito en el diccionario *Cambridge Advance Learner's Dictionary*[5] como «a small electronic device with a screen which allows you to read an electronic book, perform searches, add notes, etc».

El lector electrónico podría enmarcarse en diversos campos como, por ejemplo, el de la electrónica, ya que se trata de un dispositivo electrónico y, más concretamente, en el de la electrónica de consumo. Asimismo, este dispositivo puede incluirse también en la industria de las telecomunicaciones, pues permite la transmisión de información a distancia, bien sea a través de los libros electrónicos, bien sea a través de la consulta de noticias de diferentes medios de comunicación. En esta misma línea, si tomamos como base la Clasificación Decimal

---

[4] LA RAE permite realizar consultas lingüísticas a partir del siguiente formulario en línea: http://www.rae.es/ consultas-linguisticas/formulario.

[5] Véase la siguiente dirección URL: http://dictionary.cambridge.org/es/diccionario/britanico.

Universal (CDU)[6], podemos encuadrar los textos relacionados con los lectores electrónicos en los siguientes ámbitos: 6. Ciencias Aplicadas. Medicina. Técnica, 62. Tecnología en general. Máquinas en general, sus propiedades y características, 621. Ingeniería mecánica. Técnica en general, 621.3 Ingeniería eléctrica. Electrotecnia, 621.39 Telecomunicaciones; y también en 6. Ciencias Aplicadas. Medicina. Técnica, 65. Organización y gestión de la industria, el comercio y de las comunicaciones, 654. Organización y gestión de la telecomunicación.

Por otra parte, si nos basamos en la nomenclatura internacional de la UNESCO[7] para los campos de la ciencia y de la técnica, los textos relacionados con los lectores electrónicos se podrían encuadrar en los siguientes ámbitos técnicos: 33. Ciencias Tecnológicas, 3307. Tecnología electrónica, 3307.99 Otras (especificar); así como en 33. Ciencias Tecnológicas, 3311. Tecnología de la instrumentación, 3311.07 Instrumentos electrónicos; y también en 33. Ciencias Tecnológicas, 3325. Tecnología de las Telecomunicaciones, 3325.99 Otras (Especificar)[8].

En definitiva, podemos enmarcar al lector electrónico en distintos subcampos (el de la electrónica, el de las telecomunicaciones o el de la instrumentación, entre otros); no obstante, todos ellos se enmarcan dentro del campo de la técnica.

Por lo que se refiere a su demanda, según el portal Zona E-Readers[9], «[e]n 2011 se vendieron 356 901 dispositivos; en 2012, 699 318 *e-readers* duplicando prácticamente los del año anterior; [y, en] 2013 se vendieron 755 800 *e-readers*. [Así,] los consumidores españoles colocaban a España como el segundo país europeo que más dispositivos de tinta electrónica compraba».

Por lo que se refiere al género elegido, los manuales de instrucciones generales, Gamero Pérez (2001) distingue 30 géneros técnicos como representativos del

---

[6] La tabla de materias que establece la Clasificación Decimal Universal (CDU) puedes consultarse en la siguiente dirección URL: http://www.mcu.es/libro/docs/TablaCDU.pdf.

[7] La nomenclatura internacional de UNESCO para los campos de la Ciencia y la Tecnología, en la que nos hemos basado, se encuentra disponible en la siguiente dirección http://www.micinn.es/stfls/MICINN/Ayudas/PN_2008_2011/LIA_RRHH/FICHERO/PTA _2011/Codigos_UNESCO_2011_definitivo.pdf.

[8] A la hora de especificar, tanto en relación con la tecnología electrónica como en relación con la tecnología de las telecomunicaciones, habría que indicar que se trata del lector electrónico.

[9] Véase la siguiente dirección URL: http://www.zonaereader.com/articulo/las-ventas-de-ereaders-en-2013-siguieron-creciendo-pese-la-saturaci%C3%B3n-del-mercado-y-al-boom

mercado profesional de la traducción técnica en España, a saber, acta de reunión técnica, anuncio en medio especializado, anuncio técnico en medio general, artículo comercial, artículo divulgativo, carta técnica, certificado técnico, comunicación interna de empresa, descripción técnica, enciclopedia técnica, folleto informativo publicitario, folleto publicitario informativo, informa técnico, instrucciones de trabajo, listado de piezas, manual de instrucciones especializado, *manual de instrucciones general*, manual técnico, memoria anual, monografía divulgativa, norma laboral, norma técnica, patente, plan de estudios, plan de producción, pliego de condiciones, prospecto de medicamento, proyecto técnico, publirreportaje y solicitud de desarrollo del producto.

Entre todos los géneros técnicos que acabamos de nombrar, optamos por centrarnos únicamente en uno de ellos, por evidentes razones de espacio y extensión del trabajo, para la compilación del corpus, como ya apuntamos, el manual de instrucciones general. Lo que lo diferencia del manual de instrucciones especializado es el receptor, en función del cual variará la terminología utilizada. Así, mientras el manual de instrucciones general está dirigido al público en general, el especializado se dirige, como su propio nombre indica, a los especialistas. De esta forma, el manual de instrucciones general es un género técnico exhortativo, porque pretende regular el modo de actuar o de pensar de las personas por medio de la exhortación o la instrucción y, normalmente, persigue provocar una reacción positiva o mejorar la imagen de la empresa. Los propósitos de un manual de instrucciones general son explicar cómo funciona un determinado producto, avisar sobre posibles riesgos y accidentes y constituir un elemento publicitario, ya que una valoración positiva de un producto puede implicar una nueva compra a la misma empresa. El emisor del texto es la empresa fabricante[10] y el receptor es el usuario, en este caso, el público general. El mensaje es la descripción del producto y se trata de una situación formal con una comunicación externa. El modo del texto es escrito en papel, aunque cada vez es más común encontrar los

---

[10] En este sentido, Nord (1988: 47-48) distingue entre el emisor de un texto y el autor del mismo. El emisor sería la persona o institución que usa el texto para enviar un mensaje, mientras que el autor es la persona que lo escribe siguiendo las directrices del emisor.

manuales en soporte electrónico[11]. En la redacción, puede presentar diferencias según las variantes regionales aunque, normalmente, dentro de una empresa se suele utilizar una terminología constante y coherente, que intenta ser común a todas las variedades (cf. Gamero Pérez, 2001).

Asimismo, se usan también otras denominaciones para referirse al manual de instrucciones general como manual de usuario, modo de empleo, manual de instrucciones e instrucciones de uso (cf. Gamero Pérez, 2001). Dentro del manual de instrucciones general existen diferentes subgéneros, según la dificultad de la temática. Encontraríamos, de esta forma, manuales de pequeños aparatos y electrodomésticos, grandes electrodomésticos, aparatos de imagen y sonido, telefonía avanzada, informática y, por último, sistemas complejos. A este respecto, el manual de instrucciones del lector electrónico podría estar encuadrado en la tercera categoría: manuales de instrucciones de aparatos de imagen y sonido (cf. Gamero Pérez, 2001).

Nos hemos decidido por este género porque es uno de los más demandados en el mercado profesional de la traducción técnica (cf. ACT, 2005). Esto se debe, principalmente, a directivas como la 89/392/CEE[12], que emanan de la Unión Europea, y de obligado cumplimiento por todos los países de la Unión, en la que se expone en el punto 1.7.4.b lo siguiente:

> El fabricante o su representante en la Comunidad elaborará el manual de instrucciones, que estará redactado en una de las lenguas del país de utilización y, preferentemente, irá acompañado del mismo manual redactado en otra lengua de la Comunidad, por ejemplo la del país de establecimiento del fabricante o de su representante [...].

Asimismo, la Resolución del Consejo de 17 de diciembre de 1998 sobre las instrucciones de uso de los bienes de consumo técnicos (98/C 411/01)[13] en su artículo quinto, indica que es imprescindible asegurar la calidad en la redacción de los manuales. Precisamente para asegurar la calidad en la traducción, el uso del corpus se perfila como una herramienta de gran utilidad pues, tal y como apunta

---

[11] A este respecto, hay que puntualizar que, si bien los manuales en papel se incluyen a la hora de comprar el producto, los que se han utilizado para la compilación del corpus han sido descargados de Internet y están, por lo tanto, exclusivamente en soporte electrónico.

[12] El texto completo de esta Directiva en español está disponible en la dirección: http://eur-lex.europa.eu/LexUriServ/LexUriServ.do?uri=OJ:L:1989:183:0009:0032:ES:PDF.

[13] Puede consultarse en la siguiente dirección URL: http://www.sgpstandard.cz/editor/files/stav_vyr/dok_es/ obec_bezp/ c_411_01.pdf.

Varantola (2000) «[t]he knowledge of how to compile and use corpora is an essential part of modern translational competence».

3. Determinación de la representatividad cualitativa

El aseguramiento de la representatividad en la calidad debe realizarse siempre *a priori*. Para ello será importante tener unos criterios claros de diseño y seguir un protocolo de compilación.

3.1. Criterios de diseño

Es fundamental tener muy claro el diseño del corpus que se desea crear antes de empezar a compilar con objeto de asegurar la calidad del mismo. Así, el corpus de manuales de lectores electrónicos que pretendemos crear será un corpus *ad hoc*, pues, tal y como punta Corpas Pastor (2002), con él se persigue «reunir toda la documentación disponible sobre un tema en muy poco tiempo, ya se trate de documentar un único texto o bien de preparar todo un bloque textual». También será *electrónico* (o *virtual*), dado que los textos que lo integren se descargarán exclusivamente de la red Internet. Asimismo, será *especializado,* en este caso en el ámbito técnico y, más concretamente, en el campo de los manuales de instrucciones generales de lectores electrónicos. El corpus será *bilingüe* (inglés-español) y, por defecto, también *paralelo* (pues se integrará por textos en inglés y sus correspondientes traducciones al español) y, por ende, *monodireccional*, ya que los manuales de los productos de consumo suelen redactarse directamente en lengua inglesa, independientemente de su lugar de producción, y, a continuación, son traducidos a las diferentes lenguas de la Unión para su comercialización. También será un corpus *textual* pues se compondrá de manuales completos. Por lo que se refiere a los *límites diacrónicos*, el corpus se encuentra limitado a textos de 2004, fecha en la que se lanzó el primer lector electrónico[14], hasta el presente año 2014.

3.2. Protocolo de compilación

Una vez que se ha decidido cómo se va a diseñar el corpus, procederemos a establecer un protocolo claro de compilación en cinco fases, a saber, localización de la información, descarga, formato, codificación y almacenamiento.

---

[14] Véase la siguiente dirección URL: http://gouforit.com/la-evolucion-de-los-ereaders-sony-del-sony-librie-al-sony-prs-t3.

El primer paso consiste en la *localización de la información*. En este sentido, hemos utilizado dos tipos de búsqueda para acceder a los textos que conformarán el corpus: la *búsqueda por palabra clave*, que es aquella la realizada con buscadores, a través de *Google*[15], y la *búsqueda institucional,* que es aquella llevada a cabo en páginas de organizaciones, instituciones o empresas, de reconocido prestigio. Así, se han extraído manuales de instrucciones principalmente de las siguientes empresas internacionales: *Amazon*[16], *Sony*[17], *I-joy*[18], *Iriver*[19], *Sytech*[20], *Foxit Corporation*[21], *Tianjin Jinke Electronics*[22], *Grammata*[23], *Hanvon Technology*[24], *Nvsbl*[25], *Leer-e*[26], *Apolo XXI*[27], *Energy System*[28] y *Bookeen*[29].

---

[15] Se han utilizado las páginas de *Google España* y *Google UK* disponibles en las siguientes direcciones: http://www.google.es y http://www.google.co.uk. Se ha recurrido a ecuaciones de palabras clave como "libro electrónico", "lector electrónico" o "e-book".

[16] Es una empresa dedicada a la venta de productos tecnológicos en general. Se encuentra disponible en http://www.amazon.com.

[17] Es una empresa dedicada a la venta de productos tecnológicos en general. Se encuentra disponible en http://www.sony.es/section/home y http://www.sony.co.uk/section/home.

[18] Es una empresa dedicada a la venta de productos tecnológicos en general. Se encuentra disponible en http://www.ijoy-europe.com.

[19] Es una empresa dedicada a la venta de lectores electrónicos y dispositivos multimedia. Se encuentra disponible en http://www.iriver.com.

[20] Es una empresa dedicada a la venta de productos tecnológicos en general. Se encuentra disponible en http://www.sytech.es.

[21] Es una empresa dedicada a la venta de lectores electrónicos y programas de creación y lectura de documentos PDF. Se encuentra disponible en http://www.foxitsoftware.com.

[22] Es una empresa dedicada a la venta de lectores electrónicos. Se encuentra disponible en http://www.jinke.com.cn/Compagesql/English/index.asp.

[23] Es una empresa dedicada a la venta de libros y lectores electrónicos. Se encuentra disponible en http://grammata.es.

[24] Es una empresa dedicada a la venta de lectores electrónicos, sistemas de reconocimiento facial y *tablets*. Se encuentra disponible en http://www.hanvon.com/en.

[25] Es una empresa dedicada a la venta de lectores electrónicos, *tablets* y altavoces. Se encuentra disponible en http://www.nvsbl.es/webcontent-v2.

[26] Es una empresa dedicada a la venta de libros y lectores electrónicos. Se encuentra disponible en http://tienda.leer-e.es.

[27] Es una empresa dedicada a la venta de lectores electrónicos. Se encuentra disponible en http://www.apoloxxi.com.

La segunda fase es aquella dedicada a la *descarga* de los documentos de la página web en la en la que se encuentran alojados. En este sentido, cabe destacar que todos los documentos utilizados en el corpus se encontraban en formato PDF en sus respectivas páginas web, por lo que resultaba muy sencillo guardarlos una vez que estaban abiertos, usando simplemente la combinación «Ctrl+G». En el caso de que una página web albergara varios manuales, pudo semiautomatizarse la descarga en lote de manuales con el programa BootCat[30], programa que permite la compilación semiautomática de corpus *ad hoc*[31] a partir de los recursos disponibles en la red Internet con tan solo indicar palabras clave (o *seeds*).

El tercer paso de la compilación del corpus consiste en cambiar el *formato* de los textos descargados. Concretamente, se trata de convertir los documentos en formato PDF (.pdf) a texto plano (.txt). Como bien afirma Sinclair (1991: 21), «the safest policy is to keep the text as it is, unprocessed and clean of any other codes». Para la conversión se ha recurrido al programa ABBYY FineReader[32].

Una vez convertidos los documentos a texto plano, se procederá a su *codificación*. En este punto es imperante indicar qué criterio se ha seguido para denominar los textos: en primer lugar, el orden alfabético según el nombre comercial de los lectores; en segundo lugar, el modelo, para decidir el orden en el caso de varios lectores que pertenecen a una misma empresa. A este respecto, se han ordenado del más antiguo (2004) hasta el de última aparición (2014). Estos criterios han servido para la numeración de los lectores electrónicos: el nombre de la marca por orden alfabético así como el modelo más antiguo han sido nombrados desde el número 001 al número 100. A continuación, se indica la lengua como tercer criterio a seguir. Así, se ha utilizado EN para los manuales en inglés y ES para los manuales en español.

---

[28] Es una empresa dedicada a la venta de productos tecnológicos en general. Se encuentra disponible en http://www.energysistem.com.

[29] Es una empresa dedicada a la venta de lectores electrónicos. Se encuentra disponible en http://www.bookeen.com/en.

[30] El programa BootCat puede en la siguiente dirección URL: http://bootcat.sslmit.unibo.it.

[31] Para más información en torno al uso de BootCat para la compilación de corpus *ad hoc*, véase Gutiérrez et al. (2013).

[32] Se trata de un programa de pago que permite la conversión de diferentes formatos en formato .doc y .txt y se encuentra disponible en la dirección http://www.abbyyeu.com/es/.

Por último, con vistas a una futura ampliación temática del corpus, se ha decidido añadir las iniciales LE, de lector electrónico. En definitiva, las denominaciones de los textos que componen el corpus van desde el 001ENLE hasta el 100ENLE para los textos que forman el subcorpus en inglés de manuales de instrucciones generales originales, en TXT y PDF; y sus correspondientes traducciones, coincidentes en número, del 001ESLE al 100ESLE, para los textos que forman los subcorpus en español de manuales de instrucciones generales traducidos.

La quinta y última fase del proceso de compilación del corpus, el *almacenamiento*, consiste en guardar los textos en diferentes carpetas y subcarpetas. Para ello, primero se ha creado una carpeta llamada *E-corpus*, en la que aparece una subcarpeta referente al género, llamado *manuales de instrucciones*. Esta carpeta se subdivide, a su vez, en función del formato, PDF o TXT, y, por último, según la lengua, a saber, inglés y español (cf. Ilustración 1):

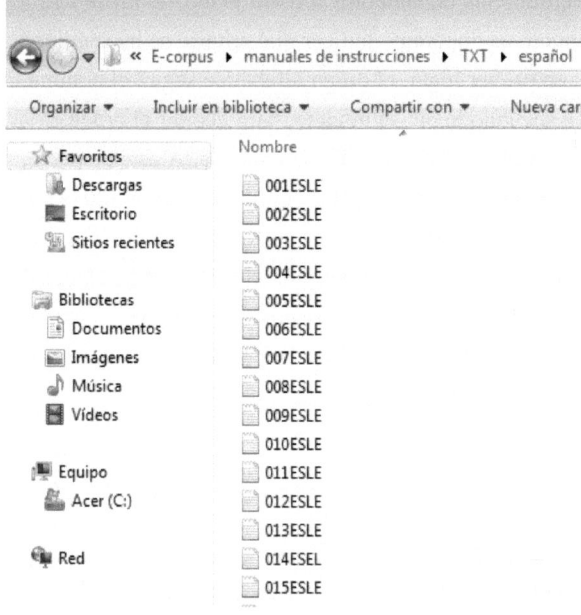

Ilustración 1. Almacenamiento del subcorpus español en formato .txt

Una vez compilado el corpus *ad hoc,* paralelo, monodireccional, electrónico y bilingüe, con 100 documentos en inglés y sus correspondientes 100 traducciones al español, y asegurada la representatividad cualitativa a través del diseño y el protocolo de compilación en cinco fases, el siguiente paso será el de comprobar la representatividad cuantitativa de la muestra compilada con el programa ReCor, diseñado para tal fin.

4. Determinación de la representatividad cuantitativa

Si repasamos algunos de los principales trabajos en los que se reflexiona en torno al tamaño mínimo que debe tener un corpus para ser representativo, sorprende observar la falta de consenso existente. Así, por ejemplo, McEnery y Wilson (2006) o Ruiz Antón (2006) sitúan en torno a un millón de palabras la cifra ideal que debería alcanzar cualquier corpus. Friedbichler y Friedbichler (2000) estiman que las cifras ente «500,000 and 5 million words per language (depending on the target field) will provide sample evidence in 97 % of language queries». Hay quienes incluso van más allá y llegan a afirmar que «more data is better data» o «the bigger the corpus the better» (cfr. Church y Mercer, 1993: 18-19 y Wilkinson, 2005: 6).

Aunque el sueño para muchos lingüistas sería disponer de colecciones gigantescas de más de diez millones de palabras para poder realizar estudios sobre la lengua en general (cfr. Wilkinson, 2005: 6), se ha demostrado que corpus de menor tamaño ofrecen resultados óptimos para áreas de especialidad (Beeby et al, 2009; Corpas y Seghiri, 2009; Seghiri, 2006, 2011 y 2014). De hecho, son cada vez más los investigadores como Bowker y Pearson (2002: 48) que subrayan que textos de menor tamaño con «few thousand and a few hundred thousand words» son igualmente útiles para el estudio de lenguas para fines específicos. En esta misma línea, Clear (1994) llega a escribir un artículo cuyo título ya es lo suficientemente explícito «I Can't See the Sense in a Large Corpus». Sin embargo, gran parte de estos autores (Church y Mercer, 1993; Clear, 1994; Bowker y Pearson, 2002; Pérez Hernández, 2002; Wilkinson, 2005) sólo ofrecen cifras orientativas. Otros investigadores, como Giouli y Piperidis (2002) van más allá y llegan a afirmar que, tras estudiar la literatura existente «[t]here is no general agreement as to what the size of a corpus should ideally be. In practice, however, the size of a corpus tends to reflect the ease or difficulty of acquiring the material (Giouli y Piperidis, 2002).

Como ya apuntábamos en la introducción del presente trabajo, se han llevado a cabo algunos intentos para establecer, con cifras exactas, el tamaño mínimo de un corpus. Algunos de los más significativos son los expuestos por Heaps (1978), Young-Mi (1995) y Sánchez Pérez y Cantos Gómez (1997), aunque, años más tarde, algunos de estos autores como Cantos (cfr. Yang et al. 2000: 21) reconocerán las deficiencias de estas propuestas al afirmar que «Heaps, Young-Mi and Sánchez and Cantos failed by using regression techniques. This might be attributed to their preference for Zipf's law».

Así las cosas, a continuación presentamos la aplicación informática ReCor, basada en el algoritmo N-Cor, que permite establecer, por primera vez *a posteriori*, el tamaño mínimo de un corpus. Para ello, partimos de la siguiente idea: si el cociente entre las palabras reales de un texto (*types*) y las totales (*tokens*) nos da cuenta de su densidad o riqueza léxica, podría desarrollarse una aplicación, basada en este algoritmo, que reflejara, el incremento del corpus («C») documento a documento (d), es decir, $Cn = d1 + d2 + d3 + ... + dn$.

De este modo, y una vez asegurada la representación cualitativa del corpus en el apartado anterior (cfr. Apartado 3), procederemos a comprobar si el corpus es representativo a nivel cuantitativo, es decir, verificaremos si se ha cubierto la terminología utilizada en este género y esta temática, todo ello a través la herramienta *ReCor*.

Esta herramienta, cuyo algoritmo N-Cor ($Cn = d1 + d2 + d3 + ... + dn$) se encuentra patentado desde 2010[33], recibe su nombre, *ReCor* por la función para la que ha sido diseñada: la representatividad de los corpus.

De este modo, y mediante una sencilla interfaz de usuario (cf. Ilustración 2), se pueden seleccionar los ficheros de entrada del corpus; además, si se desea, se puede añadir un filtro de palabras (mediante las llamadas *stop word lists*), generar tres ficheros de salida (estadístico, alfabético y de frecuencia), elegir la cantidad de palabras o n-gramas (de una a diez) que deseamos analizar y, por último, decidir si se deben filtrar o no los números que aparezcan en los textos que conforman el corpus.

En este sentido, hemos subido en primer lugar, por ejemplo, el subcorpus en inglés en texto plano (.txt) a través de la opción «Selección de los ficheros del corpus».

---

[33] Para más información véase la siguiente dirección URL: http://umapatent.uma.es/es/patent/metodo-para-la-determinacion-de-la-representa4b0.

Determinación de la representatividad cuantitativa de un corpus *ad hoc* bilingüe de manuales

En segundo lugar, aparece la opción «Filtro de entrada (Filtro de palabras)», con la que se brinda la opción al usuario de subir en un documento de texto plano (.txt) un listado palabras vacías de significado (como preposiciones, números, artículos o verbos modales, entre otros). Estos listados de palabras pueden bien confeccionarse manualmente, bien descargarse de la red Internet. Así, listados de palabras vacías de significado (*Stop Words*) en inglés pueden descargarse de *Default English Stopwords List*[34] *o English Stop Words*[35], y en español, de *Spanish StopWords*[36] o *Lista de Stopwords en español*[37]. En esta ocasión hemos decidido no subir ningún filtro de palabras con objeto de dejar la puerta abierta para realizar futuros estudios, por ejemplo, colocacionales, locucionales o fraseológicos (a través del análisis de dos o más gramas), ya que el hecho de que se suprimieran artículos o preposiciones, entre otros, a través del filtro de palabras puede alterar los resultados del estudio.

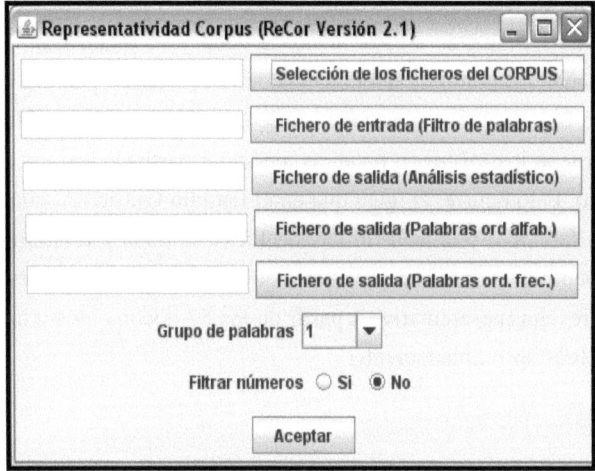

Ilustración 2. Interfaz de *ReCor* 2.1

---

[34] Disponible en la siguiente dirección URL: http://www.ranks.nl/resources/stopwords.html.
[35] Disponible en la siguiente dirección URL: http://www.textfixer.com/resources/common-english-words.txt.
[36] Disponible en la siguiente dirección URL: http://www.ranks.nl/stopwords/spanish.html.
[37] Disponible en la siguiente dirección URL: http://es.scribd.com/doc/94217611/Lista-de-stopwords-en-espanol.

En tercer lugar, el programa permite extraer tres ficheros de salida, que describiremos a continuación, una vez se hayan creado.

Seguidamente, se seleccionarán los gramas que se desean analizar que, en el presente estudio será uno (1), para conocer el tamaño mínimo del corpus grama a grama[38].

Por último, debe seleccionarse «Aceptar» para que el programa cree las gráficas y los archivos de salida.

Una vez realizados los pasos anteriores, el ReCor genera dos gráficas de representatividad (cf. Ilustración 3): por una parte, en el Estudio Gráfico A se comprueba el número de documentos necesarios para que el subcorpus en inglés sea representativo. Existe una barra vertical que mide la densidad léxica a través de la ratio entre *types* (palabras nuevas)/*tokens* (palabras totales) y la horizontal que incorpora los documentos uno a uno. Aparecen, a su vez, dos líneas: una de color rojo, que incorpora los textos en orden alfabético, y otra, azul, que los recoge en orden aleatorio. Cuando ambas líneas se unen y se estabilizan, se habrá alcanzado el tamaño mínimo de documentos de la colección. De otra parte, el Estudio Gráfico B, es idéntico al estudio gráfico A salvo en que aquí la línea horizontal comprueba los *tokens* (o palabras totales) a partir de los que el corpus es representativo. Esto ocurre, al igual que en el Estudio Gráfico A, cuando la línea roja (orden alfabético) y la azul (orden aleatorio) se unen y estabilizan. De esta forma, el subcorpus en inglés de manuales de instrucciones generales de lectores electrónicos resulta representativo a partir de los 67 documentos y unas 700 000 *tokens* o palabras aproximadamente.

---

[38] En este sentido, si se desea conocer si el corpus es representativos desde el punto de vista cuantitativo con dos o más gramas (con objeto de realizar estudios colocacionales, locucionales o fraseológicos, por ejemplo) puede seleccionarse a través de esta opción y hasta 10 gramas.

Determinación de la representatividad cuantitativa de un corpus *ad hoc* bilingüe de manuales

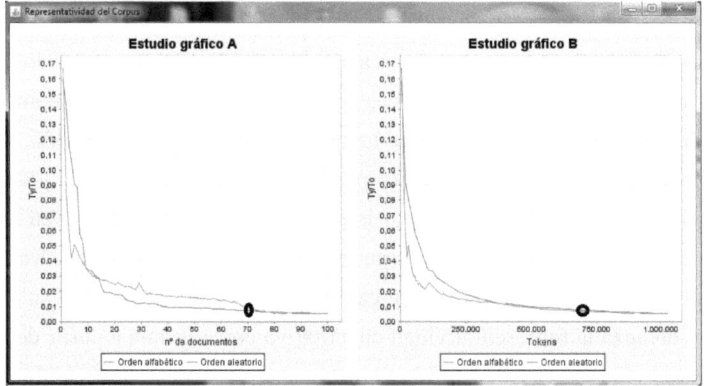

Ilustración 3. Determinación de la representatividad cuantitativa del subcorpus en inglés
(1 grama).

Procedemos de igual modo con el subcorpus en español de manuales de instrucciones generales de lectores electrónicos. Así, el sudcorpus resulta representativo a partir de los 75 documentos y los 760 000 *tokens* o palabras aproximadamente (cf. Ilustración 4).

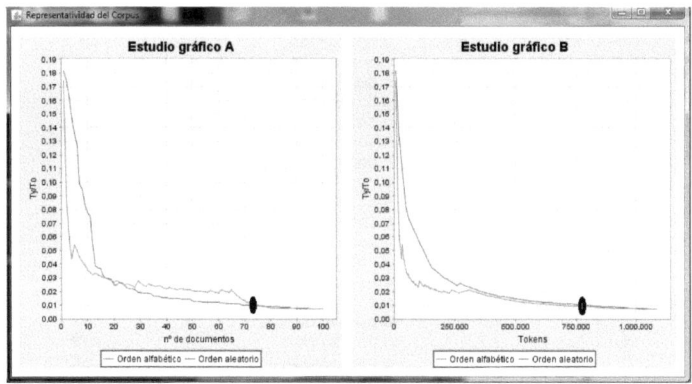

Ilustración 4. Determinación de la representatividad cuantitativa del subcorpus en español
(1 grama).

Además de las gráficas de representatividad (cf. Ilustraciones 3 y 4), el programa extrae tres ficheros de salida: un listado de palabras (en este caso, de 1 grama) ordenado alfabéticamente, un listado de palabras (1 grama) ordenado por frecuencia y, además, un análisis estadístico.

En el análisis estadístico se albergan los datos en cinco columnas, a saber, *types*, *tokens*, *types/tokens*, palabras con una aparición (V1) y palabras con dos apariciones (V2). A partir de este análisis estadístico puede observarse claramente, y con cifras exactas, cómo, en primer lugar, en el subcorpus en inglés, hay un momento en el que no entran *types* (o palabras nuevas) en el corpus y sólo entran *tokens* (o palabras repetidas), por lo que el corpus sólo aumenta en tamaño pero no en palabras nuevas o *types* y podemos, por consiguiente, observar cómo se ha cubierto la terminología de ese campo de especialidad. Así, el subcorpus en inglés alcanza la representatividad cuantitativa con 1 grama a partir de los 69 documentos y de las 707 614 palabras o *tokens*, pues no entraron palabras nuevas o *types* a partir de los 5 289 (cfr. Ilustración 5).

Por lo que se refiere al subcorpus en español, el análisis estadístico muestra que alcanza la representatividad cuantitativa con 1 grama a partir de los 75 documentos y las 764 978 palabras totales o *tokens*, pues no entraron palabras nuevas o *types* a partir de los 7 984 (cfr. Ilustración 6).

	A	B	C	D	E
59	Types	Tokens	Ty/To	V1	V2
60	5102.0	646475.0	0.008179744	126	510
61	5107.0	648977.0	0.008148208	126	481
62	5118.0	651828.0	0.008112569	126	464
63	5129.0	654184.0	0.008083353	126	438
64	5129.0	664207.0	0.007961374	126	288
65	5129.0	674098.0	0.007844557	26	368
66	5132.0	683989.0	0.007731118	26	268
67	5155.0	693880.0	0.007620914	26	268
68	5200.0	705258.0	0.007499383	27	268
69	5289.0	707614.0	0.007474414	27	268
70	5289.0	718992.0	0.007356132	26	269
71	5289.0	721622.0	0.007329322	26	269
72	5289.0	724357.0	0.007301648	26	259
73	5289.0	727174.0	0.007273362	26	230
74	5289.0	729676.0	0.007248422	26	230
75	5289.0	763124.0	0.006930721	0	255
76	5289.0	779566.0	0.006784544	0	255
77	5289.0	812013.0	0.006513442	0	255
78	5289.0	816944.0	0.006474128	0	215
79	5289.0	823886.0	0.006419577	0	92
80	5289.0	830223.0	0.006370577	0	27
81	5289.0	840246.0	0.006294585	0	27
82	5289.0	851624.0	0.006210487	0	26

Ilustración 5. Análisis estadístico del subcorpus en inglés (1 grama)

Determinación de la representatividad cuantitativa de un corpus *ad hoc* bilingüe de manuales

	I	J	K	L	M
60	Types	Tokens	Ty/To	V1	V2
61	7499.0	657461.0	0.011953561	1	820
62	7565.0	660839.0	0.01189245759	1	729
63	7565.0	698333.0	0.011253944	1	729
64	7569.0	700992.0	0.011211255	1	696
65	7575.0	706606.0	0.011299083	98	659
66	7599.0	709870.0	0.01124713	97	660
67	7600.0	711888.0	0.011059888	97	657
68	7614.0	717809.0	0.010969911	97	587
69	7624.0	718224.0	0.010298959	97	413
70	7665.0	728137.0	0.010260404	97	392
71	7784.0	731401.0	0.010217546	97	391
72	7801.0	749146.0	0.010117266	97	206
73	7905.0	752396.0	0.01007577	97	206
74	7980.0	758010.0	0.010004887	0	286
75	7984.0	764978.0	0.009561929	0	279
76	7984.0	846996.0	0.009426255	0	279
77	7984.0	861284.0	0.009269881	0	230
78	7984.0	867182.0	0.009206833	0	230
79	7984.0	870095.0	0.009176009	0	230
80	7984.0	876016.0	0.009113989	0	230
81	7984.0	879394.0	0.00907897959	0	230
82	7984.0	887139.0	0.008999717	0	230
83	7984.0	890389.0	0.008966867	0	230

Ilustración 6. Análisis estadístico del subcorpus en español (1 grama)

Asimismo, el programa extrae el listado de palabras de cada subcorpus ordenadas alfabéticamente (cfr. Ilustraciones 7 y 8):

3	Palabra	Frecuencia
4		
5	a	16644
6	ability	12
7	able	308
8	about	816
9	above	512
10	abrasion	8
11	abrasive	48
12	abrasives	4
13	abroad	4
14	absence	12
15	absolutely	4
16	absorption	8
17	abuse	8
18	accelerate	4
19	accelerated	4
20	accelerates	12
21	accept	108
22	acceptance	12
23	accepted	16
24	accepting	4
25	accepts	8
26	access	744
27	accessibility	16

1	Fichero ordenado por palabra	
2		
3	Palabra	Frecuencia
4	a	16812
5	abajo	1136
6	abarca	32
7	abarcados	8
8	abarcan	16
9	abc	16
10	abierta	16
11	abierto	164
12	abiertos	36
13	abonado	8
14	abonados	8
15	abonar	12
16	abonará	4
17	abra	444
18	abrasiva	4
19	abrasivo	20
20	abrasivos	12
21	abre	176
22	abriendo	24
23	abrieron	8
24	abrir	524

Ilustración 7. Palabras (1 grama) del subcorpus en inglés ordenadas alfabéticamente

Ilustración 8. Palabras (1 grama) del subcorpus en español ordenadas alfabéticamente

Por último, el programa extrae un fichero de salida que ordena las palabras del corpus por frecuencia donde se puede observar cómo, en primer lugar, aparecen las palabras vacías de significado (como preposiciones o artículos, por ejemplo), seguidas de los términos propios de este género y temática como *device* o *kindle* en inglés (cfr. Ilustración 9) o libro o dispositivo, en español (cfr. Ilustración 10).

Asimismo, si se desea, el programa permite comprobar la representatividad de los subcorpus desde con grupos de 2 hasta 10 palabras (o gramas) con objeto de llevar a cabo estudios colocacionales o fraseológicos, entre otros.

1	Palabra	Frecuencia
2	the	78236
3	to	43936
4	you	23556
5	and	20728
6	your	19408
7	of	17708
8	a	16644
9	kindle	16536
10	or	14852
11	device	13636
12	on	11464
13	press	9500
14	is	8696
15	for	8480
16	button	8068
17	page	7408
18	can	7140
19	will	6872
20	if	6008
21	this	5772
22	be	5764
23	select	5680
24	not	5652
25	menu	5600

1	#Palabra	Frecuencia
2	de	73780
3	el	43952
4	la	39292
5	en	29388
6	para	21828
7	y	19316
8	a	16812
9	del	16144
10	que	15004
11	o	13168
12	los	10700
13	se	10320
14	un	9672
15	una	9484
16	página	7808
17	con	7424
18	las	6776
19	puede	6380
20	si	5928
21	pantalla	5552
22	contenido	5468
23	botón	5344
24	libros	3536
25	libro	3424

Ilustración 9. Palabras (1 grama) del subcorpus en inglés ordenadas por frecuencia

Ilustración 10. Palabras (1 grama) del subcorpus en español ordenadas por frecuencia

5. Conclusiones

En este estudio se ha presentado una metodología protocolizada para la compilación de corpus *ad hoc*, esto es, aquellos destinados a cubrir la necesidades el traductor para realización de un encargo de traducción o para documentar un bloque textual, que sean representativos, fiables y de calidad. En nuestro caso hemos ilustrado esta metodología mediante la creación un corpus *ad hoc* electrónico —pues sólo se compone de textos albergados en la red Internet— y bilingüe, paralelo y monodireccional —ya que recoge un subcorpus de documentos originales en inglés y un subcorpus con sus correspondientes traducciones al español— de manuales de instrucciones generales de lectores electrónicos.

Una vez que hemos demostrado la representatividad cualitativa, a través de un diseño claro del corpus y de un protocolo propio de compilación en cinco fases —localización de la información, descarga, formato, codificación y almacenamiento—, procedimos a demostrar la representatividad cuantitativa (con 1 grama) mediante el programa *ReCor*. El mencionado programa reveló que, aunque cada subcorpus contaba con 100 documentos, el subcorpus en inglés alcanza la representatividad cuantitativa con 1 grama a partir de los 69 textos y 707 614 palabras (o *tokens*), ya que no entraron palabras nuevas (o *types*) a partir de las 5 289. Por su parte, el subcorpus en español alcanzó la representatividad cuantitativa con 1 grama a partir de los 75 textos y 764 978 palabras (o *tokens*), pues no entraron palabras nuevas (o *types*) a partir de las 7 984. De esta forma, el español necesita 2 695 *types* más que el inglés para cubrir la terminología básica de este campo de especialidad, lo que hace presuponer que el subcorpus en español tiene una macro- y microestructura más flexible y utiliza un abanico terminológico más amplio que el subcorpus en inglés. El resultado final ha sido la creación de un corpus bilingüe (inglés-español) de manuales de instrucciones generales de lectores electrónicos que es representativo tanto a nivel cualitativo como cuantitativo, listo para ser utilizado para cualquier tipo de análisis desde una perspectiva monolingüe y monocultural así como desde el punto de vista de la traducción.

6. Bibliografía

Beeby, Allison, Patricia Rodríguez Inés y Pilar Sánchez-Gijón, eds. 2009. *Corpus Use and Translating*. Ámsterdam/Filadelfia: John Benjamins. ISBN 9789027224262.

Bernardini, Silvia y Federico Zanettin, eds. 2000. *I corpora nella didattica della traduzione. Corpus Use and Learning to Translate*. Bolonia: CLUEB. ISBN 8849115598.

Church, Kenneth W. y Robert L. Mercer. 1993. Introduction to the Special Issue on Computational Linguistics Using Large Corpora. @ *Computational Linguistics*, 19 / 1: 1-24.

Clear, Jeremy H. 1994. I Can't See the Sense in a Large Corpus. @ F. Kiefer, G. Kiss y J. Pajzs. *Papers in Computational Lexicography: COMPLEX '94*. Budapest: Research Institute for Linguistics y Hungarian Academy of Sciences. ISBN 9789638461780, pp. 33-48.

Corpas Pastor, Gloria. 2002. Traducir con corpus: de la teoría a la práctica. @ J. García Palacios y M. T. Fuentes Morán, eds. *Texto, Terminología y Traducción*. Salamanca: Almar. ISBN 8474550793, pp. 189- 226.

Corpas Pastor, Gloria. 2004. Localización de recursos y compilación de corpus vía Internet: Aplicaciones para la didáctica de la traducción médica especializada. @ C. Gonzalo García y V. García Yebra, eds. *Manual de documentación y terminología para la traducción especializada*. Madrid : Arco/Libros. ISBN 8476355785, pp. 223-257.

Corpas Pastor, Gloria y Míriam Seghiri. 2009. Virtual Corpora as Documentation Resources: Translating Travel Insurance Documents (English-Spanish). @ A. Beeby, P. Rodríguez Inés y P. Sánchez-Gijón, eds. *Corpus Use and Translating*. Ámsterdam/Filadelfia: John Benjamins, ISBN 9789027224262, pp. 75-107.

Friedbichler, Ingrid y Michael Friedbichler. 2000. The Potential of Domain-Specific Target-Language Corpora for the Translator's Workbench. @ S. Bernardini y F. Zanettin, eds. *I corpora nella didattica della traduzione. Corpus Use and Learning to Translate*. Bolonia: CLUEB. ISBN 8849115598, pp. 107-116.

Gamero Pérez, Silvia. 2001. *La traducción de textos técnicos: descripción y análisis de textos*. Barcelona: Ariel. ISBN 9788434481176.

Giouli, Voula y Stelios Piperidis. 2002. *Corpora and HLT. Current trends in corpus processing and annotation*. Bulagaria: Insitute for Language and Speech Processing.

Gutiérrez, Rut, Gloria Corpas y Miriam Seghiri. 2013. Using semi-automatic compiled corpora for medical terminology and vocabulary building in the healthcare domain. @ *10th International Conference on Terminology and Artificial Intelligence: TIA 2013*. París: Université Paris 13.ISBN 9782917490259, pp. 14-19.

Heaps, Harold Stanley. 1978. *Information Retrieval: Computational and Theoretical Aspects*. Nueva York: Academic Press. ISBN 9780123357502.

McEnery, Anthony y Andrew Wilson. 2006 [2000]. *IICT4LT Module 3.4. Corpus linguistics*. Disponible en <http://www.ict4lt.org/en/en_mod3-4.htm>. [Última consulta 10/07/2014].

Nord, Christiane. 1988. *Texanalyse und Übersetzen: theoretische Grundlagen, Methode und didaktische Anwendung einer übersetzungsrelevanten Textanalyse*. Heidelberg: Groos. ISBN 9783872765987.

Pearson, Jennifer. 1998. *Terms in Context, Studies in Corpus Linguistics*, 1. Amsterdam y Filadelphia: John Benjamins Publishing. ISBN 9789027222695.

Ruiz Antón, Juan. 2006. Corpus y otros recursos lingüísticos. 1-21. <http://www.trad.uji.es/asignatura/obtener.php?letra=1&codigo=42&fichero=1098353728142>.

Sánchez-Gijón, Pilar. 2003. És la web pública la nova biblioteca del traductor? @ *Tradumàtica: Traducció i tecnologies de la informació i la comunicación*, 2: 1-7.

Sánchez Pérez, Aquilino y Pascual Cantos Gómez. 1997. Predictability of Word Forms (Types) and Lemmas in Linguistic Corpora. A Case Study Based on the Analysis of the CUMBRE Corpus: An 8-Million-Word Corpus of Contemporary Spanish @ *International Journal of Corpus Linguistics*, 2 / 2: 259-280.

Seghiri, Miriam. 2006. *Compilación de un corpus trilingüe de seguros turísticos (español-inglés-italiano): aspectos de evaluación, catalogación, diseño y representatividad*. Málaga: Universidad de Málaga.

Seghiri, Miriam. 2011. Metodología protocolizada de compilación de un corpus de seguros de viajes: aspectos de diseño y representatividad. @ *Revista de lingüística teórica y aplicada (RLA)*, 49 /2: 13-30.

Seghiri, Miriam. 2014/en prensa. Too big or not too big: Establishing the minimum size for a legal ad hoc corpus. @ *Hermes*, 53.

Sinclair, John M. 1991. *Corpus, Concordance, Collocation.* Oxford: Oxford University Press.

Varantola, Krista. 2000. Translators, dictionaries and text corpora. @ S. Bernardini y F. Zanettin, eds. *I corpora nella didattica della traduzione.* Bologna: CLUEB, pp. 117-133. ISBN 8849115598

Wilkinson, Michael. 2005. Compiling a specialized corpus to be used as a translation aid. @ *Translation Journal*, 9 /3: 1-6.

Yang, Dan-Hee, Pascual Cantos Gómez y Mansuk Song. 2000. An Algorithm for Predicting the Relationship between Lemmas and Corpus Size @ *ETRI Journal*, 22 /2: 20-31.

Young-Mi Jeong. 1995. Statistical Characteristics of Korean Vocabulary and Its Application. @ *Lexicographic Study* 5 / 6: 134-163.

Zanettin, Federico. 2002. CEXI. Designing an English Italian Translational Corpus. @ B. Ketteman y G. Marko, eds. *Teaching and Learning by Doing Corpus Analysis.* Amsterdam: Rodopi. ISBN 9789042014503, pp. 329-343.

The use of a comparable corpus:
How to develop writing applications

[Aplicaciones de ayuda a la escritura en L2 basadas en corpus comparables]

BELÉN LÓPEZ ARROYO (1) y RODA P. ROBERTS (2)
(1) University of Valladolid-ACTRES (Spain) and
(2) University of Ottawa-ACTRES (Canada)
belenl@lia.uva.es, roberts@uottawa.ca

> Scientific and professional genres have been analyzed in English for insights into rhetorical structure and information distribution (Swales 1990, 2004; Biber, Conrad & Reppen 1998 & Biber, Connor & Upton 2007 among others). However, this wealth of descriptive research has not produced particularly useful results for those writers who are not native speakers of English nor has it been «directly amenable to applied endeavours» (Rabadán 2008: 103). The aim of this paper is to describe the methodology and the tools devised by the ACTRES research group to bridge the transition between the descriptive and the procedural. The findings obtained feed into a writing application for Spanish-language writers who need to report their work in English to the global research & professional community. Custom-made comparable corpora have been compiled and analyzed for rhetorical and lexico-grammatical features of these genres in both English and Spanish. Then, cross-linguistic similarities and differences relevant for our intended users have been identified to build writing tools available as a useful and usable computer interface.
>
> **Keywords:** genre studies; corpus-based studies; contrastive studies; text generator.

1. Introduction

The ACTRES (Análisis Contrastivo y Traducción Especializada) research group, based at the University of León, but with researchers hailing from other Spanish universities such as the University of Valladolid as well as from other European and even Canadian universities, has developed the research projects entitled *Análisis Contrastivo y traducción inglés-español: aplicaciones* (HUM2005-01215), supported financially by the Ministerio de Educación y Ciencia as well as *Análisis contrastivo y traducción inglés-español (ACTRES): Aplicaciones lingüísticas para la internacionalización de la industria de transformación agroalimentaria* (LE227413).

One of the primary applications the Project is attempting to develop involves English semi-automatic writing tools for Spanish speakers. With the global dominance of English as the language of science, technology and business, non-native speakers of English are increasingly being called upon to write professionally in English. This creates problems for many. Hence the idea of creating English writing tools for non-native speakers of English.

However, the problems faced by non-native speakers as they write in English vary depending on what their first language is, because the mistakes made in English are often the result of the influence of the first language on English. This is the case not only for vocabulary and language structures, but also for writing genres, which can be somewhat different from one language to another. Therefore it is not possible to have a single English writing tool for all non-native speakers of English.

Moreover, depending on the level of knowledge of English of the non-native speakers, they may be unable to express themselves entirely in English and may need to throw in a few words or phrases in their first language. In other words, the writing application has to take into account the non-native speakers' mother tongue and provide for limited translation if necessary. What is required therefore is not just a writing template, but a translation-based writing application.

This paper deals with the use of comparable corpora to create translation-based writing applications. After briefly discussing the need for writing applications in English because of the dominance of English, we will distinguish between writing templates and translation-based writing applications, describing the latter in more detail. We will then differentiate between translation corpora and comparable corpora and indicate why the latter are more suitable for the creation of translation-based writing applications. Finally, we will demonstrate how the comparable corpora can be used to determine a rhetorical structure for a given genre, to create model lines that can be incorporated into the text by non-native speakers, and to produce a bilingual glossary. While we will refer to a number of writing applications ACTRES is working on, we will use the wine tasting notes application more particularly as an example.

2. The need for writing applications in English

As a new millennium begins, English is the common language in almost every endeavor, from science to air traffic control to the global jihad, where it is apparently the means of communication between speakers of Arabic and other languages. It has consolidated its dominance as the language of the Internet, where 80 percent of the world's electronically stored information is in English, according to Graddol (1997: 50). English dominates the business world. And the main language used in the fields of science and technology today is English. Finally, English is the language of culture. While all countries have their own actors, actresses, and singers, those that achieve global recognition are almost always English performers.

And yet not everyone is fluent in English, as the findings of a new study on the European Union have shown (Ginsburgh & Weber 2011). The European Union, which has 27 member countries and 23 official languages, carries out its official business primarily in one language — English. Yet the new study shows that barely a third of the EU's 500 million citizens speak English. The other two-thirds are linguistically disenfranchised, say the study's authors, economists Shlomo Weber, Southern Methodist University, Dallas, and Victor Ginsburgh, Free University of Brussels (ULB). «With globalization, people feel like they've been left on the side of the road. If your culture, your rights, your past haven't been respected, how can you feel like a full member of society?» says Weber (2012). «It is a delicate balance. People must decide if they want to trade their languages to increase by a few percentage points the rate of economic growth». (Swales 1990, 2004; Biber, Conrad & Reppen 1998; Biber, Connor & Upton 2007 among others).

In some places in Europe, English has invaded the workplace along with the global economy. Some Swedish companies, for example, use English within the workplace, even though they are in Sweden, because so much of their business is done through the Internet and other communications with the outside world (Mydans 2007). The use of English is by no means as widespread in a country like Spain. In fact, according to a vast new study (English Proficiency Index 2011) undertaken by EF Education First, an English-teaching company, which compiled the biggest ever internationally comparable sample of English learners with some 2 million people taking identical tests online in 44 countries, Spain was the worst performer in Western Europe (49.05 EF-EPI score, low proficiency level in 2011, although that improved somewhat to 55.89, medium proficiency level in 2012). According to the limited statistics we have been able to find on the topic, only 22% of Spain's population spoke English in 2012 (Europeans and their languages 2012).

This means that, while the need to communicate in English is as great in Spain as in most countries, the ability to do so is limited. Hence the need for writing applications in English designed for Spanish speakers.

3. Writing templates vs translation-based writing applications

Translation-based writing applications are writing templates with a difference. Most simply stated, templates are models. More specifically, writing templates are skeletal frameworks for given genres or text types. Presented below is a template for meeting minutes:

MINUTES of [*Organization name*]
Meeting date: _____
Call to order: A _____ [*kind of meeting*] meeting of the _____ [*organization name*], was held in _____ [*place, city, state*] on _____ [*date*], 20__. The meeting convened at _____ [*time*], President _____ [*name*] presiding, and _____ [*name*], secretary. [*Some small organizations choose to list attendees. This works well for boards of directors.*]
Members in attendance: [*optional item*]
Members not in attendance: [*optional item*]
Approval of minutes: Motion was made by [*name*], and seconded to approve the minutes of the _____ [*date*] meeting.
Motion carried.
Officers' reports:
  - President
  - Vice president
  - Secretary
  - Treasurer
Board and committee reports:
New business:
[*Subject title*]
Motion: Moved by [*name*] that [*state motion*].
Motion carried. Motion failed. [*leave only one of these*]
Announcements:
Adjournment: The meeting was adjourned at _____ [*time*].

_____   _____
Secretary   Date of approval
[*Organization Name*]

Table 1. Minutes template

The template includes the following:

1. The different sections of the text type (e.g. call to order, members in attendance, members not in attendance), with an indication as to whether the section is compulsory or optional;
2. Parts of sentences with blanks to fill in with words of your choice, when the content and format is fairly standard (e.g. "Motion was made by [*name*], and seconded to approve the minutes of the _____ [*date*] meeting");
3. Sections where what should be presented there is indicated but without any syntactic or semantic framework, since the content and its expression can vary considerably (e.g. Board and committee reports).

A writing template helps writers to organize material. It also helps them to develop the kinds of sentence, paragraph, and paper structure that good writers display. Templates don't simply give you advice on how to write. They show you exactly *how to do it.*

But while they provide step-by-step guidance in writing a given text type, they take for granted that the template user is fluent in the language being written. In other words, the template shows you how to write a specialized text type such as minutes, including the stock phrases or sentences found in such a text type, but it does not show you how to write the language in which the text type is written. More specifically, an English writing template is intended for English speakers who are called upon to write a specialized text in a genre with which they are not familiar.

Translation-based writing applications, like writing templates, provide step-by-step guidance in writing a given text type. But since they are intended for non-native speakers of the language of the text, they provide guidance not only in rhetorical structure (text sections) and stock phrases and sentences found in such a text type, but also in the overall vocabulary and structures required for a given text type. And since the users of these applications may have very limited knowledge of the language in which they want to write the text, the applications allow them to insert words and phrases in their native language and have the corresponding English equivalents pop up. In other words, what we have called translation-based writing applications are more detailed writing templates with a limited lexical translation component since they are intended for foreign language users. The writing applications are thus translation-based from the user point of view. And, since a translation component, however limited, always involves two specific languages, one of which is the source language and the other the target language, a translation-based writing application is restricted to speakers of one given language who wish to write in another given language.

In the case of the ACTRES project, writing applications are being created for Spanish speakers wishing to write specialized texts in English. The text types being worked on vary from scientific abstracts to meeting minutes and technical brochures, and the writing applications therefore vary considerably in rhetorical structure, vocabulary and grammatical structures. However, the same basic methodology is used to prepare all the applications. This methodology consists of the following:

- Set up a comparable corpus in Spanish and English for the given text type.
- Analyze the comparable corpus to identify the rhetorical structure of the texts both in Spanish and in English.
- Identify the most common rhetorical structure of the text type in English (while bearing in mind the similarities and differences with the most common Spanish rhetorical structure).
- Identify the commonly used structures for each of the sections of the rhetorical structure.
- Identify the common vocabulary used in the text type.
- Build a bilingual lexicon for the text type.
- Link the commonly used structures (including the vocabulary they contain) to the bilingual lexicon, which would allow users to insert words and phrases in Spanish and have them appear in English in the writing application.

It should be noted that, although the writing applications contain a translation component and are therefore translation-based from the point of view of users, the methodology used to produce them does not involve translation per se.

4. Corpora and translation-based writing applications

The starting point of creating the translation-based applications is, as indicated above, a bilingual comparable corpus. Bilingual corpora, which consist of texts in two languages, can be of two types: parallel and comparable. The ACTRES writing applications are based on comparable, rather than parallel corpora, although the latter, if easily accessible, may also be used. Before discussing the preference for a comparable corpus over a parallel corpus, we will briefly identify the key characteristics of each.

A parallel corpus is a translation corpus. It is a collection of texts, each of which is translated into another language. Translation presupposes a more or less exact match of texts in the two languages, which implies a. that the translated texts reflect the rhetorical structure of the source text, and b. that the translated texts are not always idiomatic. Also, the direction of the translation need not be constant, so that some texts in a parallel corpus may have been translated from language A to language B and others the other way around. The direction of the translation may not even be known.

A comparable bilingual corpus is one which contains similar texts in two languages. While there is as yet no agreement on the nature of the similarity, because there are very few examples of comparable corpora, it is understood that the text collections must share common features of selection from the point of view of content, genre and style. A comparable bilingual corpus allows one to compare the use of different languages in similar circumstances of communication, while avoiding the inevitable distortions introduced by the translations found in a parallel corpus.

From the descriptions of parallel and comparable corpora presented above, it is clear why the ACTRES project opted for comparable corpora. A comparable corpus allows comparison of texts in two different languages, as long as the text selection criteria are similar. The texts are authentic examples of writings in a specific genre in each language and therefore faithfully reflect the rhetorical structure of that genre in that language. Since none of the texts are translations, they all reflect, in principle at least, idiomatic use of the language in which they are written. A comparable corpus therefore allows a more accurate comparison of similar use of two different languages than does a parallel, i.e. translated, corpus. The comparable corpus of specialized texts set up for each translation-based writing application is used in almost all of the subsequent steps in the creation of the writing application (see sections 6, 7 and 8 below).

However, as indicated above, if a specialized parallel corpus is readily available, it can also be used, although to a much more limited extent. A parallel corpus could help to build a bilingual lexicon for the text type more rapidly than could a comparable corpus, although the accuracy of the lexical equivalents the parallel corpus provided would depend on the quality of the translations included.

5. Setting up a comparable corpus in Spanish and English

The challenge in setting up a good comparable corpus is determining how to find similar texts in two languages, since, as indicated above in the description of a comparable corpus, there is as yet no general agreement on the nature of the similarity.

One obvious selection criterion for the ACTRES project is text type, as each of the writing applications it is creating is intended for a given text type. Thus, for example, the wine tasting notes application requires a comparable corpus of wine tasting notes in English and in Spanish. And the meeting minutes application calls for a corpus of minutes in these two languages.

However, while certain text types imply automatically a certain content, this is not true of all text types. Thus, while all wine tasting notes involve to a greater or lesser extent the description and evaluation of a given wine and can therefore be considered reasonably similar in content, the same is not automatically true of minutes, for any meeting can cover a number of different topics.

Similarity of text type does not ensure similarity of style either, since there are variations in text types that involve variations in style. Let us use wine tasting notes as an example. Even this very narrow text type lends itself to different styles depending on whether it is integrated into a wine technical sheet prepared by a winery for oenologists and wine salesmen, or whether it is written for promotion of a wine to the general public.

From the above, it becomes clear that the criteria for similarity of texts in comparable corpora vary from one corpus to another and that the level of similarity varies as well. To achieve maximum similarity between English and Spanish wine tasting notes, we used the following selection criteria:

- Searching for wine tasting notes in the same type of source: specialized websites such as the websites for Denominations of origin in Spain that give direct and restricted access to the information written by winery oenologists, and the VQA Ontario Appellations of Origin website in English (among others) that groups together all the different Denominations of origin and hence wineries in that Canadian province.

- Using only those wine tasting notes included in wine tasting technical sheets released by wineries.
- Ensuring a balance of wine tasting notes for red wines, white wines, rosés, and sparkling wines.

The text selection criteria for the scientific abstracts application were the following:

- Using medical research abstracts in the field of cardiology;
- Selecting abstracts that appeared in high impact journals;
- Choosing abstracts written by native speakers.

While establishing and respecting these criteria did not completely eliminate differences between the English and Spanish texts, there were enough similarities for these comparable corpora to be used as the basis of analysis for the preparation of translation-based writing applications.

The size of the comparable corpora required to create such applications is another factor to be considered. In general, ACTRES's specialized comparable corpora average out to 200,000 words, meaning 100,000 words per language. While that may seem like a relatively small number, it is adequate for our purposes for a couple of reasons. First, each comparable corpus is a specialized corpus, as opposed to a general corpus that needs to be much larger. Second, what is just as important as the total number of words per language, is the number of texts per language, since these corpora are used for a text-based application: the wine tasting notes corpus, for instance, had over 700 notes in each language. In addition, since all the texts need to be individually labelled for rhetorical structure, it would be difficult to work with a much larger corpus.

Wherever possible, we select texts in electronic format to avoid the painful process of scanning. The texts are converted to .txt format before the process of analysis begins.

6. Analysis of the comparable corpus to identify the rhetorical structure of the text type in Spanish and in English

Rhetorical structure is the hierarchic organization of a text. It involves the various sections and subsections of a text, moves and steps, to use Swales' terminology (1990, 2005), and the relations between them. The rhetorical structure can vary from text to text and from language to language. But, by analysing a relatively large number of texts belonging to a specific text type, it is possible to identify the rhetorical structure of a given text type in a given language.

Such rhetorical analysis involves analysing a number of texts in a specific language in the comparable corpus, identifying the structure of each of these texts, and then comparing the different text structures to identify the most common structural elements. For the ACTRES project, the rhetorical analysis starts with the English texts, as the writing application is for English.

After examining about 100 English wine tasting notes, we were able to identify five different moves with various steps. Table 2 below shows the rhetorical structure of English wine tasting notes. The moves are marked one, two, three, etc., the steps are identified as a,b,c, etc.

1. Introductory remarks (IR)	4. Taste (TA)
2. **Appearance (AP)**	a. Flavors
a. Colour hue and depth	b. Finish
b. Clarity	c. Astringency
c. Viscosity	d. Mouthfeel
d. Effervescence	e. Body
3. **Aroma (AR)**	f. Balance
a. Fragance	5. Concluding remarks (CR)
b. Intensity	
c. Development	

Table 2. Wine tasting note rhetorical structure

These moves and steps did not always appear in the order presented above, but they constituted the main sections and subsections in the examined texts.

We next examined about 100 Spanish texts to see what differences, if any, there were in their rhetorical structure. In the case of the wine tasting notes, there were relatively few differences, but even if there had been more, we would have retained the basic rhetorical structure identified on the basis of the English texts, since users of the application would be writing in English. Identification of differences in the Spanish rhetorical structure simply allows us to foresee potential problems users may face when writing in English, problems which we have to bear in mind.

Once the rhetorical structure is identified, each of the texts in the comparable corpus is individually labelled, using a specially created computer program. The Tagger is an on-line software component designed to signal the rhetorical moves in every corpus as well as to manage and store the labelled files. The main window of the tagger provides a roll-down menu indicating the different genres that are being worked on; once a given text type is chosen, the window refreshes to show the customized set of rhetorical labels for that text type and the tool is ready to be used. See Figure 1 below.

Once the English and Spanish texts are tagged with rhetorical labels, the various moves and steps can be further compared and analysed using a specially created browser, whose search menu includes an option to analyze and contrast rhetorical structures as well as a concordancer. The browser allows the user the possibility of restricting the searches to a given move and or step/substep. See Figure 2 below.

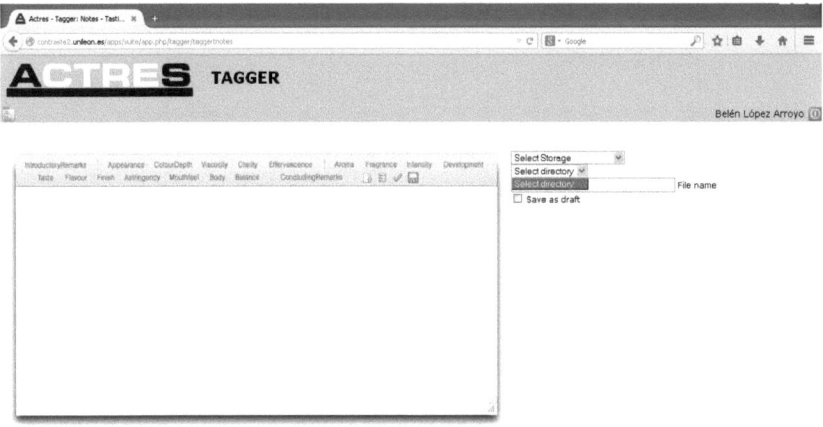

Figure 1. Tagger main window

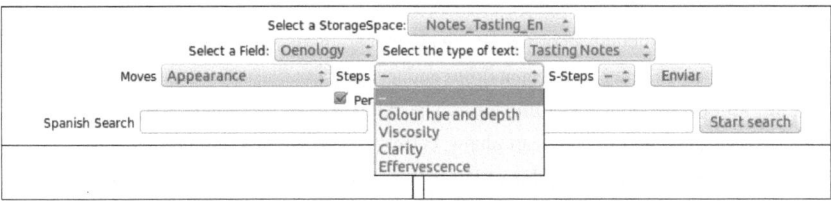

Figure 2. Concordancer Menu

7. Analysis of the English texts in the comparable corpus to identify model lines

The concordancer, specifically prepared for our needs, allows us to compare moves and steps in different texts, with the goal of identifying «model lines». Model lines, found in both writing templates and translation-based writing applications, are typical sentences and parts of sentences found in a given text type where the content and format is fairly standard. These are presented with blanks that users can fill in with words of their choice. They are derived from the comparable corpus using the following process.

By launching a query in the concordancer, the researcher first obtains a list of all the samples where a particular move occurs along with the rhetorical label. See Figure 3 below, which only presents partial results.

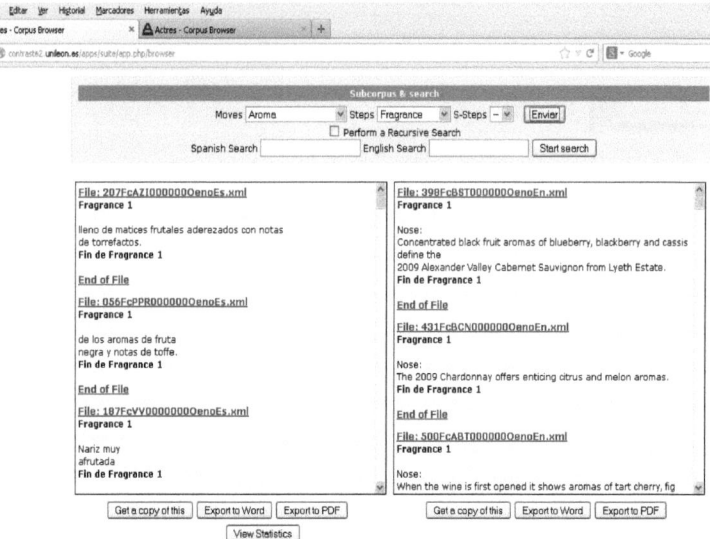

1. File 528FcSVE000000OenoEn.xml:... with a clean, pure **AROMA** of tangerine, orange, white flower, yellow plum, lemon drops and lemon grass. ...
2. File 366FcKSN000000OenoEn.xml:... The **AROMA** is filled with dark fruit such as cherries, boysenberries, elk heart plums, currents, pomegranate, cranberries, spice,...
3. File 575FcCWN000000OenoEn.xml:... with a pretty, summer rose garden **AROMA** perfectly accented by a medley of tropical fruit and lychee nuts. ...
4. File 431FcBCN000000OenoEn.xml:... Nose: The 2009 Chardonnay offers enticing citrus and melon **AROMAS**. ...
5. File 500FcABT000000OenoEn.xml:... Nose: When the wine is first opened it shows **AROMAS** of tart cherry, fig and cedar. Once it has had time to breath it demonstrates characters of red currant, blackberry, ea...
6. File 342FcBMS000000OenoEn.xml:... There are classic scents of vanilla and oak from the barrel aging. This wine has **AROMAS** of plum, black cherry and sage. The well integrated oak profile nicely compliments the fruit and spiciness of the wine....
7. File 383FcBPU000000OenoEn.xml:... Nose: Opens with **AROMAS** of ripe Bing cherries and rose petal. ...

8. File 578FcCCN000000OenoEn.xml:... with **AROMAS** of ripe apple, blossoms, stone fruit, pear and a touch of tropical fruit suggesting banana and pineapple. ...
9. File 289FcEPT000000OenoEn.xml:... The 2010 'Les Pommiers' offers **AROMAS** of Bing cherry, pomegranate and plum, with an abundance of floral and perfume notes. ...

Figure 3. Concordance lines

Based on these and other examples of expression of the fragrance of aromas, the following linguistic elements can be deduced:

    A wine can *offer/show* aromas
    Aromas can be *aromas of (cherry, fig, etc.)* or *(cherry/fig, etc.) aromas.*

This leads to the identification of the following model lines for the fragrance step of the aroma move. The model lines are grouped together on the basis of their complexity, and each model line is followed by an example from the English corpus.

1. Simplest Model Lines (Verbless sentences)

    Aromas of (*aromas*)
    Aromas of Meyer lemon, toasted nuts and fig
    Notes of (*aromas*) aromas
    Notes of raspberry and red berries
    (*Aroma a*) Elige: aroma(s)/note(s) 4 opciones: aroma, aromas, note, notes
    Sweet grapefruit and melon aromas/notes

2. Relatively Simple Model Lines

    (*Elige*: The wine, o *nombre del vino*) offers aromas of (*aromas*)
    The 2009 Far Niente Cabernet Sauvignon offers aromas of boysenberry and blackberry pie, tobacco leaf, cassis and toasted oak
    (*Elige*: The wine, o *nombre del vino*) opens with aromas of (*aromas*)
    The silky 2008 opens with aromas of white peach
    (*Elige*: The wine, o *nombre del vino*) shows aromas of (*aromas*)
    When the wine is first opened it shows aromas of tart cherry, fig and Cedar

3. More Complex Model Lines (combining fragrance with other steps):

    (*Elige*: The wine, *o nombre del vino*) is (*color*) in colour, *Elige*: displaying/showing aromas of (*aromas a*)
    Our Columbia Valley Reserve Cabernet Sauvignon is ruby red in color, displaying aromas of ripe red strawberry and sweet oak toast
    (*Elige*: The wine, o *nombre del vino*) opens with aromas of (*aromas*) that are enhanced by notes of (*describe la complejidad*)
    This wine opens with enticing aromas of honeysuckle and pear that are enhanced by notes of orange blossoms and toasted almond
    (*Aromas de*) aromas give the wine a/n *elige*: a o an (*describe la complejidad*) bouquet

Sweet grapefruit and melon aromas give the wine a(n) oak complex bouquet.
(*Elige*: The wine, o *nombre del vino*) offers describe la intensidad del vino aromas of (*aromas*)
This wine offers intense aromas of ripe blackberry and boysenberry layered with baking spices and licorice

These model lines will be offered in the wine tasting notes writing application as possibilities for the user to discuss the fragrance step of the aroma move.

8. Use of the comparable corpus to create a bilingual lexicon

As mentioned earlier, some potential users of the writing applications will have only a limited knowledge of English and may decide to introduce some words of Spanish as they try to write in English. For instance, they may want to say «aromas of blackberry» but may not know the English term for «blackberry». So they may insert «aromas of *zarzamora*». This is where the translation element of the writing application comes into play, with a bilingual lexicon offering the user one (or more) English equivalents for a word or phrase.

The bilingual lexicon has to work from Spanish into English, since the user would search for a word in his foreign language, English. However, entries for the bilingual lexicon are suggested by the model lines in English. Just sticking to the Fragrance step of the Aroma move, it becomes obvious that different types of aromas need to be repertoried. Based on the English examples identified by the concordancer, these fall into several categories: fruits, flowers, spices, foods, woods, etc. After making a list of elements contained in each of these categories, we can identify their Spanish counterparts by analyzing the same move and step in the Spanish texts using the concordance. An important feature of the lexicon is that it allows for the inclusion of phraseology as well as simple terminology. Thus, after identifying «offers aromas» and «displays aromas» as common phrases in the wine tasting language of English, the researcher looks for their phraseological equivalents in the Spanish corpus.

If a bilingual parallel corpus were available, the bilingual lexicon would be faster to create, because the English texts and their Spanish translations or the Spanish texts and their English translations could be aligned, which would allow a bilingual concordancer to immediately identify equivalents. However, as mentioned above, the quality of the lexicon would depend on the quality of the translations, whereas the use of a comparable corpus to create a bilingual lexicon, while more time-consuming and complex, ensures better quality as the texts in both languages are originals.

9. Creating the translation-based writing application

Using all the information gathered from the many steps of analysis of the comparable corpus, as presented above, the translation-based writing application, also termed generator, is created. The generator presents the moves and steps in Spanish to the user (e.g. *AROMA (obligatorio) (excepto para los usuarios que hayan elegido Color+Aroma en mov.1)*, who can then begin the writing phase. He is offered a structure in English with parts in parentheses and suggestions of the kind of lexical information that could fill the parentheses. The suggestions are in Spanish and the writer can insert Spanish terms here as the generator's dictionary will supply the English equivalent. For example, *Aromas of + (fruta, madera, especias)*.

The information that is provided to the user in bold cannot be changed. However, scroll down menus offer different options for nouns or adjectives expressing the appropriate aromas to describe the wine. So the user only has to choose the grammatical structure and «fill in the blanks» with the lexical information desired.

Thus, the generator includes the following elements:
1. the prototypical rhetorical structure showing the moves and steps to be included when writing a wine tasting note in English;
2. the lexico-grammatical patterns most frequently used in each move and step so as to solve problems of how to string words together not only correctly and acceptably but also idiomatically, aspects identified by prospective users as problematic;
3. the bilingual terminological and phraseological glossary, (with examples extracted from the corpus), which will provide not only subtechnical terms but also their most common collocations.

Thus, the generator is not an empty template, but a reliable corpus-based, computer-friendly, translation-based application that will guide Spanish speakers through the writing process in English, as illustrated below.[1]

---

[1] The wine tasting note generator produced by ACTRES has received an award in the *I Concurso Transfronterizo de Prototipos Orientados al Mercado*.

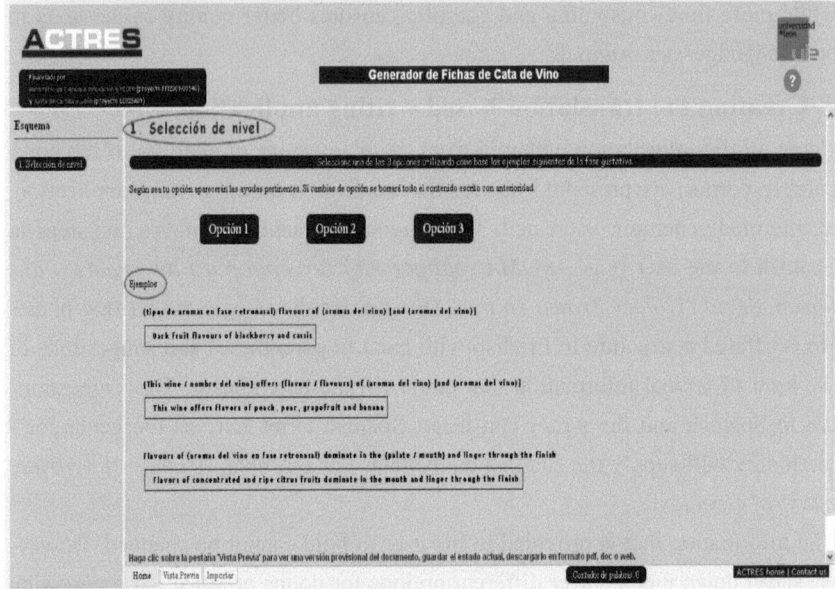

Figure 4a. Generator

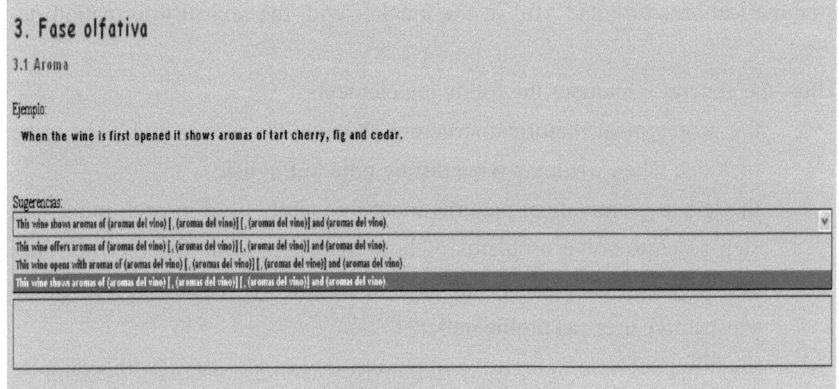

Figure 4b. Generator

10. Conclusion

In this era of globalization, not only specific discourse communities but also societies in general are demanding the development of useful and usable tools to improve cross-linguistic communication (Rabadán 2008: 106; 2008a; Quesenbery 2001; Kreitzberg & Little 2009).

As we have shown, templates are not satisfactory tools for non-native speakers of English, since they are designed to help English-speaking professionals write specific specialized genres with which they are not familiar. Non-native speakers require reliable and ready to use writing applications to guide them through the process of writing in a foreign language.

ACTRES's translation-based writing applications, which we have presented above, exemplify one specific outcome of corpus-based studies. The ACTRES project, which focuses on rhetoric, differs to some extent from the majority of corpus-based projects, which have been motivated by two major research goals (Biber, Conrad, & Reppen 1998: 5-8):

1. To describe linguistic features, such as vocabulary, lexical combinations, or grammatical features.

2. To describe the overall characteristics of a variety: a register or dialect.

While each ACTRES writing application, which deals with one given text type, involves corpus analysis of the linguistic features as well as the register characteristics associated with that text type, the primary focus is on the rhetorical structure of the text type, rather than on the two major research goals of corpus linguistics identified by Biber, Conrad, & Reppen (1998).

Another difference between the ACTRES project and many corpus-based projects is the clearly practical orientation of the former. There is no doubt that some corpus-based projects have resulted in practical applications in the form of dictionaries based on analysis of actual word use in corpora examples, such as the *Collins CoBuild English Language Dictionary* (1987), the *Longman Dictionary of Contemporary English* (1987), and the *Cambridge Advanced Learner's Dictionary* (2005), or in the form of grammars, such as the *Longman Grammar of Spoken and Written English* (Biber, Conrad, & Reppen 1999) and *Cambridge Grammar of English* (Carter & McCarthy 2006), which apply corpus-based analyses to show how any grammatical feature can be described for structural characteristics as well as patterns of use across spoken and written registers. However, many corpus-based projects have produced results, which, while interesting, have no immediate application value. This is not the case of the ACTRES project, whose goal is primarily to produce writing tools for use by Spanish professionals called upon to write specialized texts in English.

Perhaps the most significant contribution of the ACTRES project is not the writing tools produced, but the methodology it has established for corpus analysis of comparable corpora to create the writing tools. This methodology can be used by other linguists to create writing tools in English or, indeed, in any foreign language, for speakers of other languages.

11. References

Biber, Douglas. 1993. Representativeness in corpus design. @ *Literary and Linguistic Computing*, 8/4: 243-257.

Biber, Douglas, Susan Conrad & Randy Reppen 1998. *Corpus Linguistics: Investigating Language Structure and Use*. Cambridge: Cambridge University Press. ISBN 9780521499576.

Biber, Douglas et al. 1999. *Longman Grammar of Spoken and Written English*. Harlow: Pearson Education Limited. ISBN 978-0582237254.

Biber, Douglas, Ulla Connor & Thomas A. Upton, eds, 2007. *Discourse on the Move. Using Corpus Analysis to Describe Discourse Structure*. Antwerp: John Benjamins. ISBN 9789027223029.

Biber, Douglas & Susan Conrad. 2009. *Register, Genre & Style*. Cambridge: Cambridge University Press. ISBN 9780521860604.

Biber, Douglas, Randy Reppen & Edward Friginal. 2010. Research in Corpus Linguistics @ R. Kaplan, ed. *The Oxford Handbook of Applied Linguistics* (2 ed.). Oxford: Oxford University Press. ISBN 9780195384253, pp 548-570.

Cambridge Advanced Learner's Dictionary. 2005. Cambridge: C.U.P. Available at <https://dictionary.cambridge.org/dictionary/british/>. [Accessed 22 February 2014].

Carter, Ronald & Michael McCarthy. 2006. *Cambridge Grammar of English: A Comprehensive Guide; Spoken and Written English Grammar and Usage*. Cambridge: Cambridge University Press. ISBN 9780521588461.

Collins CoBuild English Language Dictionary. 1987. London & Glasgow: Collins. Available at <http://www.collinsdictionary.com/dictionary/english>. [Accessed 22 February 2014].

EF. *English Proficiency Index*. 2011. Available at <http://www.ef.com/__/~/media/efcom/epi/pdf/EF-EPI-2011.pdf%20EF >. [Accessed 7 March 2014].

European Commission. 2012. *Europeans and their languages. Report. Special Eurobarometer 386*. Brussels: European Union. Available at <http://ec.europa.eu/public_opinion/archives/ebs/ebs_243_en.pdf>. [Accessed 7 March 2014].

Flowerdew, Lynne. 2005. An Integrated Approach of Corpus-Based and Genre-Based Approaches to Text Analysis in EAP/ESP: Countering Criticism. @ *English for Specific Purposes*, 24: 321-332.

Graddol, David. 1997. *The Future of English*. London: The British Council. Available at <http://www.britishcouncil.org/learning-elt-future.pdf>. [Accessed 7 March 2014].

Ginsburgh, Victor & Sholom Weber. 2011. *How Many Languages Do we Need? The Economics of Linguistic Diversity*. Princeton NJ: Princeton University Press. ISBN 9780691136899.

Kreitberg, Charles & Ambrose Little. 2009.Usability as a core development competence @ *MSDN Magazine*. Available at <http://msdn.microsoft.com/en-us/magazine/dd727512.aspx>. [Accessed 11 August 2014].

Lane Green, Rose. 2012. English Where She Is Spoke @ *The Economist*. Available at <http://www.economist.com/blogs/johnson/2012/10/language-skills>. [Accessed 7 March 2014].

Mydans, Seth. 2007. Across Cultures, English Is the Word @ *The NYtimes*. Available at <http://www.nytimes.com/2007/04/09/world/asia/09iht-englede.1.5198685.html?pagewanted=all&_r=0>. [Accessed 7 March 2014].

Quesenbery, Whitney. 2001. What Does Usability Mean: Looking Beyond 'Ease of Use'. Available at <http://www.digitalspaceart.com/projects/cogweb2002v2/papers/whitney/whitney1.html>. [Accessed 22 February 2014].

Rabadán Álvarez, Rosa. 2008. Refining the Idea of 'Applied Extensions'. @ A. Pym, M. Schlesinger & D. Simeoni, eds. *Beyond Descriptive Translation Studies: Investigations in Homage to Gideon Toury*. Antwerp: John Benjamins. ISBN 9789027216847, pp 103-118.

Rabadán Álvarez, Rosa. 2008a. Tools for English-Spanish Cross Linguistic Applied Research @ *Journal of English Studies* 5/6: 309-324.

Scientific blogging. Science 2.0. 2012. EU Citizens Linguistically Disenfranchised by the Prevalence of English @ *Science 2.0. Join the Revolution*. Available at <http://www.science20.com/news_articles/eu_citizens_linguistically_disenfranchised_prevalence_english>. [Accessed 7 March 2014].

Southern Methodist University Research. 2012. *Vast Majority of European Union Citizens are Marginalized by Dominance of English Language*. Dallas: Southern Methodist University Press.

Swales, John. 1990. *Genre Analysis: English in Academic and Research Settings*. Cambridge: Cambridge University Press. ISBN 9780521328692.

Swales, John. 2004. *Research Genres*. Cambridge: Cambridge University Press. ISBN 9780521533348.

Cómo crear y analizar corpus paralelos. Un procedimiento con *software* accesible y económico y algunas sugerencias para *software* futuro

[How to build and analyse parallel corpora. A procedure with accessible and affordable software and some suggestions for future software]

INMACULADA SERÓN ORDÓÑEZ
Universidad Pablo de Olavide (Sevilla, España)
iseron@upo.es

> **Abstract:** The drawbacks of computer programs such as WordSmith Tools, MultiConcord and ParaConc when it comes to building and analysing—qualitatively especially—parallel corpora have been revealed by many researchers (Malmkjær 1998: 6, Bosseaux 2004, Coulthard 2005: 67). Other more appropriate applications are either linked to specific corpora or restricted in access.
> All of these obstacles can be circumvented by the procedure for building and analysing parallel corpora that is presented in this article. Such procedure, which is based on programs used in the professional translation industry (more specifically, SDLX and Examine32), offers two additional advantages: on the one hand, low cost; on the other, great flexibility, enabling use with dramatic and lyric genres, besides narrative ones.
> The procedure presented will be particularly useful for individual translation scholars wishing to build and analyse their own parallel corpora. This article not only presents it, but also suggests features for future parallel corpus building and analysis software.
> **Key words:** corpus building; corpus analysis; parallel corpora; accessible software; future software

1. Antecedentes

El análisis de textos originales en un idioma y sus traducciones correspondientes a otro(s) idioma(s) no es una tarea inusual en traductología. Cuando será un análisis en profundidad, las ventajas de alinear originales y traducciones, y de poder realizar búsquedas de concordancia en ellos, son evidentes. Sin embargo, y pese al fuerte impulso que está recibiendo desde hace algunos años la traductología basada en corpus, las herramientas informáticas para crear y analizar corpus «paralelos» en lugar de «monolingües» (Baker 1995) —por ejemplo, MultiConcord y ParaConc— son escasas y presentan considerables deficiencias (excluyendo aquellos programas que, por estar vinculados a corpus concretos o ser de acceso restringido, no están disponibles para un investigador cualquiera que desee trabajar con su propio corpus).

Los traductólogos han solido recurrir bien a esas herramientas o bien a otras para corpus monolingües en lugar de paralelos que presentan similares inconvenientes —por ejemplo, WordSmith Tools—; en ocasiones, como se verá más adelante, las han usado en combinación.

Posiblemente, la deficiencia más notable —o, al menos, que ha afectado a más investigadores— de estos dos tipos de herramientas derivados de la lingüística de corpus sea que ofrecen escaso contexto para cada resultado de una búsqueda de concordancia. Este aspecto ha sido puesto de relieve por varios autores. A finales de los años 90, Kirsten Malmkjær (1998: 6) alertaba de que:

> [...] in order to be able to provide any kinds of *explanation* of the data provided by the [parallel] corpus, rather than mere statistics, analysts really need substantially more context than computers tend to search and display.[1]

Algunos años más tarde, Robert James Coulthard (2005: 67) llamaba la atención sobre el mismo problema en una revisión de los programas informáticos que permiten consultar corpus paralelos:

> [...] there are certain problems with existing parallel corpus software, the most significant of which is the lack of scope provided by the viewing window and the restricted context that this results in.[2]

El problema de la escasez de contexto puede ilustrarse fácilmente, con fines de concreción, mediante los tres programas mencionados hasta el momento, que se encuentran entre los más conocidos y usados. MultiConcord no ofrece contexto más allá del párrafo de la coincidencia. ParaConc ofrece solo varios párrafos. Por último, WordSmith Tools, hasta muy recientemente, permitía al usuario ampliar el contexto, más allá del renglón de la coincidencia, de dos en dos renglones (Olohan 2004: 73), pero su ventana de resultados no tenía barra de desplazamiento y, cuanto más se ampliara el contexto, más probabilidades había de

---

[1] «[...] para poder ofrecer cualquier tipo de *explicación* de los datos proporcionados por el corpus [paralelo], en lugar de meras estadísticas, los analistas verdaderamente necesitan notablemente más contexto del que los ordenadores tienden a explorar y mostrar.» (traducción propia)

[2] «[...] el software existente para corpus paralelos presenta algunos problemas, el más importante de los cuales es la falta de espacio de la ventana de visualización y el restringido contexto resultante.» (traducción propia)

Cómo crear y analizar corpus paralelos

que no todos los resultados quedaran visibles (suponiendo que antes de la ampliación del contexto todos los resultados estuvieran visibles, lo que no siempre ocurría). Su versión 5.0, lanzada en 2008, incluía leves mejoras en la ampliación de contexto; no obstante, no ha sido hasta su versión 6.0 (2012) cuando el programa ha incorporado barra de desplazamiento.

La incapacidad para realizar búsquedas de concordancia simultáneamente en más de cuatro textos alineados (Serón Ordóñez 2012: 408, respecto a ParaConc) o la imposibilidad de alinear textos dramáticos por réplica (Bandín 2007: 28, respecto a Translation Corpus Aligner 2) son otras de las deficiencias lamentadas. En relación con la primera, conviene subrayar que cuatro textos no son más que un original y tres traducciones, lo que trae a colación la defensa de Malmkjær (1998) del análisis de tantas traducciones de un original como sea posible, basada en que la selección de los textos traducidos para su inclusión en un corpus paralelo puede afectar en demasía a los resultados de la observación y en que un corpus paralelo bitextual «still only provides, for each instance, the result of one individual's introspection, albeit contextually and cotextually informed»[3] (1998: 6). Al filo del cambio de siglo, la investigadora instaba a empezar a complementar los estudios de grandes corpus paralelos bilingües de orientación cuantitativa con corpus más pequeños con el mayor número de traducciones de un mismo original que fuera posible (Malmkjær 1998: 6).

Las limitaciones expuestas han llevado a algunos investigadores y pequeños grupos de investigación a crear sus propias herramientas. Por citar un ejemplo, Coulthard (2005), quien califica en general a MultiConcord de insatisfactorio (Coulthard 2005: 11), desarrolló una aplicación para analizar corpus (véase la figura 1) y la combinó con WordSmith Tools, Google Desktop Search y TweakGDS (la primera para fines estadísticos y las otras dos para la búsqueda de archivos en su corpus —TweakGDS restringió las búsquedas de Google Desktop Search a su corpus, desde su ordenador completo—).

---

[3] «solo proporciona, para cada caso, el resultado de la introspección de un individuo, aunque informado contextual y cotextualmente» (traducción propia).

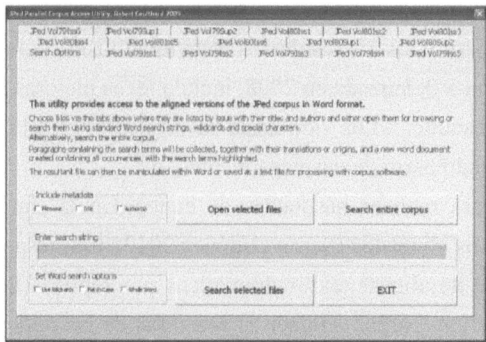

Fig. 1. Ventana de búsqueda de la herramienta de búsqueda en corpus paralelos desarrollada por Robert J. Coulthard (Coulthard 2005: 68)

El procedimiento de creación y análisis de corpus que se presenta en este artículo es otra solución, que no implica nuevo software y se caracteriza por su bajo coste económico y su gran capacidad para ser adaptada a diferentes proyectos. Con ella, se pretende facilitar a otros investigadores la creación y el análisis de sus propios corpus. No en vano, la falta de herramientas adecuadas para crear y analizar corpus paralelos puede haber tenido consecuencias de tanto alcance en traductología como ralentizar la incorporación de los estudios de corpus a la disciplina, como ha reconocido Berber Sardinha (2002: 20).

El siguiente apartado se dedica a describir esta nueva solución. En el tercer apartado, se consideran sus posibilidades de adaptación, así como sus limitaciones. Por último, en el cuarto apartado, dedicado a las conclusiones, se ofrecen algunas ideas para avanzar hacia el desarrollo de programas que, por un lado, permitan a investigadores individuales y pequeños grupos de investigación crear sus propios corpus paralelos y, por otro, les faciliten su análisis; concretamente, se indican prestaciones que tales programas deberían incluir.

2. La solución

A diferencia de las aplicaciones que hasta la fecha se han venido utilizando con más frecuencia en traductología para la creación y el análisis de corpus, el procedimiento que se presenta en este artículo no procede de la lingüística de corpus, sino del sector profesional de la traducción; específicamente en el sentido de que combina los programas SDLX (versión 2005 [SDL International, 1997-2005]) y Examine32 (versión 3.31a [Aquila Software, 1993–2002]). El primero es un sistema de gestión de memorias de traducción; el segundo, una aplicación de búsqueda en archivos que los traductores utilizan para realizar búsquedas terminológicas en glosarios.

Tanto SDLX como Examine32 son programas accesibles. Este último es *shareware* y se puede usar gratuitamente durante un periodo de evaluación de 30 días. Una vez concluido tal periodo, para continuar usándolo, debe adquirirse una licencia cuyo precio actual es 28 €. El programa está disponible para su descarga en el sitio web <http://www.examine32.com/>.

En lo que se refiere a SDLX, desde finales de la década de 2000 forma parte del paquete del sistema de memorias de traducción Trados, lo que lo ha llevado a los ordenadores de un elevado número de traductores profesionales y centros de formación de traductores, como universidades.

La combinación que a continuación se hace de ambos programas permite realizar búsquedas de concordancia en tantos textos alineados como se desee, así como visualizar tanto contexto como sea necesario para cada resultado de una búsqueda. Además, la visualización de los resultados resulta considerablemente más cómoda que en otras aplicaciones. Por ejemplo, la ventana de resultados muestra cada segmento que incluye una coincidencia junto con sus segmentos «paralelos» (véase la figura 2); en cambio, en ParaConc, cada coincidencia aparece junto con las demás coincidencias del mismo texto, lo que dificulta la comparación de original y traducciones (véase la figura 3, en página siguiente).

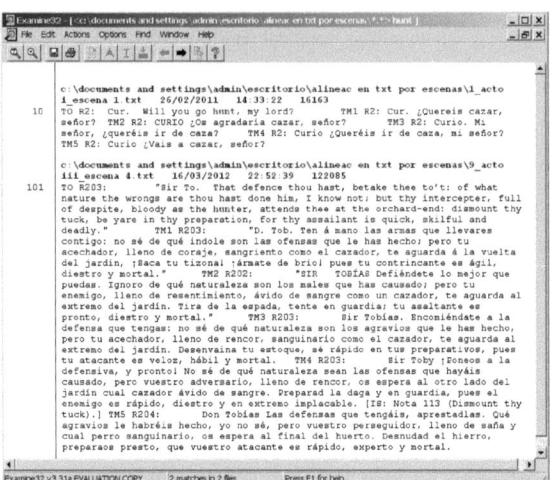

Fig. 2. Resultados de una búsqueda a través de Examine32
en un corpus de seis textos

Los siguientes subapartados describen el procedimiento paso a paso, incidiendo en otras de sus ventajas cuando estas salen a relucir. Cada subapartado se corresponde con una de sus cinco fases:
1. alineación;
2. exportación;
3. agrupación en un solo archivo de todos los textos alineados (para corpus de más de dos textos);
4. realización de ajustes para enriquecer los resultados de las búsquedas de concordancia; y
5. análisis.

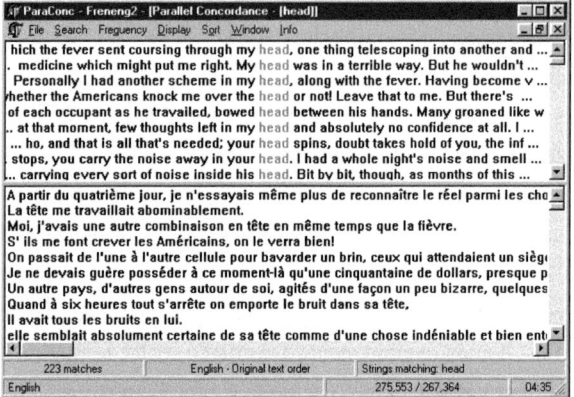

Fig. 3. Resultados de una búsqueda a través de ParaConc en un corpus bitextual (Barlow 2003: 30)

De la misma manera que la tercera fase solo será necesaria cuando el corpus vaya a incluir más de dos textos alineados (por ejemplo, un texto original —en adelante, «TO»— y dos traducciones de dicho texto —o *textos meta*; en adelante, «TM»—), algunos de los ajustes incluidos en la cuarta fase pueden resultar innecesarios según el proyecto, y otros son de naturaleza optativa.

Naturalmente, el procedimiento debe ir precedido de la digitalización de los textos en caso de que estos no se encuentren en formato electrónico. Si bien describir un proceso de digitalización no entra dentro de los objetivos de este artículo, conviene especificar que los textos que se vayan a alinear deberán estar en un formato legible por ordenador (como el formato de Microsoft Word .doc), razón por la cual si hay textos en formato de imagen (sean o no resultado de una digitalización), deberán someterse a un proceso de reconocimiento óptico de caracteres (OCR, por sus siglas en inglés). ABBYY FineReader es un programa eficaz tanto para el reconocimiento óptico de caracteres como para la corrección posterior de los fallos cometidos por este reconocimiento (para más detalles acerca de ambos procesos y de cómo se pueden llevar a cabo con ABBYY FineReader, véase Serón Ordóñez 2012: 382-383).

2.1. Fase 1: alineación

La alineación la realiza automáticamente SDL Align, el módulo de alineación de SDLX. Este programa admite el formato .doc en los archivos para alinear, a diferencia de aplicaciones como WordSmith Tools, MultiConcord y ParaConc, que requieren un formato de solo texto (como .txt), el cual conllevaría la pérdida de formato como la negrita o la cursiva ya en esta fase inicial.

También la segmentación por párrafos, en lugar de oraciones, de SDLX coloca a este programa en una posición de ventaja.[4] La segmentación por párrafos será especialmente útil para textos dramáticos que se quieran alinear por réplica, o textos líricos que se quieran alinear por estrofa, por poner dos ejemplos. Continuando con este último, para que el programa reconozca cada estrofa, simplemente hay que asegurarse de que al final de cada verso haya un salto de línea (↵), y al final de cada estrofa, una marca de párrafo (¶). De la misma manera, en el caso de un texto dramático, en el cuerpo del texto, las marcas de párrafo estarían ubicadas al final de cada réplica (véase la figura 4).

---

[4] WordSmith Tools alinea únicamente por oraciones. MultiConcord alinea también por oraciones, aunque de un modo que permite visualizar párrafos alineados. La alineación se efectúa «en el momento» cada vez que se realiza una búsqueda de concordancia. El programa busca coincidencias y, al detectar una coincidencia en un párrafo determinado, comienza a alinear las oraciones de ese párrafo con las del párrafo «paralelo» hasta llegar a la oración en la que se encuentra la coincidencia. Los resultados, que solo pueden verse uno a uno, muestran la oración de la coincidencia y la oración del otro texto que, según los cálculos del programa, es equivalente (funcionalmente). Los párrafos en los que se encuentran ambas oraciones pueden verse entonces con un solo clic, aunque tener que hacer clic para ver cada párrafo añadiría un paso innecesario a investigaciones no interesadas en la alineación por oraciones. En lo que respecta a ParaConc, si bien permite alinear por párrafos y por oraciones, es superado por SDLX en facilidad de manejo.

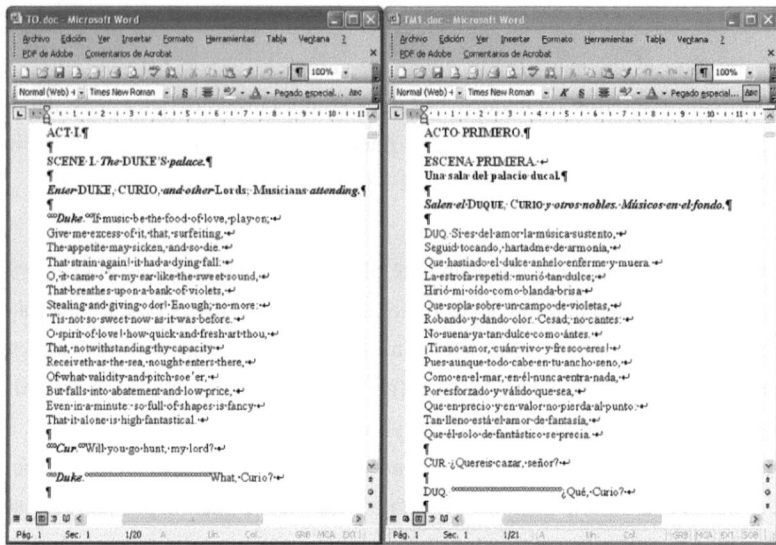

Fig. 4. Distribución de saltos de línea y marcas de párrafo
para la alineación por párrafos (réplicas) de un TO y un TM teatrales

El reemplazo automático de todas las marcas de párrafo por saltos de línea y la sustitución posterior de algunos saltos de línea concretos por marcas de párrafo pueden agilizar enormemente la preparación de los textos para la alineación por párrafos (véase para más detalles Serón Ordóñez 2012: 383-386).

Si se crean documentos con una estructura de párrafos (u oraciones, en el caso de la alineación por oraciones) idéntica, los resultados de la alineación serán óptimos, es decir, no requerirán ninguna corrección manual. Esto es especialmente útil con traducciones que no se correspondan formalmente con el TO a nivel de párrafo (u oración) debido a supresiones o adiciones. Para conseguirlo, se pueden introducir párrafos (u oraciones) vacíos donde se omitió en una traducción un párrafo (u oración) (véase la figura 5, donde «IS» representa las iniciales de la autora de este artículo); o se pueden separar con saltos de línea párrafos de una traducción que en el original formaban un solo párrafo (véase la figura 6). El resultado de estas operaciones demuestra que la falta de correspondencia párrafo por párrafo (u oración por oración) entre una traducción y su TO no es óbice para que estos textos se puedan alinear automáticamente (*cf.* Bandín 2007: 28).

Cómo crear y analizar corpus paralelos

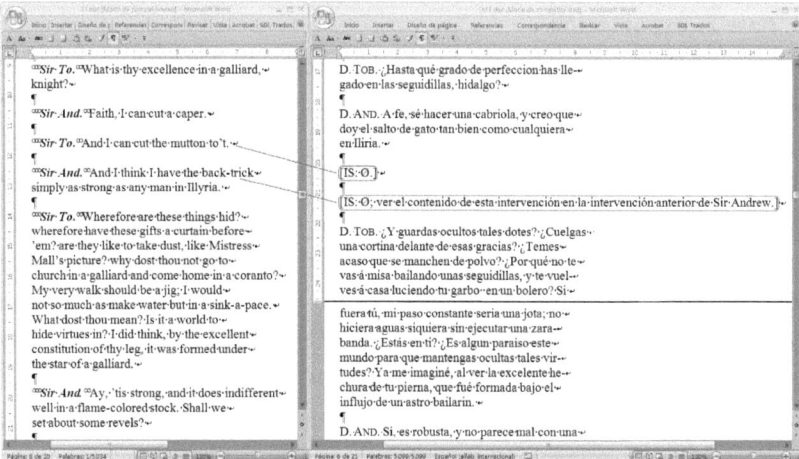

Fig. 5. Dos párrafos «vacíos» creados en una traducción
en lugares en los que se omitían párrafos (réplicas) del original

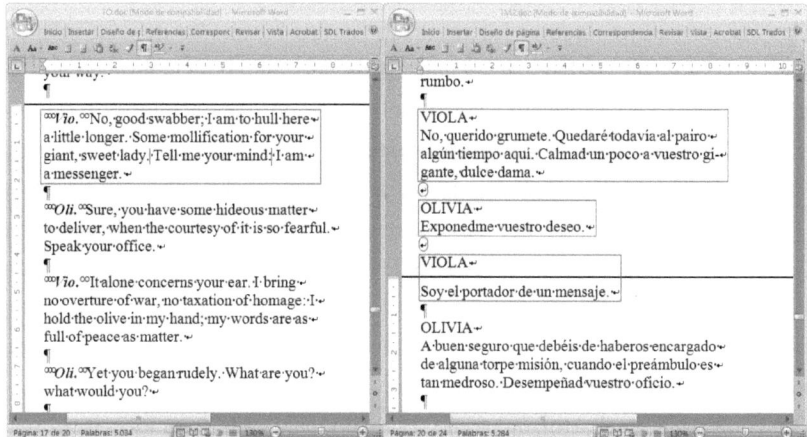

Fig. 6. Varios párrafos de una traducción que se corresponden
con un solo párrafo en el original, separados con saltos de línea

Un inconveniente de SDL Align es que no permite alinear más de dos textos a la vez, de modo que en caso de que haya que alinear más de dos textos, deberán alinearse por pares (TO-TM1, TO-TM2, etcétera).[5]

---

[5] Tradicionalmente los alineadores no han podido alinear más dos textos simultáneamente.

2.2. Fase 2: exportación

Una vez que los textos estén alineados, será necesario exportar el resultado de la alineación a un archivo de Microsoft Excel especificando que TO y TM queden delimitados por una tabulación. La exportación se realiza en SDL Maintain, módulo de SDLX con el que se abren los archivos de alineación en forma de memorias de traducción. En el menú «TM» (Translation Memory, memoria de traducción) de dicho módulo, se debe seleccionar «Export» (exportar). Aparecerán una serie de ventanas en las que es preciso seleccionar las siguientes opciones según vayan apareciendo: «Delimited File» (archivo delimitado), «Tab» (tabulación), «Source» (original) y «Target» (traducción). Los demás parámetros de exportación deben permanecer tal como están. El TO ocupará la primera columna de una hoja del archivo de Excel creado y el TM, la segunda.

Si el corpus fuese bitextual, con esto su creación habría concluido, a falta de posibles ajustes para enriquecer los resultados de las búsquedas de concordancia (véase 2.4), así como, tal vez, de la conversión del archivo de alineación en formato de Excel (.xls) a formato «Texto (delimitado por tabulaciones) (.txt)», necesaria a veces para una visualización óptima de los resultados. Para realizar esta conversión, basta con abrir el archivo .xls, hacer clic en «Guardar como» y elegir «Texto (delimitado por tabulaciones) (.txt)» en la lista desplegable «Guardar como tipo», dentro del cuadro de diálogo «Guardar como». Este guardado debe ser posterior a la realización, en su caso, de algunos de los ajustes mencionados (véanse 2.4.1, 2.4.2 y el segundo párrafo de 2.4.4). Como se detallará más adelante, las búsquedas de concordancia se realizarán en Examine32, y en un corpus bitextual arrojarán como resultado, para cada coincidencia, el segmento original seguido del segmento meta.

2.3. Fase 3 (para corpus de más de dos textos alineados): agrupación de los textos en un solo archivo

Con un corpus de más de dos textos, para que Examine32 muestre todas las traducciones de un segmento original tras ese segmento, hay que reunir en una sola hoja de Excel todos los textos, ubicando cada uno en una columna, tal como se puede apreciar en la figura 7. Para ello, basta con copiar las columnas correspondientes de los archivos que se hayan creado mediante la exportación.

Cómo crear y analizar corpus paralelos

Fig. 7. Resultado de la alineación de seis textos en Excel (I)

2.4. Fase 4: realización de ajustes para enriquecer los resultados de las búsquedas de concordancia

Si Examine32 hace búsquedas en un archivo como el de la figura 7, o en su versión en formato .txt, los resultados no son como los mostrados en la figura 2, sino como los que se muestran a continuación en la figura 8, que corresponden a la misma búsqueda de la figura 2.

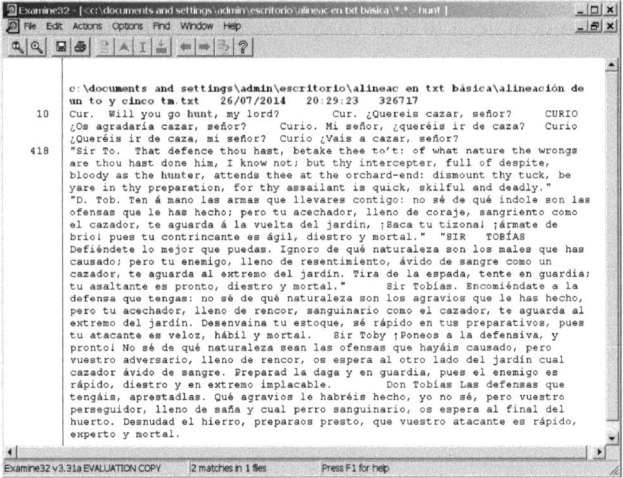

Fig. 8. Resultados de una búsqueda a través de Examine32 cuando no se ha realizado ningún ajuste tras la exportación (y agrupación en un solo archivo) de los textos alineados

Como puede observarse, las diferencias entre las figuras 2 y 8 son notables, y estriban en la cantidad de información que aparece sobre los segmentos de los dos resultados obtenidos. La figura 8 solo proporciona un dato acerca de tales segmentos: su posición en el archivo en el que se ha realizado la búsqueda, que figura a la izquierda del resultado pertinente (véanse los números *10* y *418*) y corresponde al número de línea en dicho archivo (o, lo que es lo mismo, al número de fila en el archivo de Excel de origen). En cambio, la figura 2 ofrece mucha más información. Identifica cada segmento indicando: *a*) a qué texto pertenece (TO, TM1, TM2, etc.);[6] *b*) el acto en el que aparece (I o III, según el resultado); *c*) la escena (1 o 4); *d*) su número de réplica dentro del acto si es una réplica (2 en todos los textos en el primer resultado; en el segundo, 203 en los casos del TO y de los TM 1, 3 y 4, 202 en el caso del TM2, y 204 en el del TM5); y *e*) su número de segmento (o fila en el archivo de Excel de origen) dentro de la escena (10 o 101), dato que puede ser útil si el segmento no constituye una réplica. Además, en la figura 2 consta que la réplica 203 del TM4 tiene asociada una nota relativa a la expresión «Dismount thy tuck» del TO. Para que las búsquedas en Examine32 arrojen todos estos datos, se han realizado ajustes que se describen seguidamente junto con otras mejoras, esencialmente la incorporación de las notas completas al archivo de alineación multitextual en formato .xls.

2.4.1. *Identificación del texto (punto* a*) anterior)*

La identificación del texto se ha hecho posible añadiendo seis columnas más al archivo de alineación multitextual en formato .xls, una por texto. Cada columna debe ir situada junto a la columna de su texto respectivo (en el corpus de ejemplo, se colocó justo antes de dicha columna) y debe contener en todas sus filas un código que identifique este texto (como *TO*, *TM1*, *TM2*, etc., que son los códigos del corpus de ejemplo). Cada segmento del texto que aparezca en la ventana de resultados irá precedido de ese código, como muestra la figura 2 (frente a la 8).

---

[6] Puesto que el orden en el que aparecen los segmentos siempre es el mismo (TO, TM1, TM2, TM3, TM4 y TM5) y viene determinado por el orden de los textos en el archivo de Excel de origen, esta información está presente de algún modo en la figura 8. No obstante, hacerla explícita facilita considerablemente la tarea del investigador y evita confusiones respecto al texto al que pertenece un segmento concreto.

2.4.2. Identificación de la réplica (punto d) anterior)

Si en cada columna adicional se numeran los segmentos que constituyen réplicas añadiendo al código del texto el número correspondiente (*TO R1*, *TO R2*, etc., donde *R* equivale a *réplica*), cada réplica que se visualice en la ventana de resultados aparecerá numerada, como se puede apreciar en la figura 2.

La figura 9 muestra las seis columnas adicionales en su forma final. Obsérvense los códigos de texto y los números de réplica.

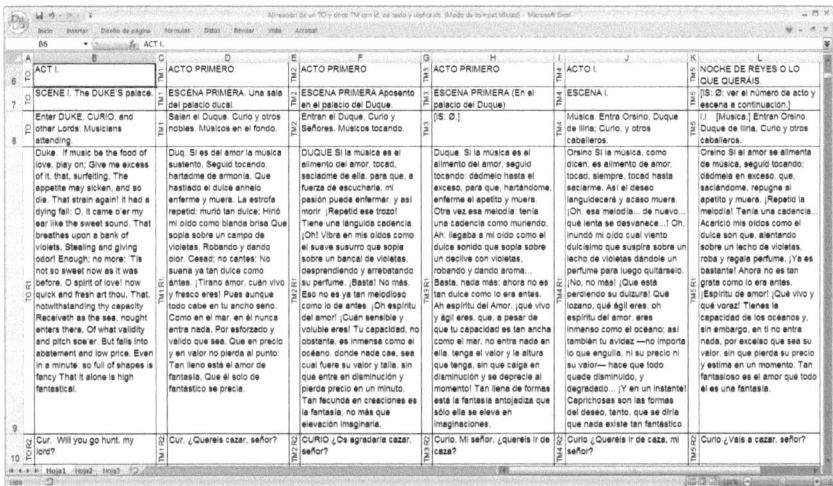

Fig. 9. Resultado de la alineación de seis textos en Excel (II)
(después de añadir los códigos de texto y números de réplica)

2.4.3. Identificación del acto y de la escena y del número de segmento dentro de la escena (puntos b), c) y e) anteriores)

Distribuyendo el contenido del archivo de alineación multitextual (o bitextual, en caso de que el corpus sea bitextual) en formato .txt (o .xls, si no se va a realizar la conversión a .txt) entre diferentes archivos de manera que cada uno contenga solo la alineación de una escena, se mostrarán el acto, la escena y el número de segmento dentro de la escena en la ventana de resultados, siempre que cada nombre de los nuevos archivos identifique por número de acto y escena la escena que incluye el archivo en cuestión (ejemplo: *Acto 1_Escena 1.txt*). El acto y la escena de cada segmento de los resultados aparecerán en la ruta de archivo que preceda en negrita al segmento.

Cuando busca en varios archivos colocados dentro de una misma carpeta, Examine32 muestra los resultados ordenados según, primero, el nombre del archivo, y, después, la posición en el archivo. Sin embargo, si se utilizan números romanos en lugar de arábigos para, por ejemplo, el número de acto, interpretará que *Acto II* precede a *Acto I* y mostrará los resultados del segundo acto antes de los del primero. De ahí que en la figura 2 un número arábigo preceda al número de acto en cada nombre de archivo (como *1_Acto I_Escena 1.txt*, que se muestra en la figura del siguiente modo: «1_acto i_escena 1.txt»). Ese número arábigo ha posibilitado que Examine32 muestre los resultados por acto (y, a continuación, escena, etc.) pese a que los actos lleven numeración romana.

Respecto al número de segmento, puesto que el número que aparece a la izquierda de cada resultado indica la posición del resultado en el archivo en el que se ha realizado la búsqueda, si cada archivo incluye solo una escena, indicará la posición en la escena de la que se trate.

2.4.4. Incorporación de las notas

Cuando el texto de un segmento meta tiene asociadas notas, lo indican llamadas de nota. Sin embargo, las notas, al no formar parte de la alineación, deben consultarse por separado, dirigiéndose, por ejemplo, a la carpeta que contenga el texto digitalizado, o a una carpeta que reúna todos los paratextos de este.

Puesto que las notas son unos paratextos relacionados de forma particularmente estrecha con los textos, puede estimarse conveniente darles un tratamiento especial: incorporarlas al/a los archivo(s) de alineación. Esta incorporación se puede realizar copiando el texto completo de cada nota en el segmento correspondiente, si bien en caso de que existan numerosas notas, el proceso consumirá una gran cantidad de tiempo. Una alternativa es realizar la incorporación única y exclusivamente en el archivo de alineación multi o bitextual en formato .xls, mediante la incrustación de las notas en los segmentos pertinentes a través de enlaces a las páginas digitalizadas que las contengan. Estos enlaces se pueden mostrar fácilmente en el archivo .xls como iconos de documentos (véase la figura 10, en la que aparecen en forma de iconos una nota del TM3 y otra del TM4). Al hacer doble clic en uno de estos iconos, se abre el documento, que muestra la nota en su página del TM (véase la figura 11).

Cómo crear y analizar corpus paralelos

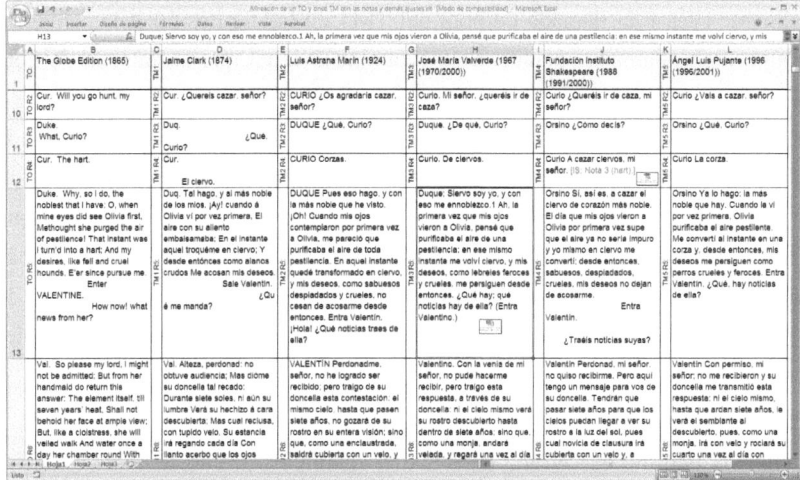

Fig. 10. Resultado de la alineación de seis textos en Excel (III)
(después de añadir las notas)

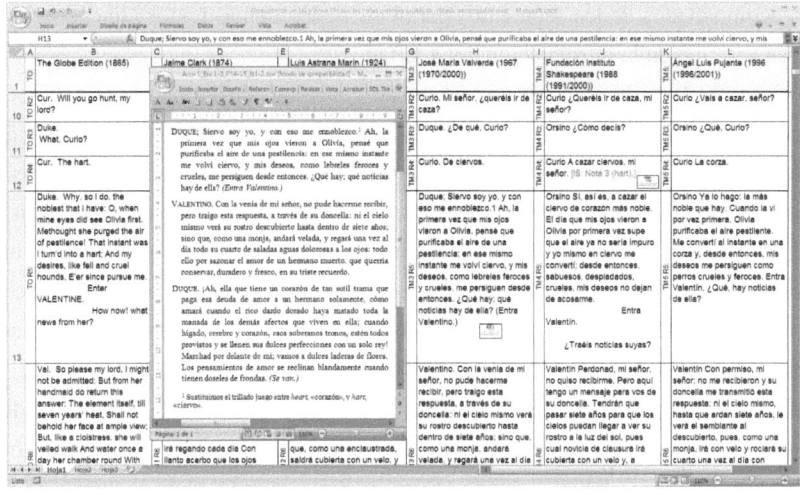

Fig. 11. Ventana con el texto de una nota (del TM3),
abierta desde el archivo de Excel de la alineación

En las ediciones bilingües, es posible que las notas a la traducción (y las llamadas de nota correspondientes) se encuentren todas en el texto original, en página opuesta a la del texto meta. Es el caso del TM4 del corpus de ejemplo. Puesto que el TO de la edición bilingüe a la que pertenece dicho TM no formaba parte de tal corpus, las llamadas de nota se introdujeron en el archivo de Excel manualmente (véase la llamada de nota del TM4 en las figuras 10 u 11, en color naranja; dicha llamada aparecería en Examine32 igual que la llamada de nota que se muestra en la figura 2).[7]

Nótese que, en las figuras 10 y 11, la primera fila está inmovilizada, lo que la mantiene visible en todo momento mientras se consultan los textos alineados en formato de Excel. Para cerrar la exposición de los ajustes, conviene señalar que no solo la introducción de enlaces a las notas, sino también todos los demás ajustes (dirigidos a la consulta a través de Examine32), mejoran la consulta de los textos alineados en el archivo de Excel, la cual puede ser un buen complemento a aquella a través de Examine32.[8]

2.5. Fase 5: análisis

Examine32 permite buscar en tantos textos «paralelos» como se desee, y muestra en su ventana de resultados todas las coincidencias. Tal como reflejan las figuras 2 y 8, estas aparecen resaltadas en sus segmentos respectivos, los cuales van acompañados de los segmentos paralelos de los demás textos alineados, como se anticipó en la introducción del apartado 2.

El contexto de cada coincidencia se puede consultar sin limitaciones con solo hacer doble clic sobre el renglón de la coincidencia. Este doble clic —equivalente a pulsar el icono «View file» [ver archivo]— abre el archivo de alineación correspondiente en formato de solo texto en una nueva ventana de Examine32, a la altura del segmento en cuestión y con la coincidencia resaltada con un subrayado intermitente, además de con la letra negrita y el color azul que la destacaban en la ventana de resultados (véanse las figuras 12 y 13; en esta última no se puede apreciar el carácter intermitente del subrayado).

Otras opciones parecidas de Examine32 son «Launch» (abrir) y «Editor» (editor), del menú «Actions» (operaciones). La primera abre el archivo de alineación en el programa que lleve asociado (Excel o Bloc de notas);[9] la segunda, en el

---

[7] Una llamada de nota no introducida de forma manual es, naturalmente, el número *1* que aparece en la réplica 5 del TM3 en las figuras 10 y 11. Esta llamada de nota se mostraría tal cual en Examine32.

[8] Nótese que MultiConcord, al efectuar la alineación en el momento en el que se realiza una búsqueda de concordancia (véase la nota 4), no permite visualizar los textos alineados, visualización que puede ser de gran utilidad en investigaciones de tipo cualitativo.

[9] Conviene aclarar que el programa admite otros formatos de entrada, como .doc y .htm.

Cómo crear y analizar corpus paralelos

programa de edición de textos elegido por el usuario. Estas otras opciones presentan la desventaja de no resaltar la coincidencia.

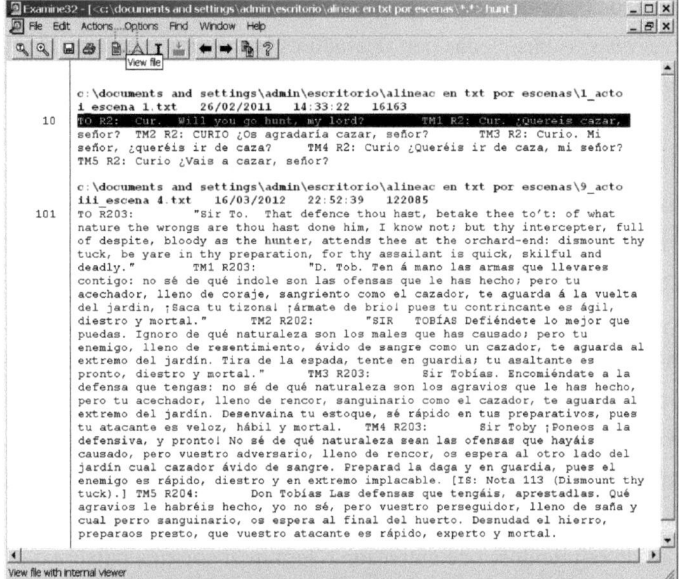

Fig. 12. Opción de Examine32 para ver más contexto

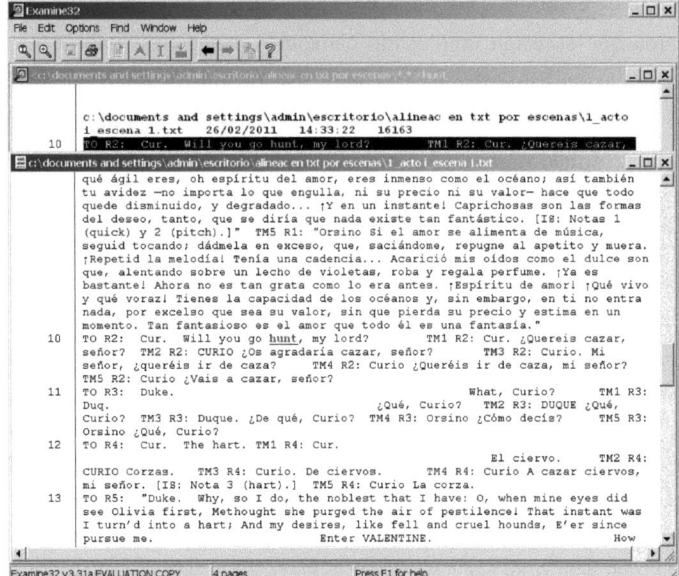

Fig. 13. Contexto adicional en Examine32

183

Examine32 también permite guardar y editar los resultados de las búsquedas (mediante la opción «Save As» [guardar como] del menú «File» [archivo]). En cuanto a los tipos de búsquedas, la aplicación distingue en primer lugar entre *logical searches*, o búsquedas con operadores booleanos (véase la figura 15), y *text searches*, o búsquedas simples (véase la figura 14). Ambos tipos de búsquedas permiten hacer las siguientes elecciones entre opciones de búsqueda alternativas: buscar o no en subcarpetas de la carpeta indicada; incluir o no en la búsqueda los archivos que formen parte de archivos comprimidos; buscar en todos los archivos o solo en algunos que se especifiquen mediante el nombre completo y/o la extensión; no distinguir entre mayúsculas y minúsculas o tenerlas en cuenta; buscar todas las palabras/expresiones que contengan el texto especificado (como las inglesas *amend* y *mended* y la española *enmendar*, además del también vocablo inglés *mend*, si se introduce «mend») o solo las palabras/expresiones que se correspondan al cien por cien con el texto especificado (*mend* en el ejemplo anterior); y buscar o no empleando caracteres especiales que, bien dan al programa la orden de buscar las líneas (en nuestro procedimiento, las filas de segmentos) que empiezan o terminan con una palabra o expresión concreta, o bien sustituyen a diversos caracteres o conjuntos de caracteres posibles (a modo de comodín). Por ejemplo, la búsqueda de «mend[^a]», si se indica al programa que se están empleando caracteres especiales (habría que marcar para ello la casilla «Regular Expression» [expresión regular]), arrojaría como resultado todas las coincidencias de «mend» no seguido de una *a* (es decir, excluiría de los resultados *enmendar*).

La búsqueda con operadores booleanos (OR, AND, NOT y XOR) permite, además, indicar la distancia máxima o mínima entre hasta cuatro palabras o expresiones que se buscarán usando los operadores AND, NOT o XOR. Dicha distancia puede ser de desde un número determinado de caracteres hasta el archivo completo, pasando por un número determinado de líneas (en nuestro procedimiento, filas de segmentos).[10]

---

[10] El operador AND busca fragmentos de texto en los que se encuentren tanto la primera palabra/expresión buscada (véase la figura 15) como la que sigue a este operador; NOT, en cambio, busca fragmentos de texto en los que se encuentre la primera palabra/expresión pero no la que sigue a NOT; por último, XOR busca fragmentos de texto en los que se encuentre solo una de las dos palabras/expresiones, sea cual sea. El cuarto operador (OR), pa-

Cómo crear y analizar corpus paralelos

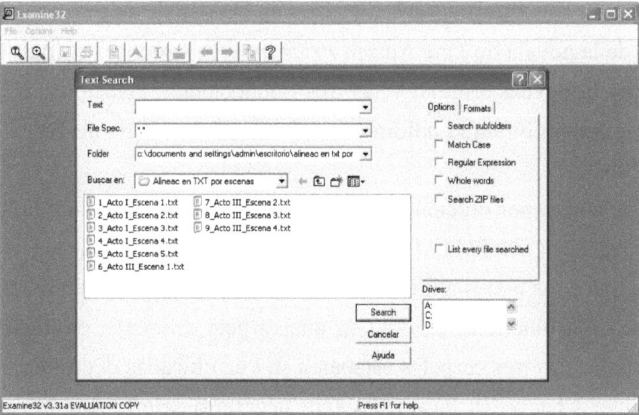

Fig. 14. Cuadro de diálogo de búsqueda simple de Examine32

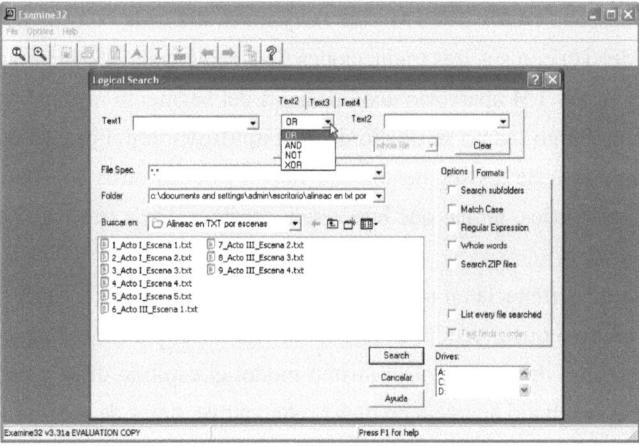

Fig. 15. Cuadro de diálogo de búsqueda con operadores booleanos de Examine32

3. Posibilidades de adaptación y limitaciones del procedimiento descrito

Como se ha demostrado, el procedimiento descrito es válido para textos dramáticos o líricos además de narrativos. Más allá de este tipo de diferencias entre proyectos, sus posibilidades de adaptación son amplias y deben estudiarse en relación con cada proyecto en particular. A continuación se describe, a modo de ejemplo, la adaptación a un proyecto para el cual fue simplificado.

ra el que la búsqueda teniendo en cuenta la proximidad carece de sentido, busca todas las coincidencias de las palabras/expresiones.

El proyecto (Jiménez Carra 2007) consistía en el análisis de tres traducciones al castellano de la novela de Jane Austen *Pride and Prejudice*. El corpus iba a estar formado por la novela original y las tres traducciones seleccionadas, de modo que sería «paralelo bilingüe unidireccional» en terminología de Baker (1995) y Laviosa (2002).

Cada TM se alineó por oraciones con el TO, de modo que resultaron tres archivos de alineación (TO-TM1, TO-TM2 y TO-TM3). La agrupación en un solo archivo de todos los textos alineados se sustituyó por la ubicación de cada archivo de alineación bitextual (en .xls) en una carpeta diferente, en lugar de en la misma carpeta. Las tres carpetas estaban a su vez ubicadas dentro de otra, en la que Examine32 hacía las búsquedas (era necesario seleccionar la opción que permite buscar en subcarpetas, «Search subfolders» [buscar en subcarpetas]). El programa buscaba en los tres TM y el TO y mostraba cada coincidencia de una expresión del TO con sus tres traducciones. Las coincidencias encontradas no en el TO sino en los TM aparecían acompañadas del segmento original correspondiente; sin embargo, como resultado de la simplificación del procedimiento, no iban acompañadas de los segmentos equivalentes de los otros dos TM, los cuales, de ser necesarios, tenían que buscarse a continuación a través del segmento original.

El texto al que pertenecía un resultado (TO o TM1/2/3) aparecía especificado en la ruta de archivo que precedía en negrita al resultado, porque a cada carpeta se le dio un nombre descriptivo. Del mismo modo, el capítulo de la novela al que pertenecía el resultado aparecía en dicha ruta, ya que, antes de guardar los archivos de alineación en sus carpetas respectivas, se dividió cada archivo por capítulos y se dio a cada uno de los archivos resultantes un nombre descriptivo. Por poner un ejemplo, si la novela hubiera tenido 5 capítulos, en la carpeta del TM1 habría habido 5 archivos, cada uno con un capítulo alineado.

Otra aplicación del procedimiento, en este caso sin simplificar, es la de Serón Ordóñez (2012), donde se utilizó para analizar cinco versiones castellanas de la comedia de Shakespeare *Twelfth Night*. El corpus que se creó con este objetivo es precisamente el que ha servido ejemplo en el apartado 2, un corpus también paralelo bilingüe unidireccional. Mientras la investigación de Jiménez Carra era de tipo cualitativo, la de Serón Ordóñez combinaba métodos cualitativos y cuantitativos, los segundos fundamentalmente para la selección de las traducciones a analizar.

El procedimiento al que se dedica este artículo, desarrollado por la autora del artículo —quien lo adaptó para Jiménez Carra (2007)—, no está concebido para realizar estadísticas, ni posee otras funciones tradicionales de los programas propios de la lingüística de corpus, como la ordenación de los resultados según las palabras que anteceden o siguen a las coincidencias. No obstante, parece claro que llena un hueco en la traductología basada en corpus. No en vano, incorpora las funciones de búsqueda de la herramienta de búsqueda en corpus paralelos desarrollada por Robert J. Coulthard (véase la figura 1), sin que sea preciso usar esa herramienta y otras dos —Google Desktop Search y TweakGDS— solo para las búsquedas.

4. Conclusiones

La traductología basada en corpus ha avanzado notablemente en las últimas décadas. Prueba de ello son los números especiales de revista y las múltiples monografías de los que ha sido objeto recientemente (como Campenhoudt y Temmerman 2011 y Neumann, Čulo y Hansen-Schirra 2011, entre los primeros, y Kruger, Wallmach y Munday 2011, Zanettin 2012, Oakes y Ji 2012 y Straniero-Sergio y Falbo 2012 entre las monografías). Sin embargo, aún se puede observar la carencia de herramientas adecuadas para crear y analizar corpus paralelos, especialmente en los proyectos cuyos recursos son más limitados (tesis doctorales, pequeños proyectos colectivos, etcétera). Valga recordar el caso de Coulthard (2005), quien, por considerar insatisfactorio el programa MultiConcord, creó su propia aplicación de análisis de corpus y la tuvo que combinar con otros tres programas (Google Desktop Search y TweakGDS más WordSmith Tools); o considérese Bosseaux (2004), donde se utiliza MultiConcord para realizar búsquedas de concordancia después de haber empleado para otras tareas (en concreto, para la obtención de estadísticas y la elección de términos que analizar) un programa que también realiza búsquedas de concordancia: WordSmith Tools (ceñido a corpus monolingües).

El procedimiento presentado en este artículo es una solución para muchos de los problemas detectados en el software existente. Sus principales ventajas en este sentido son posiblemente que permite realizar búsquedas en tantos textos integrantes de un corpus paralelo como se desee, que ofrece tanto una cómoda visualización de los resultados como ilimitado contexto, y que presenta posibilidades de adaptación (no solo a diversos géneros textuales sino también a diferentes niveles de exigencia, entre otros factores); además, admite formatos de entrada diferentes de .txt y posibilita la adición de metadatos y otra información. Todo ello con software accesible.

Especialmente indicado para análisis de tipo cualitativo, no ofrece algunas de las prestaciones que incluyen las aplicaciones derivadas de la lingüística de corpus; sin embargo, por si solo —así como combinado con estas— puede ser de gran utilidad para numerosas investigaciones basadas en corpus paralelos. No en vano, los llamamientos a combinar métodos cuantitativos con métodos cualitativos (como Malmkjær 1998) siguen plenamente vigentes (véase Zanettin 2013), al igual que las siguientes palabras de Stig Johansson a favor de corpus pequeños creados con esmero, pronunciadas por primera vez en 1991 y reiteradas por el investigador en 2004: «Something may still be said for smaller, carefully constructed corpora which can be analysed exhaustively in a variety of ways»[11] (Johansson 2004: 12).

En cualquier caso, de cara al futuro, es de desear que se desarrollen aplicaciones que incluyan las prestaciones antes mencionadas, que permitan alinear (y luego exportar de manera ventajosa) más de dos textos simultáneamente, y tal vez que incluso incorporen prestaciones provenientes de la lingüística de corpus. Al fin y al cabo, «progress relies on the refinement of [...] practical tools for corpus construction and investigation»[12] (Zanettin 2012: 206).

---

[11] «Aún queda algo que decir a favor de corpus pequeños creados cuidadosamente que puedan analizarse de forma exhaustiva de diversas maneras» (traducción propia). La similitud entre esta afirmación y la siguiente de Zanettin (2013: 31) habla por sí sola: «together with sophisticated ways of handling quantitative data, corpus-based translation research profits from conducting in-depth analyses on small, scrupulously collected samples» («junto con formas sofisticadas de manejar datos cuantitativos, la investigación en traducción basada en corpus se beneficia de realizar análisis en profundidad de pequeñas muestras recogidas meticulosamente»; traducción propia).

[12] «el avance depende del perfeccionamiento de las herramientas [...] prácticas para la construcción e investigación de corpus» (traducción propia).

5. Bibliografía

Aquila Software. 1993-2002. Examine32 (versión 3.31a) [programa informático]. Southborough: Aquila Software.

Baker, Mona. 1995. Corpora in Translation Studies. An overview and some suggestions for future research. *@ Target* 7/2: 223-243.

Bandín Fuertes, Elena. 2007. *Traducción, recepción y censura de teatro clásico inglés en la España de Franco. Estudio descriptivo-comparativo del Corpus TRACEtci (1939-1985)*. Tesis doctoral inédita, Universidad de León.

Barlow, Michael. 2003. *ParaConc: a concordancer for parallel texts (draft 3/03)* [manual de programa informático]. [s. l.]. Disponible en <http://www.athel.com/paraconc.pdf>. [Última consulta 21/07/2014].

Berber Sardinha, Tony. 2002. Corpora eletrônicos na pesquisa em tradução. *@ Cadernos de Tradução*, 1/9: 15-59.

Bosseaux, Charlotte. 2004. *Translation and narration. A corpus-based study of French translations of two novels by Virginia Woolf*. Tesis doctoral inédita, University College London.

Campenhoudt, Marc Van y Rita Temmerman, eds, 2011. Les corpus et la recherche en terminologie et en traductologie / Corpora and research in terminology and Translation Studies. @ Meta 56/2: número especial. Disponible en <http://www.erudit.org/revue/meta/2011/v56/n2/>. [Última consulta 26/7/2014].

Coulthard, Robert James. 2005. *The application of corpus methodology to translation. The JPED parallel corpus and the Pediatrics comparable corpus*. Trabajo de fin de máster, Universidade Federal de Santa Catarina, Florianópolis.

Jiménez Carra, María Nieves. 2007. *Análisis y estudio comparativo de tres traducciones españolas de* Pride and Prejudice. Tesis doctoral inédita, Universidad de Málaga.

Johansson, Stig. 2004. Corpus linguistics—past, present, future. A view from Oslo. *@* J. Nakamura, N. Inoue y T. Tabata, eds. *English corpora under Japanese eyes*. Amsterdam: Rodopi. ISBN 9042018828, pp. 3-24.

Kruger, Alet, Kim Wallmach y Jeremy Munday, eds, 2011. *Corpus-based Translation Studies. Research and applications*. Londres: Continuum. ISBN 9781441115812.

Laviosa, Sara. 2002. *Corpus-based Translation Studies. Theory, findings, applications*. Amsterdam: Rodopi. ISBN 9042014873.

Malmkjær, Kirsten. 1998. Love thy neighbour. Will parallel corpora endear linguists to translators? *@ Meta* 43/4: 534-541. DOI 10.7202/003545ar. Disponible en <http://www.erudit.org/revue/meta/1998/v/n4/003545ar.html?vue=resume>. [Última consulta 26/7/2014].

Neumann, Stella, Oliver Čulo y Silvia Hansen-Schirra. 2011. Parallel Corpora. Annotation, Exploitation, Evaluation. *@ Translation: Computation, Corpora, Cognition* 1/1: número especial. Disponible en <http://www.t-c3.org/index.php/t-c3/issue/view/1>. [Última consulta 26/7/2014].

Oakes, Michael P. y Meng Ji, eds, 2012. *Quantitative methods in corpus-based translation studies. A practical guide to descriptive translation research*. Amsterdam: John Benjamins. ISBN 9789027203564.

Olohan, Maeve. 2004. *Introducing corpora in Translation Studies*. Londres: Routledge. ISBN 0415268850.

SDL International. 1997-2005. SDLX (versión 2005) [programa informático]. Maidenhead: SDL International.

Serón Ordóñez, Inmaculada. 2012. *Las traducciones al español de* Twelfth Night *(1873-2005). Estudio descriptivo diacrónico*. Tesis doctoral inédita, Universidad de Málaga. Disponible en <http://riuma.uma.es/xmlui/handle/10630/7301>. [Última consulta 20/7/2014].

Straniero-Sergio, Francesco y Catarina Falbo, eds, 2012. *Breaking ground in corpus-based Interpreting Studies*. Berna: Peter Lang. ISBN 9783034310710.

Zanettin, Federico. 2012. *Translation-driven corpora. Corpus resources for descriptive and applied Translation Studies*. Manchester: St. Jerome. ISBN 9781905763290.

Zanettin, Federico. 2013. Corpus methods for descriptive Translation Studies. @ *Procedia - Social and Behavioral Sciences* 95: 20-32. DOI 10.1016/j.sbspro.2013.10.618. Disponible en <http://www.sciencedirect.com/science/article/pii/S1877042813041384>. [Última consulta 29/7/2014].

Corpus-based knowledge management systems for specialized translation: bridging the gap between theory and professional practice

[Sistemas de gestión del conocimiento basados en corpus para traductores especializados: de la teoría a la práctica]

ANABEL BORJA ALBI and ISABEL GARCÍA-IZQUIERDO

Universitat Jaume I (Castelló, Spain), Gentt group[1]
borja@uji.es, igarcia@uji.es

Abstract: This article presents a corpus-based tool conceived as an online knowledge system which will permit the 'reusability' of electronic translation resources (both conceptual and linguistic) by highly specialized translators. These resources have been organised into an online platform aimed at legal and medical translators. Corpus-based studies represent a major advance in the field of DTS, but most projects have been geared towards teaching and research and focused on linguistic and textual issues, which are of great importance for translators but are insufficient for professional translation work. The GENTT research team, in collaboration with medical and legal translators, health professionals and lawyers, medical and law associations and public bodies and institutions, has therefore developed the JUDGENTT and MEDGENTT web platforms, designed to offer professional translators and writers of highly specialized texts of this kind a range of linguistic, conceptual and legislative resources to facilitate the process of documentary research, drafting and translation. These platforms allow the automatisation of the process of retrieval, indexation, semi-controlled writing and computer-assisted translation of specialised texts, taking into account the professional needs, habits and processes of the final users of these texts.

Key words: textual corpus; legal translation; medical translation; corpus based knowledge systems; document management systems; specialized terminology

---

[1] This article is part of the following research projects: 2010-2012 (FFI2009-08531/FILO), funded by the Spanish Ministry of Science and Innovation (MICINN), GENTT Group; 'Análisis de necesidades y propuesta de recursos de información escrita para pacientes en el ámbito de la Oncología' (FFI2012-34200), funded by the Ministry of Economy and Competitiveness, GENTT Group; and LEMATRAD 2014-15, funded by USE, Universitat Jaume I.

1. Introduction

The knowledge society, as it has come to be known, provides and at the same time demands rapid access to information. This demand is particularly pressing in the field of highly specialized communication and translation, where experts perform a task of linguistic (and cultural) mediation which very often requires them to implement a wide range of conceptual, terminological and discursive competences in a very limited space of time.

In the last few decades numerous publications in the field of Translation Studies have been devoted to analysing the benefits of using electronic corpora, both for research and for teaching. Following Biel 2010:

> Corpus-based translation studies were developed in the mid 1990s and have continued to be intensely applied in the last decade. They mark a shift from the analysis of the ST-TT relation (i.e. equivalence, accuracy) to TTs as independent texts on their own, emphasizing the importance of translated texts in receiving cultures. This shift from the ST to the TT has been referred to by Pym as a 'paradigm shift' in translation studies (2004).

Authors such as Toury (1995), Baker (1993), Laviosa (1998) and Corpas (2008), among others, used this methodology to investigate such diverse issues as the norms that constrain translational behaviour, language regularities, and translation universals (explicitation, disambiguation and simplification, etc.). Corpora, both multilingual parallel (Beeby et al., 2009; Borja et al., 2013; García-Izquierdo, 2005; Gavioli, 1996; Zanettin, 2012) and monolingual comparable (Biel, 2010; Bowker, 1998; Laviosa, 2002 and 2003; Ordóñez, 2009) have also been extensively used for translator training. All these studies highlight the wide range of possibilities this tool can offer for students, trainers and practitioners.

The use of corpora has undoubtedly given a great impetus to Descriptive Translation Studies, for exploring both the product and the process. As Malmkjaer (2003: 119) points out:

> The use in Translation Studies of methodologies inspired by corpus linguistics has proved to be one of the most important gate-openers to progress of the discipline since Toury's re-thinking of the concept of equivalence.

This fruitful line of work has also played a very important role in the field of LSP, as evidenced by studies such as those of Aijmer (ed.), 2009 and Sinclair (ed.), 2004, to cite just two examples from the extensive literature on the subject. As Sinclair (2004: 1) remarks: '[…] in studying corpora we observe a stream of creative energy that is awesome in its wide applicability, its sublety and its flexibility.' Indeed, many pioneering publications in the field of Corpus-based Translation Studies (Baker, 1993; Laviosa, 2002) draw directly on the work of authors such as Sinclair. Although they do not address translation issues, the insight they provide on specialized types of language has had a great impact on the research currently being developed in the field of specialized translation.

2. Corpus-based tools for professional translators

Despite the fact that Corpus-based Translation Studies (CTS) is now recognized as a major paradigm within the discipline of Translation Studies, relatively little effort has been devoted to developing corpus-based tools designed to assist freelance professional translators in their daily work.

Laviosa (2003: 115) argues that professional translators can benefit from the new developments in corpus-based research:

> [...] they can draw on the insights provided by descriptive studies into the differences and similarities between languages, the strategies adopted by translators, the patterning of translational language independently of the source language, as well as the most common translation equivalents.

Some remarkable studies have been published on the use of corpora by professional translators (Corpas Pastor, 2007; Varela Vila, 2009; Zanettin, 2002, among others) and on the compilation of DIY ad-hoc corpora for translators (Zanettin, 2002; Varantola, 2003) but, in practice, there are relatively few corpus-based resources available for specialized translators, and access to existing corpora is very often restricted, especially in the case of legal texts, due to confidentiality issues.

Translators in international organisations do make use of terminological databases and translation memories, which they share through their Intranet and are based essentially on exploiting the corpora made up of their own original and translated texts. Most professional practitioners of highly specialized translation, however, do not work in international organisations and continue to rely on traditional textual/linguistic, terminological and conceptual reference tools (García-Izquierdo and Conde, 2012).

The solutions that traditional corpora can offer translators are, of course, vital, as we have already pointed out, but other issues have still to be addressed, such as subject-field understanding, choice of exact term or phraseology in specialized discourse, and awareness of specialized genre conventions and schemata, among others. Moreover, the time pressure to which professional translators are subject makes it necessary to use tools specially designed for each professional community of specialist translators (legal, medical, technical, pharmaceutical, etc.), going beyond the structure of traditional corpora. In our opinion, all these requirements could be answered by corpus-based expert knowledge management systems tailor-made to meet the real needs of specialized translators (Borja, 2005 and 2013), as we shall see in the following sections.

3. Our experience with corpora for specialized translation: The GENTT corpus 2.0

In 2000 the GENTT research group, following the trend towards Corpus-based Translation Studies mentioned above, began compiling and subsequently analysing a database in the form of a comparable corpus of original texts used in professional legal, medical and technical domains (García-Izquierdo, 2005). We later extended its scope to include parallel texts that would enable us to apply contrastive analysis techniques. The working languages chosen were Spanish, Catalan, English, French and German. This corpus was initially intended for teaching and research.

The GENTT corpus is organized on the basis of a structure aimed at facilitating the textual 'acculturation' of the specialized writer or translator by means of a large number of comparable texts (the same genres in different languages, not the same texts translated) that the user can retrieve very easily by using different search parameters in an advanced search engine. Previous studies by the research group (García-Izquierdo, 2002; Borja, 2005; García-Izquierdo, 2007 and 2011; Borja, García-Izquierdo and Montalt, 2009, among others) have demonstrated the usefulness that the notion of 'textual genre'(as a complex concept combining formal, communicative and cognitive considerations) can be a powerful tool for accessing and 'reusing' the linguistic and extra-linguistic information technical writers and translators need for managing highly specialised communication. Following Ezpeleta (2012:139), the acquisition of competence in genre and genre systems can be considered an effective means of acquiring the abilities needed by linguistic mediators of professional texts, such as translators, since it facilitates their socialisation as communication agents in highly specialised domains.

The structure of this multilingual specialized corpus is, thus, underpinned by GENTT's genre trees. The definition of the trees of genres (or textual mapping) for each specialized field is based on constant observation of the socio-professional world and takes into account the opinions of expert users; in addition, we perform an empirical analysis of the corpus texts compiled. Each genre identified is included in the taxonomy of genres with details of its distinctive characteristics at various levels (Gentt genre matrix). Usually, when a genre is identified and described, at least one sample of it is uploaded to the corpus, and then further examples of that genre are collected and uploaded. The GENTT 2.0 corpus could be described as a 'genre sample corpus' or 'genre example corpus', since its aim is the quality rather than the quantity of the items it includes. That is, the objective is not to construct a corpus that provides the greatest possible number of words, but a corpus that provides the greatest possible number of textual occurrences with at least five sample texts of each genre and in several languages. Further information can be found at http://www.gentt.uji.es.[2]

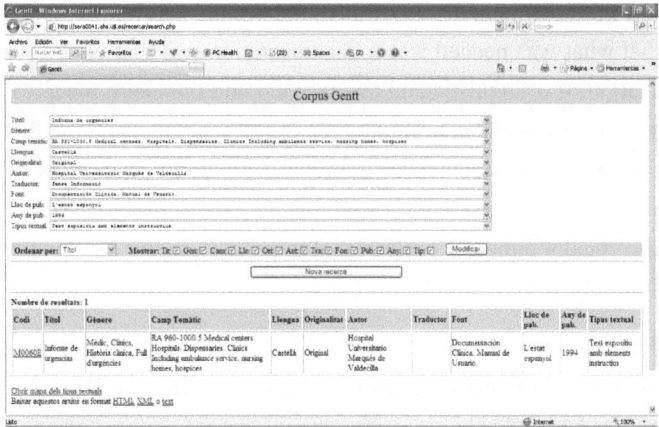

Figure 1. The GENTT 2.0 corpus

For over a decade we have been using this corpus with excellent results in undergraduate and postgraduate university teaching. The GENTT corpus provides

---

[2] Because of copyright restrictions it cannot be accessed freely, but researchers can apply for a special authorisation.

a user-centred interface that enables learners and teachers alike to exploit the texts in very specific ways. Personalized corpora and subcorpora can be designed in order to select appropriate texts for a particular teaching requirement and analyse them accordingly. Advanced search or classification criteria may also be implemented according to the user's needs (by genre, working language, etc.), thus fostering creativity and collaboration among its users.

On the other hand, this sample corpus has given rise to numerous research studies that address the study of specialized genres, genre systems and colonies, frequency analyses and concordances in specific genres (Aragonés, 2009; Borja et al., 2009; Del Pozo, 2014; García-Izquierdo and Borja, 2008; García-Izquierdo and Montalt, 2009; García-Izquierdo, 2009; Ordóñez, 2009, among others).

As a result of this research, the team conducted qualitative and quantitative studies, through surveys and interviews (García-Izquierdo, 2012; García-Izquierdo and Conde, 2012; Muñoz Miquel et al. 2012), which revealed that although researchers and future translators valued the compilation of the GENTT corpus and the potential advantages it offers, professional translators in the specialized fields examined made little use of electronic corpora, as they considered that the information these contained was of interest but only relevant to certain issues, and felt that what was needed was a documentation tool that would supplement the information of a linguistic and textual kind and the genre matrices with another more contextual and conceptual type of information, enabling them to carry out comprehensive documentary research. We therefore decided to develop an applied research Project which would enable us to design corpus-based resources specifically aimed at professional translators, as we shall explain in the next section.

4. From traditional corpus-based resources to interactive dynamic expert knowledge management systems: the JUDGENTT and MEDGENTT Platforms

The use of the GENTT 2.0 corpus both for the teaching of specialized translation and for research has certainly produced very fruitful results, as can be seen from the numerous publications members of the team have produced in the last decade (see www.gentt.uji.es). However, following the maxim that every methodological process has to go through a series of stages, we decided to go a step further, as indicated above, and begin to engage in what have been termed action research projects, through which the results of our research could be directly transferred to the professional sector.

Since 2009 GENTT has developed various action research projects aimed at improving the working processes of specialized translators by designing an intelligent documentation management system that makes it possible to automate processes of retrieval, indexing, semi-controlled composition and assisted translation of texts generated in highly specialized fields. From that point, the team started conducting qualitative studies on the habits and needs of professionals in the fields involved. Our new objective was to expand the GENTT 2.0 corpus and turn it into a corpus-based platform that would incorporate additional resources and from which new target users (professional specialized translators) could more effectively reuse and retrieve the information that they identified (according to the surveys and focus groups we conducted) as most relevant and useful for enhancing the quality and efficiency of their translation processes.

The concept of reusability, which comes from Computer Science, began to be adopted in Linguistics from the 1980s, when various research groups put forward projects and activities aimed at reusing linguistic resources in order to save costs (Göpferich, 2006). In our view, reusability is open to two interpretations. On the one hand, it refers to reusing existing linguistic resources, which are used by computer applications to generate new resources. On the other, it applies to the construction of linguistic resources, whether by creating them or by using sources generated from other existing resources, which can in turn be reused in various applications and theoretical frameworks and by different types of users (human and/or mechanical).

4.1. Needs analysis for the design and implementation of new GENTT corpus-based resources

To define the design of the new tools we took two professional communities, legal translators and medical translators, as our sample, and proceeded to carry out a needs analysis of their information requirements. These requirements are not the same for all translators. They vary depending on the field of specialization, and even in the same field we find differences depending on the subdomain. Legal translators who work for law firms do not have the same information requirements as those who work in the criminal courts, nor do they use the same conceptual reference material or work with the same types of documents (contracts and commercial documents in the first case and court documents, such as judgments or letters of request, in the second), terminology or normative references.

We focused our research on two particularly sensitive disciplinary areas, such as the medical and legal fields, where professional translators, albeit with different levels of recognition or status (Pym et al. 2012) and a constant struggle to professionalize their community (in the case of both legal and medical translation), perform a task of undeniable social importance.

From a methodological point of view, we used a mixed approach: qualitative, in that we carried out the needs analysis by means of personal interviews and surveys, and quantitative, because in the final stages we relied on corpus analysis methods and statistical calculations. This phase was crucial to our research, as the results obtained from consulting users had to give us a clear and precise idea of how they use and perceive expert knowledge management requirements. To ensure the quality and accuracy of the results, we enlisted the help of experts in statistics applied to research on socio-professional habits, who supervised the formulation of questionnaires, the conduct of interviews and the statistical treatment of the data. Experts in documentation management also collaborated in this phase.

During this stage of the project we also analyzed the role played by the concept of genre, from a theoretical perspective, in the document management tasks required by the populations in the sample. Our dialogue with the potential users being studied enabled us to establish a catalogue of the most commonly used genres and the most commonly translated ones. This information was vital for deciding on the type of documents that should be included in the new corpora on which the platform is based. Moreover, it helped us to determine the appropriate degree of specificity or granularity of the classification of genres into subgenres, sub-subgenres, etc., in order for it to be effective in each particular domain.

To arrive at a scientific assessment of the role of the various textual genres in these professional communities and to gauge their information and documentation management needs, we needed to know the answers to the following questions: What multilingual documentation management systems did they use (if they used any)? How do professionals (lawyers, doctors and legal and medical translators) refer to the texts they work with? How familiar are they with the genres that are already commonly used in their communications? Does genre awareness exist among users? Do the ways in which users refer to genres coincide with those we use in our research group? Which are the genres most often used in each language? Which genres are most frequently translated and into which languages? With which communicative function or situation do users relate the genres identified?

The results of this phase for each of the socio-professional communities taken as the sample provided us with:

1. An inductively validated list or catalogue of the genres most commonly used in the two communities studied.
2. An inductively validated list or catalogue of the genres most commonly translated in the two communities studied.
3. A list of defining features of the genre, including not only the descriptors used by the GENTT group in previous studies but also the additional metadescriptors that users identified as relevant for their communicative purposes.
4. A series of document management requirements, which we have used as specifications for designing the new GENTT Platforms.

On the basis of the data obtained in the needs analysis phase we revised the genre trees for the legal and medical domains we had defined in the GENTT 2.0 corpus and proceeded to complete the classification of genres for these subcorpora and to refine their descriptive summaries (GENTT Genre Matrix).

In the interviews and focus groups that we conducted with legal and medical translators and experts in these fields they provided us with a wealth of textual materials, which enabled us to expand our multilingual comparable and parallel corpora. They also advised us on the most authoritative sources of information for their disciplines: handbooks, rules and regulations, quality standards, specialised websites, discussion forums, etc., which we then included in the platforms.

4.2. Web architecture and interface design/implementation

Since the main object of our platform was to enhance the efficiency of translation in terms of quality and speed, we integrated all the resources identified as relevant for specialised translators in the needs analysis phase into a single platform. In non-automated translation systems such as the one we were working on, efficiency of translation depends on speed of information retrieval: terminology mining, phraseology mining, identification of genre schemata and understanding of specialized concepts. The necessary speed and quality of the information mining process can only be achieved by integrating the various corpus-based and non-corpus-based resources available into a single tool. This tool should also use a reliable metalanguage that indicates the provenance of the information in every search so that users can judge its reliability for themselves.

All the GENTT platforms have the same web architecture. They have been developed using Drupal as a platform (database, corpus, html resources, etc.), with a Lucene and Solr text search engine library.

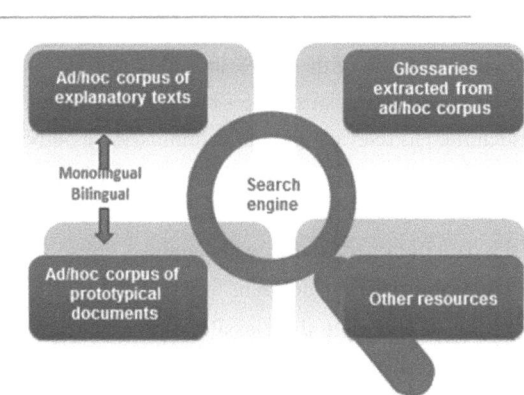

Figure 2. Web architecture of the GENTT platforms

They contain an *ad hoc corpus of explanatory texts for the discipline* (handbooks, manuals, good practice guidelines, rules and regulations) and an *ad hoc corpus of prototypical genres for the discipline*, which includes full-text documents used in professional practice. These corpora are multilingual, comparable and parallel. They are made up of *monolingual corpora* and *bilingual corpora*. They comprise genuine professional documents (originals and translations), from which personal details have been removed, and forms or precedents, as well as all kinds of reference materials. These corpora are the main database for the platforms' advanced search engine. The search utility permits retrieval of complete collections of texts organized by genre, subject matter, etc. These collections (or subcorpora) can be incorporated by professional translators into their translation memories or used as

DIY corpora for other purposes. The languages in each platform depend on the frequencies of language combinations identified during the needs analysis (up to now, English, French, German and Spanish for The JUDGENTT platform and English and Spanish for the MEDGENTT platform).

A series of specialized *glossaries* have been created by extracting terminology from each platform's corpus of texts. There are monolingual and bilingual glossaries. All entries are accompanied by a definition (in monolingual glossaries), a proposed equivalent or explanation (in zero equivalence cases) in the other language (in bilingual glossaries) and the context from which they have been extracted.

The GENTT Platforms have a user-friendly single interface with four tabs at the top for accessing textual resources, terminological resources, conceptual resources and other resources. As we have said, these resources are different for each field and subfield of specialization and are generated by exploiting the corpora of prototypical texts and explanatory and normative texts, the terminological databases and the genre matrixes compiled by our team in collaboration with translators and experts in each field of specialization.

Figure 3 (p. 202) shows the interface of the JUDGENTT platform devoted to criminal court translators. By clicking on the first tab we access the list or catalogue of legal documents in the GENTT platform interface for court translators, which includes information on four legal systems (France, Germany, United Kingdom and Spain). Note that for legal translation we organize the information and resources not by language but by legal system[3], whereas in the MEDGENTT platforms texts are classified by language (see Figure 4, p. 202). By clicking on each of the genres in the catalogue a genre matrix appears with genological information and links to a number of samples of the document.

The third tab at the top accesses the section containing conceptual information, which varies enormously from one field to another. As an example, the platform devoted to criminal court translators includes information relating to the four national systems selected on: 1) courts hierarchy; 2) rules and regulations; 3) participants in criminal proceedings; 4) outline summaries of judicial processes and their phases; and 5) classification of criminal offences and penalties (see Figure 5, p. 203).

---

[3] For a more detailed description of the JUDGENTT platform see Borja, 2013.

Perhaps the most important contribution this tool offers is the *integrated search engine* (right top corner), which covers all sections of the site and retrieves results of various types depending on the search criteria selected in the advanced search window: monolingual, bilingual, language combination, authentic/form, only legislation, genre (see Figure 6, p. 203).

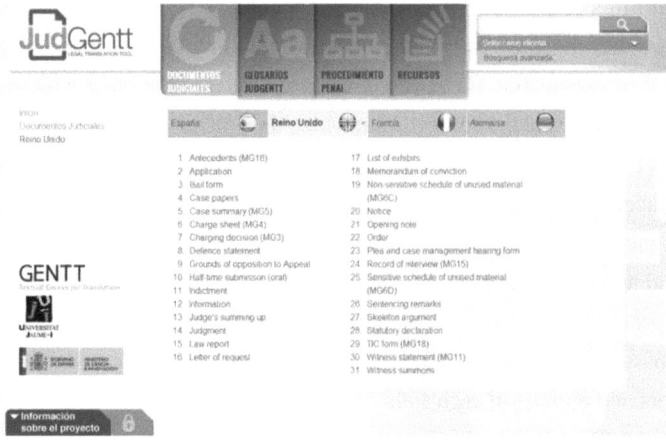

Figure 3. Catalogue of criminal court documents for the United Kingdom. JUDGENTT platform

Figure 4. Catalogue of medical-legal documents English/Spanish. MEDGENTT platform

Corpus-based knowledge management systems for specialized translation

Figure 5. Criminal courts procedure section containing conceptual/contextual resources. JUDGENTT platform

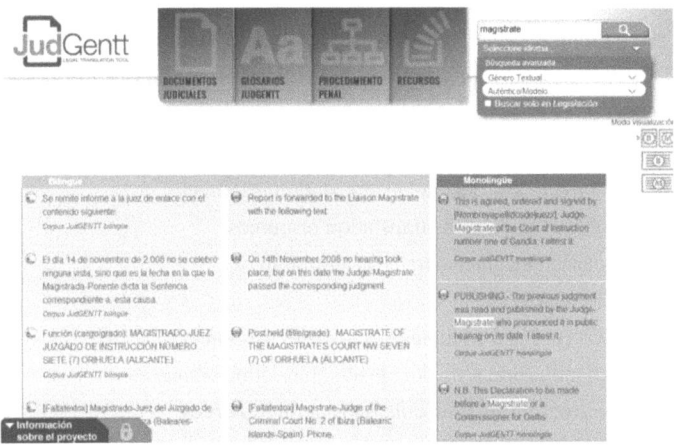

Figure 6. Search engine results page. JUDGENTT platform

Finally, there is a *Resources for translators* section, which includes a subsection for *Bibliography* and another for *Links*, with connections to useful web pages, web portals for specialized translators, discussion forums for specialized translators and experts in the field in question, electronic terminological resources relevant to the field of specialization, etc.

Figure 7: Resources for medical-legal translators. MEDGENTT platform

So far we have developed two integrated platforms, JUDGENTT and MEDGENTT, which currently include the following subplatforms:

- JUDGENTT platform
    - Criminal court documents translation resources
    - Company law documents translation resources
    - Contract documents translation resources
    - Notarial documents translation resources
- MEDGENTT platform
    - Medical-legal documents translation resources
    - Patient information documents translation resources
    - Research study protocols translation resources
    - Pharmaceutical product information documents translation resources

The structure of our web platforms makes it possible to extend the scope of our tools to cover other relevant fields of Law and Medicine, other languages and language combinations, other legal systems, etc. It is interactive, so it can be customized to the specific needs of individual users who can add new material to the corpora and create their own subcorpora, among other utilities. As we mentioned before, to promote integration with CAT tools the platform corpora are set up in such a way that translators can incorporate contents to the various existing memory systems or CAT tools. It should be emphasised at this point that translators will need to be trained in the use of these tools and academic institutions now have a responsibility to acquaint translation students with the powerful IT resources currently available (CAT Tools), so they will be capable of making creative and skilful use of the corpus-based tools that will undoubtedly continue to proliferate in the near future.

5. Conclusion

Corpus-based research in Translation Studies is moving forwards towards the creation of dynamic, collaborative and integrated resources for highly specialized translators. In this article we have presented the progress of the GENTT group's corpus-based research over the last fifteen years, and in particular one of its most recent results: direct application to the professional world through the GENTT platforms. We have described and discussed the theoretical concepts underlying this resources, the selection and organization of contents, the web architecture and the user-friendly interface that make it possible to retrieve data and information using a range of different search criteria. The textual corpora contained in the platforms' databases are underpinned by the concept of genre, a complex concept, combining formal, communicative and cognitive considerations.

Obviously there is a great deal still to be done, because highly specialized translation poses ever greater challenges in terms of the conceptual knowledge the translator has to handle and the requirement of using extremely precise terminology and phraseology as well as being aware of genre schemata and achieving greater textual naturalness. Genre-based corpora are a highly valuable source for the information mining process constantly performed by professional translators. For all these reasons, corpus-based online resources that include conceptual, textual and terminological information and can be integrated with CAT tools such as the one discussed here constitute a very productive line of research with a clear and direct application to society, bridging the gap between academia and the professional world.

6. References

Aijmer, Karin, ed. 2009. *Corpora and Language Teaching*. Amsterdam: John Benjamins. ISBN 9789027223074.

Alcaraz Varó, Enrique et al. eds. 2007. *Las lenguas profesionales y académicas*. Barcelona: Ariel lenguas modernas. ISBN 9788434481220.

Aragonés Lumeras, Maite. 2009. *Estudio descriptivo multilingüe del resumen de patente: aspectos contextuales y retóricos*. Berna: Peter Lang. ISBN 9783039117710.

Baker, Mona. 1993. Corpus Linguistics and Translation Studies: Implications and Applications. @ M. Baker, G. Francis and E. Tognini-Bonelli, eds. *Text and Technology: In honour of John Sinclair*. Amsterdam: John Benjamins. ISBN 9789027221384, pp. 233-250

Beeby, Allison et al. eds. 2009. *Corpus Use and Translating*. Amsterdam: John Benjamins. ISBN 9789027224262.

Biel, Lucja. 2010. Corpus-Based Studies of Legal Language for Translation Purposes: Methodological and Practical Potential. @ C. Heine & J. Engberg, eds. *Reconceptualizing LSP*. Online proceedings of the XVII European LSP Symposium 2009. Aarhus 2010. ISBN 9788778824745.

Borja Albi, Anabel. 2005. Organización del conocimiento para la traducción jurídica través de sistemas expertos basados en el concepto de género textual. @ I. García-Izquierdo, ed. *El género textual y la traducción. Reflexiones teóricas y aplicaciones pedagógicas*. Berna: Peter Lang. ISBN 9783039106769, pp. 37-67.

Borja Albi, Anabel. 2013. A genre analysis approach to the study of court documents translation. @ L. Biel & J. Engberg, eds. *Research models and methods in legal translation. Linguistica Antverpiensia, New Series – Themes in Translation Studies (LANS – TTS)* 12: 33-53. Available at <https://lans-tts.uantwerpen.be/index.php/LANS-TTS/article/view/235>. [Last accessed 16/10/2014]

Borja, Anabel, Conde, Tomás, Juste, Natividad & Pilar, Ordóñez. 2013. A genre-based approach to the teaching of Legal and Business English: the GENTT specialized corpus in the LSP classroom. @ E. Bárcena, T. Read & J. Arús, eds. *Technological and methodological innovation in teaching and processing specialized linguistic domains.* New York: Springer-Verlag (Serie: Eductional Linguistics). ISBN 978331902222-2, pp. 117-196.

Borja Albi, Anabel, García-Izquierdo, Isabel & Vicent Montalt. 2009. Research Methodology in Specialized Genres for Translation Purposes. @ *The Interpreter and Translator Trainer*, St. Jerome. Special Issue on Doctoral Research (I. Mason guest editor) 3/1: 57-79. ISBN 9781905763122.

Bowker, Lynne. 1998. Using Specialized Monolingual Native-Language Corpora as a Translation Resource: A Pilot Study. @ S. Laviosa, ed. *L'Approche basée sur le corpus/The Corpus-Based Approach. META* 43/4: 631-651.

Cabré, María Teresa. 2002. Textos especializados y unidades de conocimiento: metodología y tipologización. @ J. García Palacios & C. Fuentes, eds. *Texto, terminología y traducción*, Salamanca: Ediciones Almar. ISBN 9788474550795, pp. 15-36

Corpas Pastor, Gloria. (2007). Lost in Specialised Translation: The Corpus as an Inexpensive and Under-Exploited Aid for Language Service Providers. *Translating and the Computer 29. Proceedings of the ASLIB Conference*. Londres: Aslib. ISBN 0851424856, pp. 1-18.

Corpas, Gloria. 2008. *Investigar con corpus en traducción. Los retos de un nuevo paradigma*. Frankfurt am Main, Berlin & New York: Peter Lang. ISBN 9783631584057.

Del Pozo, Maribel. 2014. Analysis of Charterparty Agreements from Textual Genre and Translation Points of View. *META* 59/1: 160-175.

Ezpeleta Piorno, Pilar. 2012. Metagenres and medicinal product information. @ A. Borja Albi & L. Gallego Borghini. *Panacea* 13/36: 327-332, ISSN: 1537-1964.

García-Izquierdo, Isabel. 2002. El género: plataforma de confluencia de nociones fundamentales en didáctica de la traducción. @ *Discursos, Série Estudos de Traduçao* 2: 13-21. ISSN 1647-1202.

García-Izquierdo, Isabel. 2005. Corpus electrónico, género textual y traducción. Metodología, concepto y ámbito de la Enciclopedia electrónica para traductores GENTT. @ *META*, 50/4: CD-ROM. Available at <http://www.erudit.org/livre/meta/2005>. [Last accessed 16/10/2014].

García-Izquierdo, Isabel. 2007. Los géneros y las lenguas de especialidad. @ E. Alcaraz et al. eds. *Las lenguas profesionales y académicas*. Barcelona: Ariel. ISBN 9788434481220, pp. 119-125.

García-Izquierdo, Isabel. 2009. *Divulgación médica y traducción: el género Información para pacientes*. Berna: Peter Lang. ISBN 9783039116980.

García-Izquierdo, Isabel. 2011. Investigating Professional Languages through Genres. @ T. Suau & B. Pennock, eds. *Interdisciplinarity and languages: current issues in research, teaching and professional applications and ICT. Selected Papers* (Contemporary Studies in Descriptive Linguistics, 30). Berna: Peter Lang. ISBN 9783034302838, pp. 125-145.

García-Izquierdo, Isabel. 2012. La investigación cualitativa en traducción especializada: una mirada a los ámbitos socioprofesionales. @ S. Cruces et al. eds. *Traducir en la frontera*. Granada: Atrio. ISBN 9788415275077, pp. 603-619.

García-Izquierdo & Anabel Borja. 2008. A multidisciplinary approach to Specialized writing and Translation. @ *LSP & Professional Communication* 8/1: 39-65. ISSN: 1601-1929.

García-Izquierdo & T. Conde. 2012. Investigating Specialized Translators: Corpus and Documentary sources. @ *Ibérica* 23: 131-157. ISSN 1139-7241.

García-Izquierdo & T. Conde. forthcoming. Necesidades documentales del traductor médico en España. @ *TRANS, Revista de traducción*. ISSN 11372311.

Gavioli, Laura. 1999. Corpora and the Concordancer in Learning ESP. An Experiment in a Course for Interpreters and Translators. @ G. Azzaro and M. Ulrych, eds. *Lingue a Confronto. Atti del XVIII Convegno AIA, Genova*, vol. 2. Trieste: EUT, pp. 331-343.

Göpferich, S. 2006. Modifications in documentation processes and their impact on the work of technical communicators and translators and their training. @ *LSP & Professional Communication* 6/1: 38-51. ISSN: 1601-1929.

Laviosa, Sara. ed. 1998. The Corpus-based Approach: A New Paradigm in Translation Studies. @ *META* 43/4: 474–479. Available at <http://www.erudit.org/revue/meta/1998/v43/n4/003424ar.pdf>. [Last accessed 16/10/2014].

Laviosa, Sara. 2002. *Corpus-Based Translation Studies. Theory, Findings, Applications*. Amsterdam: Rodolpi. ISBN 978-9042014879.

Laviosa, Sara. 2003. Corpora and the translator. @ H. Sommers, ed. *Computers and Translation*. Amsterdam: John Benjamins. ISBN 978902721640, pp. 105-117.

Malmkjaer, Kirsten. 2003, On a pseudo-subversive use of corpora intranslation training. @ F. Zanettin, S. Bernardini and D. Stuart, eds. *Corpora in Translator Education*. Manchester: Saint Jerome. ISBN 9781900650601, pp. 119-134.

Muñoz Miquel, Ana, Vicent Montalt & Isabel García Izquierdo. 2012. La investigación socioprofesional y la competencia traductora aplicadas a la pedagogía de la traducción médica. @ S. Cruces et al. eds. *Traducir en la frontera*. Granada: Atrio. ISBN 9788415275077, pp. 103-120.

Ordóñez, Pilar. 2009. The GENTT corpus of Specialized Genres: A valuable Tool for Professional Translators. @ LL. Gea Valor, I. García-Izquierdo & A. J. Esteve, eds. *Linguistic and Translation Studies in Scientific Communication*. Bern: Peter Lang. ISBN 9783034300698, pp. 219-242.

Pym, Anthony et al. 2012. *Studies in Translation and Multilingualism. The Status of the Translation Profession in the European Union*. Available at <http://ec.europa.eu/dgs/translation/publications/studies/translation_profession_en.pdf>. [Last accessed 16/10/2014].

Sinclair, John. ed. 2004. *How to Use Corpora in Language Teaching*. Amsterdam: John Benjamins. ISBN 9789027222824.

Toury, Gidéon. 1995. *Descriptive Translation Studies and Beyond*. Amsterdam: John Benjamins. ISBN 9789027216847.

Varantola, Krista. 2003. Translators and disposable corpora. @ F. Zanettin, S. Bernardini & D. Stewart, eds. *Corpora in Translator Education*. Manchester/ Northampton: St. Jerome. ISBN 978-1900650601, pp. 55-70.

Varela Vila, Tamara. 2009. Córpora 'ad hoc'en la práctica traductora especializada: aplicación al ámbito de las enfermedades neuromusculares. @ P. Cantos Gómez & A. Sánchez Pérez, eds. *A Survey on Corpus-based Research/Panorama de investigaciones basadas en corpus*. Asociación Española de Lingüística del Corpus (AELINCO). ISBN: 9788469221983, pp. 814-831.

Zanettin, Federico. 1998. Bilingual Comparable Corpora and the Training of Translators. @ S. Laviosa, ed. 1998. *L'Approche basée sur le corpus/The Corpus-Based Approach. META*

43/4: 616-630. Available at <http://www.erudit.org/revue/meta/1998/v43/n4/004638ar.pdf>. [Last accessed 16/10/2014].

Zanettin, Federico. 2002. DIY Corpora: The WWW and the Translator. @ B. Maia; J. Haller & M. Urlrych, eds. *Training the Language Services Provider for the New Millennium.* Oporto: Facultade de Letras, Universidade do Porto. ISBN 9789027216663, pp. 239-248.

Zanettin, Federico. 2012. Translation-Driven Corpora. Corpus Resources for Descriptive and Applied Translation Studies. Manchester: St. Jerome. ISBN 978-1905763290.

Estudio basado en corpus de las traducciones del alemán al vasco

[Corpus based study of German-Basque translations]

ZURIÑE SANZ, NAROA ZUBILLAGA e IBON URIBARRI
Universidad del País Vasco/Euskal Herriko Unibertsitatea (UPV/EHU, España)
zurine.sanz@ehu.es, naroa.zubillaga@ehu.es, ibon.uribarri@ehu.es

Abstract: The aim of this paper is to present the Aleuska corpus, a parallel and multilingual corpus created to analyse translations from German into Basque. Due to sociolinguistic factors, translations into Basque have specific features, and we compiled our corpus paying attention to those characteristics. When studying translations made from German into Basque, we find both, direct translations (made directly from German into Basque) and indirect ones (made indirectly through the Spanish version). In order to analyse those bitexts and tritexts, our parallel corpus is a trilingual corpus aligned at sentence level. Due to the fact that the available tools for creating and managing corpora did not suit our needs, we developed our own program. This way we could create the Aleuska corpus and do searches in it. Up to the present, researches based on this corpus have analysed translational behaviour in the mentioned linguistic combination, paying special attention to the two laws proposed by Toury, the law of growing standardisation and the law of interference, both in direct and indirect translations.

Keywords: corpus based translation studies; descriptive translation studies; standardisation; interference; German; Basque

1. Introducción

Los estudios de traducción basados en corpus (CBTS en sus siglas en inglés) ofrecen al investigador una metodología de trabajo empírica para realizar investigación de forma sistemática en Estudios de Traducción. De acuerdo con Corpas (2008: 216), en menos de una década, todas las ramas de los Estudios de Traducción, especialmente la descriptiva, se han beneficiado del trabajo realizado en la lingüística de corpus. Estudios basados en corpus bien diseñados y organizados conducen a un desarrollo cualitativo y cuantitativo de la disciplina.

Xiao y Yue (2009) ofrecen una visión de los CBTS fundada en el mapa de los Estudios de Traducción diseñado por Holmes y Toury (Xiao y Yue 2009: 243). Dado que nuestro planteamiento va a ser descriptivo, nos centraremos en la rama descriptiva de los Estudios de Traducción y dejamos de lado las otras dos ramas, la aplicada y la teórica. Según estos autores, la línea de investigación iniciada por Baker, que se centra en el producto, es la que más resultados ha aportado hasta ahora. Baker y sus colegas de la Universidad de Manchester crearon el TEC, Translational English Corpus, y muchas investigaciones se han basado en el mismo para buscar los universales de la traducción (Laviosa 1998, por ejemplo). Xiao y Yue llegan a decir que «the majority of product-oriented translation studies attempt to uncover evidence to support or reject the so-called translation universal hypothesis» (2009: 244). Otros investigadores, como por ejemplo Kenny (2001), reconocen el valor de corpus monolingües, pero señalan que este tipo de estudios resultarían muy beneficiados si contaran también con los textos fuente:

> Thus while monolingual translational corpora have been invaluable in attempts to describe the specific nature of translated text and to pinpoint aspects of the styles of individual translators (and not just original authors), some researchers (Laviosa 1998b: 565; Puurtinen 1998: 529) have argued that studies based on them may sometimes need to be supplemented by an analysis of the relevant source texts (Kenny 2001: 62).

Otra línea de investigación se centra en el proceso de traducción. Este tipo de estudios se basan normalmente en corpus paralelos que permiten al investigador comparar los textos fuente y meta. Utka (2004), por ejemplo, basándose en un corpus paralelo inglés-lituano formado por textos legales generados por la Unión Europea con tres versiones para cada texto meta (el primer borrador del traductor, la versión intermedia y la traducción final), señala casos de «normalization, systematic replacement of terminology and influence by the original language» (Xiao and Yue 2009: 246). En referencia al desarrollo de este tipo de corpus paralelos, Ji (2010) menciona que debido al coste y a los problemas de copyright, el tipo de corpus más usados son los «small-scale topic-specific parallel corpora» (2010: 6) y que «the usefulness of this type of DIY corpus, when studied in conjunction with larger-scale comparable corpora, translational or non-translational, may be maximally extended» (2010: 6).

En tercer lugar, los estudios basados en corpus orientados a la función de las traducciones no son tan frecuentes, «possibly because the marriage between corpora and this type of research, just like corpus-based discourse analysis (e.g. Baker 2006), is still in the 'honeymoon' period» (Xiao and Yue 2009: 247).

En nuestro caso, siendo investigadores del área de Traducción e Interpretación de la Universidad del País Vasco que trabajan en el marco del grupo de investigación TRALIMA/ITZULIK1, estamos desarrollando estudios de traducción basados en corpus en la combinación lingüística alemán-vasco con el objetivo final de llegar a conclusiones contrastadas sobre las características de estas traducciones y el comportamiento de los traductores. Por un lado, comparamos los textos fuente con los textos meta, basándonos en un corpus paralelo, y en ese sentido atendemos al proceso de traducción. Por otro lado, nuestras investigaciones también se ocupan del producto, ya que nos centramos en los textos meta y su contexto cultural con el objetivo de explicar ciertos aspectos de nuestra realidad traductora. Por ello, hacemos referencia también y usamos en nuestras investigaciones algunos corpus monolingües vascos, un campo de trabajo que se inició ya en los años 80.

El primer corpus vasco monolingüe fue creado en 1984, y aunque ha habido una larga pausa hasta la creación del siguiente en 2002, la actividad en este campo ha sido frenética en la última década. Por ejemplo, ETC (Egungo Testuen Corpusa)[2], accesible desde 2013, contiene 204.9 millones de palabras. De esta forma, es el mayor corpus vasco monolingüe y funciona como un corpus de referencia para la lengua vasca.

Sin embargo, dado que no existía ningún corpus que conectara las lenguas con las que queríamos trabajar (alemán y vasco), tuvimos que crear nuestro propio corpus. Para ello nos basamos en un trabajo previo de catalogación de la producción de traducciones del alemán al vasco. Desde 2003 mantenemos y actualizamos el catálogo de traducciones Aleuska, que recoge todas las traducciones de textos alemanes al vasco. Tras descartar las traducciones de textos poéticos y dramáticos, nos centramos en los textos literarios (narrativa infantil y juvenil como texto más representativo del catálogo, y narrativa para adultos) y filosóficos. Por otro lado, ya en el momento de la catalogación quedó claro que nos enfrentábamos a una situación compleja, con traducciones indirectas y directas (o al menos, supuestamente directas, ya que en esta fase sólo nos podíamos basar en los paratextos para clasificar el tipo de traducción). Debido a ello nuestro corpus se compone de bitextos alemán-vasco y tritextos alemán-español-vasco. En el desarrollo del corpus convergen los trabajos independientes pero estrechamente vinculados de tres investigadores.

[1] GIC 12_197, IT728-13, UFI 11_06, UPV/EHU.
[2] Se encuentra en esta página web: http://www.ehu.es/etc/.

Naroa Zubillaga analiza las traducciones de literatura infantil y juvenil alemana al vasco, y en su tesis doctoral ha indagado en las características de la traducción del lenguaje informal de este género textual centrándose en las traducciones de insultos y maldiciones, por un lado, y las partículas modales alemanas por otro (Zubillaga 2013). Debido a que estos textos tienen un receptor doble, el lector final y los adultos relacionados con la educación de los menores, el tipo de lenguaje usado en las traducciones suele estar adaptado con frecuencia. O'Sullivan por ejemplo relaciona las restricciones pedagógicas con la eufemización del lenguaje ofensivo en la literatura infantil y juvenil: «Besonders deutlich erkennbar sind sprachpädagogische Normen der Zielkutur in der Tilgung von Beleidigungen oder Beschimpfungen»[3] (O'Sullivan 2000: 212). Investigadores como Marcelo, que ha analizado la traducción al español de obras de la autora alemana Christine Nöstlinger, incide en la misma tendencia:

> una comparación de muchos libros y de sus traducciones nos mostraría cómo los traductores cambian insultos por palabras más suaves o simplemente los eliminan [...]. Todo esto depende por supuesto de las características de cada cultura y de los tabúes existentes e imperantes en cada una de ellas (Marcelo 2007: 146).

Por otro lado, las partículas modales alemanas son típicas del lenguaje informal y también suelen ser estandarizadas en las traducciones (Helbig 1988: 12; Prüfer 1995: 16). En cuanto a la lengua vasca, no hay trabajos significativos sobre la traducción del lenguaje informal, salvo el trabajo de Barambones (2012) relativo a la traducción de productos audiovisuales para niños y jóvenes. En su estudio concluye que «children's and teenagers' slang is scarcely used [in the Basque translations], perhaps due to the fact that in practice most of these idiomatic expressions are borrowings from Spanish» (Barambones 2012: 166-167).

Por otra parte, Zuriñe Sanz centra su investigación en la traducción de unidades fraseológicas alemanas al vasco (Sanz 2013). La traducción de estas estructuras polilexémicas relativamente estables e idiomáticas en mayor o menor medida ha sido objeto de muchos estudios desde los años 70. Los trabajos se han realizado teniendo en cuenta varias combinaciones lingüísticas, tipos de unidades fraseológicas y metodologías. Por ejemplo, Higi-Wydler (1989) analiza 3.700 unidades fraseológicas extraídas de traducciones literarias del alemán al francés y Se-

---

[3] «Las normas relativas a la pedagogía lingüística de la cultura meta son claramente reconocibles en la eliminación de insultos y maldiciones» (traducción propia).

gura (1998) analiza fraseologismos en traducciones literarias del alemán al español y viceversa. En cuanto a tipos de fraseologismos, Ji (2010) examina expresiones compuestas por cuatro caracteres chinos al español y van Lawick (2006) se centra en somatismos. En cuanto a la metodología, aunque los CBTS empiezan a tomar fuerza en este ámbito, Marco (2009: 843) reconoce que muchos estudios aún «move within the narrow limits of manual analysis».

Finalmente, Ibon Uribarri ha desarrollado un subcorpus de textos filosóficos alemanes y sus traducciones al vasco. Aunque la filosofía alemana es un campo de genera muchas traducciones a otras lenguas, no es un tipo textual que haya recibido mucha atención hasta ahora en los Estudios de Traducción. Uribarri ha publicado varios trabajos sobre la censura en las traducciones de textos filosóficos alemanes en España durante la dictadura franquista. Este subcorpus seguirá siendo desarrollado y se espera que pronto se puedan alcanzar algunos resultados basados en su análisis.

Las tres líneas de investigación trabajan en el marco de la rama descriptiva de los Estudios de Traducción, se acercan a los textos traducidos desde perspectivas diferentes pero complementarias, y toman como marco de referencia teórico las leyes de la traducción propuestas por Toury (2012), la ley de la estandarización y la ley de la interferencia.

Toury define la ley de estandarización con la observación «in translation, items tend to be selected on a level which is *lower* [énfasis en el original] than the one where textual relations have been established in the source text» (Toury 2012: 305). Sin embargo, en el contexto vasco, la estandarización se encuentra con otra norma, el proceso de normalización de la lengua vasca y la creación de un estándar de la lengua vasca. Se trata de un fenómeno reciente, ya que el uso de la lengua vasca se limitaba sobre todo al ámbito privado hasta hace unas décadas y no estaba presente en la vida pública, mediática, académica, etc. En estas últimas décadas, la lengua ha ampliado sus usos con el desarrollo de su variedad estándar, y la traducción ha sido un elemento esencial en el éxito de este proceso. Sin embargo, cuando se trata de traducir lenguaje informal, los traductores se encuentran con una situación compleja: el lenguaje informal real muestra mucha interferencia del español por un lado y de los dialectos vascos por otro. Esto lleva a que los traductores huyan de esos dos extremos y tiendan a activar el vasco estándar y ofrecer así un registro más neutral que el texto original. En resumen, aunque la estandarización afecta a las traducciones a la lengua vasca, estas traducciones están aún más condicionadas por el empuje de la construcción de una variedad estándar de la lengua vasca (Barambones 2012). Por ejemplo, en su subcorpus trilingüe Zubillaga ha encontrado que los insultos y las maldiciones son frecuentemente eufemizados en las traducciones y la función pragmática de las partículas modales alemanas sólo se mantiene en el 15% de los casos.

Además de la ley de estandarización, Toury propone también la ley de la interferencia, según la cual «[...] phenomena pertaining to the make-up of the source text tend to force themselves on the translators and be transferred to the target text» (Toury 2012: 310). Cuando habla de la interferencia, parece que sólo tiene en cuenta la interferencia directa del texto original sobre la traducción, pero parece lógico considerar otro tipo de situaciones, como la que llamamos interferencia indirecta. De hecho, Toury trata las traducciones indirectas en otro apartado de su importante libro (Toury 1995: 129-146) y creemos que estas situaciones también hay que considerarlas al hablar de interferencia. Por ejemplo, *Pippi Långstrump,* traducido del sueco al inglés y luego del inglés al español, puede mostrar rastros en la traducción española tanto de la versión intermedia inglesa como de la versión original sueca. Sin embargo, nuestra hipótesis es que no es lo mismo traducir *Pippi Långstrump* del inglés al español y del inglés al vasco. Porque en el segundo caso la traducción la produce un traductor diglósico, para un lector diglósico en un entorno diglósico usando herramientas intermedias. En resumen, creemos que en el caso de lenguas minoritarias en situaciones de diglosia puede darse una interferencia indirecta e incluso diglósica en este sentido: al traducir esta obra al vasco, la interferencia del español en la traducción puede ser incluso más relevante que la interferencia del inglés o el sueco.

En relación con este tipo de interferencia indirecta, hemos encontrado casos de interferencia diglósica textual, en el sentido de que el traductor vasco casi siempre tiene una versión española a mano, de la que puede echar mano en mayor o menor medida. Puede ser que el traductor no haga uso de la traducción intermedia y entonces tendríamos en principio una traducción directa; pero en el extremo opuesto, el traductor puede traducir directamente desde la versión intermedia sin contar para nada con el original. Sin embargo, lo que vemos en muchos casos es algo más complejo que se aleja de los dos extremos que acabamos de describir: el traductor usa el texto original *y* la versión española (y quizás alguna otra) en grados varios según el caso. Se podría hablar entonces de que en estos casos tenemos un texto fuente complejo, un texto compilado que puede incluir varios textos pero que pivota en torno al texto intermedio español.

> Hypothetically identified relationships may also give rise to the assumption that a target text drew on a text in a language other than the assumed one, or on more than one source text, in more than one language (Toury 1995: 72).

Significativamente, es raro encontrar referencias a textos fuente compilados en los paratextos, de manera que estas situaciones complejas resultan invisibles y la categorización de las traducciones se limita normalmente a la dicotomía simplificadora de traducciones directas e indirectas.

En segundo lugar, se puede hablar de una interferencia diglósica instrumental, en el sentido de que las fuentes de documentación y otras herramientas que usa el traductor en su trabajo son frecuentemente intermedias. Muchas traducciones del alemán al vasco fueron realizadas cuando no había ningún diccionario alemán-vasco. Ahora disponemos de uno relativamente pequeño que no cubre todas las necesidades de los traductores[4]. Pello Zabaleta, hasta hace poco uno de los pocos traductores que traducía directamente del alemán al español, subraya la complejidad de las traducciones del alemán al vasco debido a esta falta de diccionarios apropiados: «Alemanetik eta itzultzen dugunok, lehendabizi alemanetik gaztelerarakoa ikusi behar dugu, eta ondoren gazteleratik euskararakoa, eta ondoren euskaraz begiratu behar dugu ea konforme dagoen»[5] (Zabaleta 1995).

En tercer lugar, se puede hablar también de una interferencia diglósica cognitiva, en el sentido de que los traductores vascos son normalmente bilingües diglósicos en diverso grado y usan tanto la lengua dominante (español o francés) como la lengua meta de sus traducciones, el vasco. Por tanto, su escritura en lengua vasca está mediada por la lengua dominante. Los traductores activan sus dos lenguas en su trabajo y esto puede dejar huella en el texto meta. En su investigación sobre la traducción de somatismos alemanes al vasco, Zuriñe Sanz ha

---

[4] En 2006 Elena Martínez publicó un diccionario vasco-alemán / alemán-vasco, y se ha vuelto a editar en 2010 con algunas mejoras. La versión más reciente tiene 32,400 entradas en ambas direcciones.

[5] «Al traducir del alemán y otras lenguas extranjeras primero hay que consultar un diccionario alemán-español, luego uno español-vasco y, finalmente, mirar el resultado en lengua vasca para ver si es apropiado» (traducción propia).

encontrado evidencia de este tipo de interferencia en su subcorpus trilingüe (Sanz 2013). El siguiente ejemplo muestra este tipo de interferencia. La expresión *gastar dinero a manos llenas* en la versión intermedia española es una traducción cercana al original *Geld mit vollen Händen ausgeben*. Sin embargo, la versión meta en vasco no sigue el fraseologismo alemán original, sino que calca otra expresión fraseológica española, *arrojar, o echar, algo por la ventana*, produciendo una expresión atípica en vasco con evidentes muestras de esa interferencia del español. De modo interesante, la traducción añade *esaera den bezala* (según el dicho), siguiendo al original, pero con el problema de que la versión vasca no recoge en realidad ningún dicho.

Texto original	Texto puente	Texto meta
Ich fing an, Geld auszugeben - mit vollen Händen, wie man sagt (Roth 1936).	Comencé a gastar dinero a manos llenas, como suele decirse (Roth 1981).	Hasi nintzen dirua leihotik botatzen, esaera den bezala (Roth 2003). [Empecé a echar el dinero por la ventana, como dice el dicho]

Tabla 1. Ejemplo de interferencia diglósica cognitiva

En resumen, los traductores vascos no viven aislados. Al contrario, viven en una situación cultural en la que el vasco y el español (el francés, en el caso del País Vasco francés) conviven en una situación de bilingüismo diglósico. Por tanto, los traductores pueden consultar las traducciones realizadas al español, la mayoría de las obras de referencia que usan son en español y, además, su propia estructura cognitiva diglósica puede interferir en su labor traductora. Este tipo de interferencia es muy relevante para estudios cognitivos de traducción, y está siendo investigado en los últimos años en estudios sobre adquisición de lenguas y multilingüismo bajo la etiqueta CLI (*cross-linguistic influence*).

Un problema importante al que nos hemos enfrentado es la falta de herramientas adecuadas para crear un corpus que pudiera servir como base para explorar una situación tan compleja. En investigaciones previas[6] habíamos utilizado otros programas como *Wordsmith Tools*, pero los problemas que nos planteaban a la hora de alinear textos complejos a nivel de frase de manera ágil y rápida nos llevó a diseñar nuestra propia herramienta. Disponíamos de un programa de alineación muy elemental que se había desarrollado en el marco de

---

[6] En la producción del corpus multitextual TRACEKantKrV, que consiste de 7 fragmentos de la *Kritik der reinen Vernunft* de Immanuel Kant y cinco traducciones diferentes al español.

los proyectos de investigación TRACE (*TRACEaligner*) y lo hemos podido desarrollar en los últimos años gracias al respaldo del grupo de investigación en traducción TRALIMA/ITZULIK. Hemos mejorado el programa para que pueda trabajar con multitextos y no sólo bitextos, cosa que es esencial en nuestro contexto; hemos adaptado las funciones de re-alineación para facilitar al máximo el proceso; hemos programado una herramienta para generar un corpus virtual y, finalmente, hemos dotado al programa con un motor de búsquedas complejo. El desarrollo de esta herramienta, que esperamos pronto esté disponible para la comunidad investigadora, es una parte esencial de nuestro trabajo de investigación.

2. Construyendo el corpus Aleuska

Dado que nuestro objetivo es realizar un análisis descriptivo en una combinación lingüística prácticamente virgen hasta el momento, desde el inicio el proyecto siguió las recomendaciones metodológicas realizadas para este tipo de estudios por van Gorp y Lambert (1985). Antes de nada el primer paso era estudiar los datos preliminares, y para lograrlo se creó un catálogo de las traducciones de textos alemanes al vasco usando el programa Filemaker. El catálogo Aleuska fue iniciado en 2003 y se ha ido ampliando y actualizando en esta última década buscando en muchas bases de datos locales e internacionales como el Index Translationum[7], Deutsche National Bibliothek[8] o la base de datos de las bibliotecas públicas del País Vasco[9]. En este momento el catálogo contiene unas 700 entradas (Uribarri 2009). Además de los datos usuales en este tipo de catálogos, como título original, autor, traductor, año de la traducción, editorial, hemos puesto especial atención en catalogar las traducciones como directas o indirectas. Para ello hemos partido de los datos paratextuales disponibles en el momento de la catalogación, y se trata por supuesto de una clasificación inicial que el posterior análisis textual deberá confirmar o refutar. Usamos la categoría de supuesta traducción directa, y de esta manera ampliamos el concepto de Toury de *assumed translation* (Toury 1995) al tipo de traducción.

---

[7] http://portal.unesco.org/culture/en/ev.php-URL_ID=7810&URL_DO=DO_TOPIC&URL_SECTION=201.html.
[8] http://www.dnb.de/DE/Home/home_node.html.
[9] http://www.katalogoak.euskadi.net/cgi-bin_q81a/abnetclop/O9406/ID0cbc23a1/NT1?ACC=111&LANG=en-US.

Una vez analizado el catálogo se establecieron criterios para seleccionar qué textos serían incorporados a los tres subcorpus que íbamos a construir. Por un lado, usamos unos criterios generales comunes: tuvimos en cuenta traducciones indirectas y supuestas traducciones directas; mantener una variedad equilibrada entre autores fuente y autores meta, y también editoriales; seleccionamos traducciones realizadas a partir de 1980, ya que nuestra intención era hacer un estudio sincrónico sobre la realidad contemporánea de la traducción del alemán al vasco. Luego, siguiendo los intereses de investigación más específicos de cada investigador se han creado tres subcorpus diferentes: un subcorpus de textos de literatura infantil y juvenil alemanas y sus traducciones (AleuskaHGL), un subcorpus de textos de narrativa alemana y sus traducciones (AleuskaPhraseo) y un subcorpus de textos filosóficos alemanes y sus traducciones (AleuskaFilo). AleuskaPhraseo incorpora algunos textos presentes en AleuskaHGL. Como se puede ver en la tabla 1 el primer subcorpus contiene 80 textos: 38 textos relativos a 19 traducciones supuestamente directas y 42 textos relativos a 14 traducciones indirectas; el segundo contiene 110 textos: 68 textos relativos a 34 supuestas traducciones directas y 42 textos relativos a 14 traducciones indirectas; y el tercer corpus contiene 33 textos y sus correspondientes traducciones directas.

	AleuskaHGL	AleuskaPhraseo	AleuskaFilo	Total
Traducciones directas	19x2= 38	34x2= 68	33x2= 66	78x2= 146
Traducciones indirectas	14x3= 42	14x3= 42		22x3= 66
Autores originales	18	30	13	
N° de palabras	1.276.280	3.529.533	1.213.261	5.511.204[10]

Tabla 2. Características de los subcorpus AleuskaHGL, AleuskaPhraseo y AleuskaFilo

2.1. Acceso a los textos

Se intentó primero obtener los textos ya en formato digital (pdf o rtf). Se rastreó su accesibilidad en internet (en el proyecto Gutenberg, por ejemplo, para los originales) y también pedimos poder acceder a los textos digitalizados a las editoriales locales o a los traductores directamente. En los casos en los que no pudi-

---

[10] Dado que los corpus de Zubillaga y Sanz comparten algunos textos, el número total de palabras no se corresponde con la suma de los tres corpus.

mos acceder a los textos digitalizados, tuvimos que escanear los textos. Esto retarda mucho el trabajo, ya que supone mucho tiempo.

2.2. Preparación de los textos

Los textos que obtuvimos digitalizados los convertimos al formato txt sin dificultades. Los textos escaneados tuvieron que ser corregidos, dada la presencia de errores de todo tipo en los textos en alemán, español y vasco. La corrección de algunos errores de formato recurrentes como dobles espacios o dobles saltos de párrafo resultaba muy laboriosa, pero pudimos trabajar con un técnico informático que generó un programa basado en Access (TRACEcleaner) para poder solucionar ese tipo de errores de manera automática. Por desgracia ese programa no podía solucionar los errores propiamente textuales, cuya corrección resultó por eso bastante laboriosa.

Una vez limpiados los textos se pudo tener una visión más exacta del corpus en conjunto: el corpus consiste de 5.511.204 palabras, de las cuales, 2.722.000 palabras pertenecen a los textos fuente alemanes, 2.298.472 a las traducciones al vasco (al ser una lengua aglutinante siempre refleja un menor número de palabras que el alemán) y el resto, 490.732 palabras, a las traducciones puente en español. Es probablemente el mayor corpus paralelo alineado con lengua fuente alemán realizado en España.

2.3. Etiquetado y alineación de textos

El próximo paso importante es alinear los textos, para luego poder hacer búsquedas específicas y sistemáticas en el conjunto textual. La alineación implica varios pasos: primero se etiquetan los textos, luego se alinean los textos automáticamente siguiendo la etiquetación inicial, y finalmente hay que reajustar la alineación, ya que la alineación automática en los casos de textos literarios no suele ser del todo perfecta. La figura 1 muestra la interfaz de nuestro programa, en su versión más reciente, con las funciones de etiquetado y alineación en la parte superior izquierda.

Figura 1. Interfaz de *TRACEaligner*

Cada texto se etiqueta automáticamente a nivel de frase y parágrafo en un archivo XML, que además incluye unos metadatos (título, autor, traductor, código de identificación, lengua, tipo de traducción, género textual). Introducir los metadatos es esencial para una gestión productiva posterior del corpus. En la figura 2 (pág. 223) tenemos un ejemplo de un archivo XML etiquetado.

Una vez que los textos están etiquetados, nuestro programa ofrece la alineación automática de dos o más textos. La versión original del programa solo alineaba bitextos, la versión 2.0 ya alineaba tritextos y la actual 3.0 puede alinear varios textos simultáneamente. El programa, por tanto, alinea a nivel de frase siguiendo el etiquetado previo. Podemos ver el resultado en la figura 3 (pag. 223). Dado que en las traducciones se pueden producir desajustes en la estructura de frases, en especial en traducciones literarias, puede que nos encontremos con desajustes en el alineado, y por tanto hace falta re-alinear los textos manualmente.

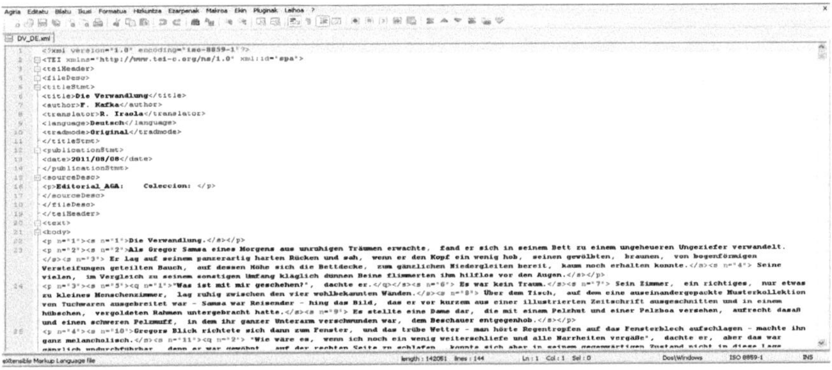

Estudio basado en corpus de las traducciones del alemán al vasco

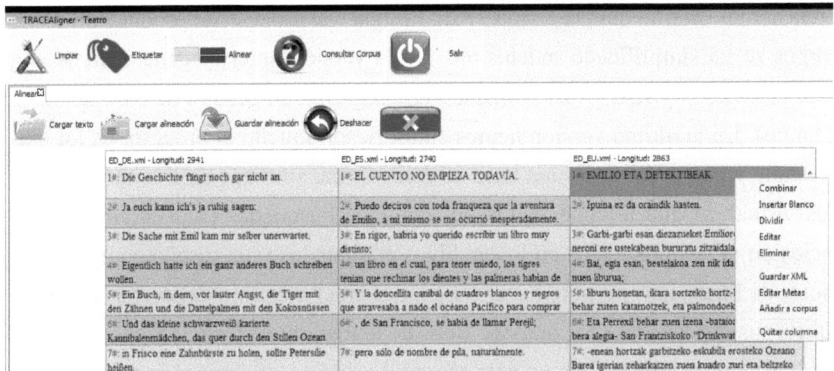

Figura 2. Archivo XML de un texto etiquetado

Figura 3. Alineamiento automático de archivos XML

Dada la necesidad de re-alinear los textos y la dificultad que suponía este paso en programas similares ya existentes (*Wordsmith Tools*, por ejemplo), hemos incluido en nuestro programa opciones de edición, como *combinar*, *dividir*, *añadir línea*, *eliminar*, *editar*, con el objetivo de que la re-alineación a nivel de frase sea lo más cómoda y rápida posible. Esta fase es esencial porque solo así lograremos que en las búsquedas que se realicen después en el corpus tengamos resultados pertinentes de modo sistemático. El resultado se puede ver en la figura 4 (pág. 224).

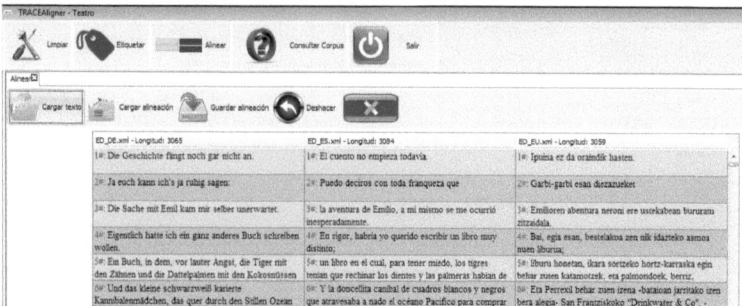

Figura 4. Re-alineamiento manual de acuerdo con el texto fuente

2.4. Producción del corpus y búsquedas

En la actual versión del programa *TRACEaligner* el proceso de producción de un corpus se ha simplificado muchísimo. En la versión anterior generábamos una base de datos MySQL física utilizando un programa de gestión de base de datos (xampp). En la última versión hemos simplificado mucho el proceso, de tal manera que ya no generamos una base de datos física, sino que producimos un corpus virtual, al que le conectamos un motor de búsquedas (*search engine*). La inclusión de los metadatos en los archivos etiquetados y un diseño complejo del motor de búsquedas permite hacer búsquedas en el conjunto del corpus o definir subcorpus específicos (por autores, tipos de textos, traductores, lenguas) y realizar búsquedas simples (con un sólo término) o búsquedas complejas (combinando hasta tres términos). La interfaz del motor de búsqueda se puede ver en la figura 5.

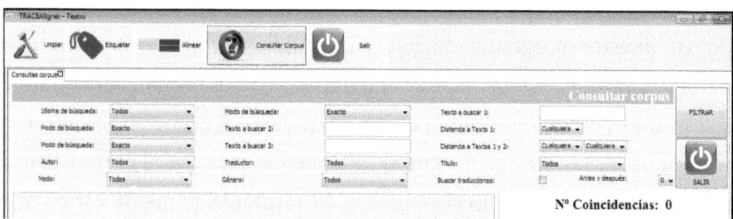

Figura 5. Motor de búsqueda

Finalmente, en la figura 6 mostramos el resultado de una búsqueda. En este ejemplo hemos hecho una búsqueda de los términos *Nagel* y *Kopf* en combinación. La primera columna contiene el código del texto, el segundo el texto alemán original, el tercero el texto intermedio español (cuando existe), y el cuarto el texto meta en vasco. Otro importante aspecto de la interfaz de búsquedas es que permite ver los resultados contextualizados, es decir, existe la opción de recibir las búsquedas con la frase que contiene los elementos buscados y sus correspondencias, o también se pueden visualizar una o dos frases anteriores y posteriores a la frase que contiene los elementos buscados.

DEKB	es wurde noch ungemütlicher, denn Trude B. konnte sich nicht verkneifen, den alten Freund, während sie weiterhin in ihrer Kaffeetasse rührte, mit den Worten zu begrüßen "Hallo Herrenbesuch".		oraindik gogorrago izan zen. Trude B. k ezin izan bait zuen isilik gorde, bere kafeari eragiten zion bitartean, adiskide zaharra "kaixo jaun -bisitari" batekin agurtzea.
DEKB	"Ich nehme an", sagte Bloma verlegen, "Trude hat mal wieder den **Nagel** auf den **Kopf** getroffen".		- Dirudienez -esan zuen lotsati Blornak-, orain ere Trudek iltzeari buru -buruan jo dio.
DEKB	"Ja", sagte Sträubleder, "fragt sich nur, ob das immer taktvoll ist".		- Bai -esan zuen Sträublederrek-, baina ez dakit hori egiaz beti zuhur den.
DKVG	Du wolltest bloß nicht zugeben, daß du um ein Haar abgestürzt wärst!".	¡Tú lo que no querías era admitir que no te has estrellado por un pelo!	Onartu nahi ez zenuena zera zen, txiripaz ez duzula muturra lurraren kontra apurtu!
DKVG	Daß Anton mit seiner Überlegung den **Nagel** auf den **Kopf** getroffen hatte, merkte er an der Reaktion des Vampirs:	Por la reacción del vampiro Antón se dio cuenta de que con su observación había dado en el clavo:	Banpiroaren erreakzioaz, Anton bete -betean asmatu zuela ohartu zen:
DKVG	ein verlegenes Grinsen huschte über sein Gesicht.	una tímida sonrisa irónica se deslizó hasta su rostro.	irri barre ironiko ttiki bat piztu zitzaion aurpegian.

Figura 6. Ejemplo de una búsqueda con *TRACEAligner*

3. Algunos resultados

Aunque el objetivo principal de este artículo es describir el proceso de creación del corpus y las principales características del mismo, a continuación expondremos algunos de los resultados obtenidos de los trabajos de investigación de Zubillaga y Sanz, quienes han hecho uso de este corpus trinlingüe.

Tal y como hemos comentado, Zubillaga se ha centrado en el análisis de los insultos y las maldiciones y de algunas partículas modales alemanas. A fin de realizar el análisis de la traducción de los insultos, se ha basado en la lista de Scheffler (Scheffler 2000), quien publica una relación de los insultos alemanes más frecuentes tanto para hombres como para mujeres. Tras realizar las búsquedas y clasificar los insultos y las maldiciones en diferentes grupos (Zubillaga 2013: 71), ha observado los cambios que ha sufrido el tono tanto en las traducciones directas como en las indirectas. A la vista de los resultados, la eufemización del tono, y por tanto, la estandarización, es un fenómeno general, aunque en mayor medida en traducciones indirectas:

	Traducciones directas	Traducciones indirectas
Insultos descriptivos	38%	52%
Insultos personales	30%	46%
Maldiciones	44%	66,5%

Tabla 3. Análisis de las traducciones de los insultos y las maldiciones

Los resultados obtenidos en el análisis de las traducciones de las partículas modales alemanas no son tan significativos. Concretamente, Zubillaga se ha centrado en la observación de las traducciones de las partículas *ja* y *eben/halt*[11]. Estas partículas modales aportan a los enunciados un significado ilocutivo, un matiz que a menudo no se mantiene en las traducciones. Según el análisis de Zubillaga (2013: 99-110), el porcentaje de casos en los que no se ha mantenido el matiz de las partículas en las traducciones es muy alto, 84% en el caso de *ja* y 83% en el caso de *eben* o *halt*. Por tanto, en el caso de las partículas alemanas, también resulta evidente el grado de estandarización. La comparación de traducciones directas e indirectas, sin embargo, no ha dejado ver diferencias tan grandes como en el caso de los insultos y las maldiciones. Es más, las traducciones indirectas han recogido un poco más la traducción de las partículas, aunque la diferencia no resulta demasiado significativa: en el caso de *ja*, las traducciones indirectas recogen la traducción de la partícula un 1% más, y en el caso de *eben*, un 7% más. Parece que en el caso de las partículas alemanas, la intermediación de un texto puente haya ayudado a mantener un poco más la traducción de las partículas.

Además de la estandarización, se han observado casos de interferencia. Por un lado, se han identificado interferencias textuales de la versión puente en las traducciones indirectas. Esto era de esperar, pues las traducciones indirectas se han realizado sin tener en cuenta el texto original en alemán, por lo que las interferencias que presenta el texto meta provienen del texto puente. Sin embargo, se han encontrado algunos ejemplos de posibles interferencias de una lengua puente también en las traducciones supuestamente directas. El siguiente ejemplo corresponde a una traducción directa. Nos resultó llamativo que el traductor vasco escogiera traducir *Depp* (tonto) como *mamu* (fantasma):

Texto original	Texto meta
Die sind mit mir umgegangen wie mit dem *letzten Deppen*. (Härtling 1989) [Me han tratado como si fuese *el último tonto* (significado: el tonto más tonto)]	*Azkeneko mamua* banintz bezala portatu zaizkit. (Härtling 1992) [Se han portado conmigo como si fuese *el último fantasma*]

Tabla 4. Ejemplo de interferencia en una traducción directa

Pensamos que tal vez la traducción directa pudiera no ser tan directa, por lo que consultamos la versión española (pues no la teníamos incluida en el corpus). Sin embargo, el texto en español traduce *Depp* como *mono* («se han portado conmi-

---

[11] *Eben* se utiliza más en el norte de Alemania y *halt*, en cambio, en el sur.

go como si fuera *el último mono»*). De todos modos, nos parece igualmente sospechoso que el traductor vasco utilizase *mamu* (fantasma), sobre todo teniendo en cuenta que la palabra fantasma no se suele utilizar generalmente como insulto en vasco. Así, y aunque para asegurar esto necesitaríamos seguir investigando y analizando, pensamos que se puede tratar de una interferencia cognitiva (en este caso concreto, interferencia de la expresión *ser un fantasma* del español).

En el caso de Sanz, el objeto de estudio han sido las unidades fraseológicas (UFs), y dentro de este campo tan amplio, el análisis se ha centrado en los fraseologismos somáticos (es decir, aquellos que están formados por elementos que designan partes del cuerpo humano) y en los binomios. En este artículo, presentamos los resultados obtenidos del análisis traductológico de los somatismos, concretamente los que están formados con los equivalentes de la palabra mano tanto en alemán (*Hand*) como en vasco (*esku*).

En términos generales, de los fraseologismos somáticos alemanes que hemos extraído (301 unidades en total), la mayoría (alrededor del 60%) se han traducido por otro somatismo en la lengua de llegada, ya sea por una UF similar o diferente. Este no es un dato llamativo, si lo comparamos con los resultados de otras investigaciones (Marco 2013; Oster y van Lawick 2013) que analizan la traducción de fraseologismos somáticos del inglés y del alemán al catalán. Sin embargo, lo que llama la atención en nuestro análisis es el número de copias tanto directas —cuando el resultado del texto meta es una copia de la UF del texto original— como indirectas —cuando lo que se copia es una UF de otra lengua que no sea la original. De los 52 casos encontrados, sólo mencionaremos, a modo ilustrativo, tres ejemplos de copias.

El primer ejemplo representa un caso de copia directa en el que la UF se traduce de forma literal. En este caso, dada la transparencia del somatismo, dicha literalidad no provoca incoherencia en el texto meta, como puede ocurrir en otros casos. El somatismo alemán en cuestión es *sich mit Händen und Füßen gegen etw wehren* que literalmente significa «defenderse con manos y pies», y el equivalente español que encontramos en el diccionario idiomático bilingüe alemán-español es *oponerse/resistirse a algo con todas sus fuerzas*. Tal y como se ha indicado, *eskuekin eta hankekin defendatu* es una traducción literal de la UF alemana.

Texto original	Texto meta
Er *wehrt sich* tapfer und wild *mit Händen und Füßen*, aber es hilft nichts, es geht über ihn (...) (Döblin 1929). [Se defiende valiente y salvajemente con pies y manos, pero no le sirve de nada, es más fuerte que él].	*Eskuekin eta hankekin defendatzen da* sendo eta gogor, baina alferrik da, bera baino gehiago da (...) (Döblin 2000). [Se defiendo con fuerza con manos y pies, pero en vano, es más que él (...)].

Tabla 5. Ejemplo de copia directa en la traducción de somatismos

En segundo lugar, en el texto original podemos ver la UF alemana *jmdm rutscht die Hand aus* que literalmente significa «resbalársele a alguien la mano» y cuyo equivalente fraseográfico en español según el diccionario idiomático alemán-español sería *escapársele/írsele a alguien la mano*. En otras palabras, el significado fraseológico de este somatismo es, tal y como podemos observar en el diccionario fraseológico alemán Duden 11, darle a alguien una bofetada («jmd. gibt jmdm. eine Ohrfeige»). En el texto meta en vasco, la combinación de palabras *eskuak alde egin*, que literalmente significa «escapársele a alguien la mano», no representa una UF en vasco. No hemos encontrado esta expresión ni en diccionarios ni en el corpus que hemos mencionado en el apartado primero de este artículo (el corpus ETC). Además, creemos que la UF en español, *escapársele/írsele a alguien la mano*, ha influido en cierta forma en la traducción al vasco, y que esta traducción, que hemos calificado como copia indirecta, es uno de los resultados de la situación de bilingüismo diglósico que hemos mencionado en líneas anteriores.

Texto original	Texto meta
Kann jedem mal passieren, daß *ihm die Hand ausrutscht*, wenn er in Rasche ist (Döblin 1929). [A cualquiera puede pasarle que se le vaya la mano cuando está furioso].	Edonori gertatzen zaiok, amorrazita dagoenean *eskuak alde egitea* (Döblin 2000). [Le puede pasar a cualquiera que cuando está furioso se le escape la mano].

Tabla 6. Ejemplo de copia indirecta en la traducción de somatismos

El tercer ejemplo hace referencia al fraseologismo alemán *die Hand ins Feuer legen*, cuyo equivalente formal en español es un fraseologismo similar: *poner la mano en el fuego*. En nuestro corpus, dicha UF alemana aparece tres veces, y tres traductores diferentes lo han traducido al vasco de la misma forma. Veamos uno de los ejemplos:

Texto original	Texto meta
Auch sie hätten, wenn sie in unsere Lage gekommen wären, um kein Haar anders gehandelt. *Dafür lege ich die Hand ins Feuer*. (Preußler 1958).	Gure egoeran aurkitu izan balira, guk bezala, berdin-berdin, jokatuko zuten. *Eskua sutan jarriko nuke!* (Preußler 1987)].

[Si hubieran estado en nuestro lugar, no habrían actuado de ninguna otra forma distinta. Pongo la mano en el fuego].	[Si se hubieran encontrado en nuestra situación, habrían actuado como nosotros, igual igual. ¡Pondría la mano en el fuego!].

Tabla 7. Ejemplo de interferencia doble en la traducción de somatismos

Lo que ocurre es que la traducción en vasco es una copia literal tanto del fraseologismo alemán *die Hand ins Feuer legen* como del español *poner la mano en el fuego*, y que a pesar de que en los diccionarios vascos se pueden encontrar otras opciones, opciones fraseológicas (como por ejemplo *lepoa egin, jugarse el cuello*), en los tres casos encontrados en el corpus AleuskaPhraseo se ha copiado la UF alemana (o española). A diferencia del segundo caso, hay que mencionar que aunque en el corpus vasco que recoge textos del siglo XX (*XX. mendeko euskararen corpus estatistikoa*) no hemos encontrado ninguna ocurrencia de *eskua sutan jarri*, en el corpus del siglo XXI (en el ETC), sí que hemos encontrado algunos casos, sobre todo en los textos de prensa y en el corpus de una serie de televisión vasca (Goenkale). En este caso, el uso del calco fraseológico *eskua sutan jarri* parece que está más extendido que el ejemplo anterior. Sea como fuere, otra vez resulta imprescindible tener en cuenta la situación en la que se realizan las traducciones para poder describir el comportamiento traductor.

Mediante los ejemplos que hemos expuesto en esta sección hemos intentado, por una parte, mostrar cómo hemos utilizado el corpus y la herramienta de búsqueda para extraer información del corpus, y por otra parte, reflejar cómo ha sido el análisis del comportamiento traductor en el marco de los proyectos de investigación en cuestión. Los datos extraídos del proyecto de Zubillaga muestran el grado de estandarización que sufren algunos de los elementos del lenguaje no formal, y el ejemplo de la tabla 4 representa una posible interferencia diglósica. Los demás ejemplos extraídos del proyecto de Sanz representan casos de interferencia, no sólo de la lengua original (como se puede ver en el ejemplo de la tabla 5), sino también interferencias de otras lenguas, como es el español en nuestro caso (tablas 6 y 7).

Si bien es cierto que nuestro objetivo ha sido analizar el comportamiento traductor en la combinación de lenguas alemán-vasco, el corpus digitalizado y la herramienta de búsqueda podrían usarse con otros fines en otros proyectos de investigación. Lo que queda claro es que el proceso de creación del corpus es una inversión a largo plazo que puede tener diversas aplicaciones en el futuro.

4. Algunas conclusiones

El objetivo de nuestro artículo es explicar y presentar las motivaciones y los pasos dados en la construcción de nuestro corpus Aleuska y también ofrecer algunos resultados de investigación obtenidos hasta la fecha. Gracias a una labor de equipo conjuntamente con el informático que ha apoyado todo el desarrollo técnico, hemos sido capaces de crear un programa fácil de manejar que nos permite trabajar con un corpus paralelo multilingüe y seguir ampliando su tamaño en el futuro. Nuestro trabajo está dando unos primeros frutos, que ya evidencian la presencia de la estandarización y de la interferencia en las traducciones del alemán al vasco. Estos resultados iniciales (los que se refieren, por ejemplo, a los distintos tipos de interferencia) serán contrastados en los próximos años con más estudios. En la parte técnica, nuestro programa es ya una herramienta adecuada para construir corpus multilingües con objetivos de investigación en Estudios de Traducción y en el futuro esperamos integrar elementos de análisis textual en el mismo.

En un futuro próximo se integrarán los tres subcorpus en un único corpus Aleuska con al menos seis millones de palabras. Este corpus será la base para futuras investigaciones empíricas sobre la traducción de textos alemanes al vasco y también prevemos que pueda dar lugar a otro tipo de resultados tanto en la rama aplicada de los Estudios de Traducción (lexicografía, lingüística contrastiva, didáctica de la traducción) como en la rama teórica (profundización en los temas de la estandarización y la interferencia). Planteamos también que nuestro corpus y los trabajos que se basan en el mismo sean un modelo para similares trabajos en otras combinaciones lingüísticas con el vasco como lengua meta, con lo que se pueda ampliar el espectro hacia una visión más amplia de la traducción a la lengua vasca.

Agradecimiento

Quisiéramos agradecer a Iñaki Albisua su labor en los últimos años en el desarrollo y la mejora de los programas informáticos que han hecho posible nuestro trabajo.

5. Bibliografía

Barambones, Josu. 2012. *Mapping the dubbing scene. Audiovisual translation in Basque television*. Bern: Peter Lang. ISBN 9783034302814.

Corpas, Gloria. 2008. *Investigar con corpus en traducción: los retos de un nuevo paradigma*. Frankfurt am Main: Peter Lang. ISBN 9783631584057.

Döblin, Alfred. 1929. *Berlin Alexanderplatz: Die Geschichte vom Franz Biberkopf*. Berlin: Fischer Verlag.

Döblin, Alfred. 2000. *Berlin Alexanderplatz: Franz Biberkopfen istorioa* (traductor: Antton Garikano). Euba: Ibaizabal. ISBN 9788483253854.

Duden 11. 1998. *Redewendungen und sprichwörtliche Redensarten. Idiomatisches Wörterbuch der deutschen Sprache*. Mannheim et al.: Dudenverlag. ISBN 9783411041121.

Härtling, Peter. 1989. *Fränze*. Weinheim: Beltz&Gelberg. ISBN 3407800339.

Härtling, Peter. 1989. *Franze* (traductor: Xabier Mendiguren). Donostia: Elkar. ISBN 978-8479172398.

Helbig, Gerhard. 1988. *Lexikon deutscher Partikeln*. Leipzig: VEB, Verlag Enzyklopädie Leipzig. ISBN 3324003105.

Higi-Wydler, Melanie. 1989. *Zur Übersetzung von Idiomen: ein Beschreibung und Klassifizierung deutscher Idiome und ihrer französischen Entsprechungen*. Bern: Peter Lang. ISBN 3261041005.

Kenny, Dorothy. 2001. *Lexis and Creativity in Translation*. Manchester: St. Jerome. ISBN 9781900650380.

Ji, Meng. 2010. *Phraseology in Corpus-based Translation Studies*. Frankfurt am Main: Peter Lang. ISBN 9783039115501.

Lambert, José y Hendrik van Gorp. 1985. On describing translations. @ T. Hermans, ed. *The manipulation of literature: studies in Literary Translation*. London/Sydney: Croom Helm. ISBN 9780709912767, pp. 42-53.

Laviosa, Sara. 1998. Core patterns of lexical use in a comparable corpus of English narrative prose. @ *Meta*, 43/4. Disponible en <http://id.erudit.org/revue/meta/1998/v43/n4/003425ar.pdf>. [Última consulta 27/5/2014].

Martínez, Elena. 2006. *Euskara-alemana / alemana-euskara hiztegia*. Donostia: Elkar. ISBN 9788497839396.

Marcelo, Gisela. 2007. *Traducción de las referencias culturales en la literatura infantil y juvenil*. Frankfurt am Main: Peter Lang. ISBN 9783631547267.

Marco, Josep. 2009. Normalisation and the Translation of Phraseology in the COVALT Corpus. @ *Meta*, 54/4. Disponible en <http://www.erudit.org/revue/meta/2009/v54/n4/038907ar.html>. [Última consulta 27/5/2014].

Marco, Josep. 2013. La traducció de les unitats fraseològiques de base somàtica en el subcorpus anglès-català. @ L. Bracho, ed. *El corpus COVALT: un observatori de fraseologia traduïda*. Aachen: Shaker Verlag. ISBN 9783844014945.

O'Sullivan, Emer. 2000. *Kinderliterarische Komparatistik*. Mörlenbach: Universitätsverlag C. Winter Heidelberg. ISBN 9783825310394.

Prüfer, Irene. 1995. *La traducción de las partículas modales del alemán al español y al inglés*. Frankfurt am Main: Peter Lang. ISBN 9783631482599.

Roth, Joseph. 1936. *Beichte eines Mörders*. Amsterdam: Allert de Lange.

Roth, Joseph. 1981. *Confesión de un asesino* (traductor: Juan José del Solar). Barcelona: Bruguera. ISBN 9788402078124.

Roth, Joseph. 2003. *Hiltzaile baten aitormena* (traductor: Matías Múgica). Pamplona: Igela. ISBN 9788487484506.

Sanz, Zuriñe. 2013. Korpusbasierte Übersetzungsanalyse von Hand-Somatismen (Deutsch-Baskisch). @ M. Fabčič, S. Fiedler y J. Szerszunowicz, eds. *Phraseologie im interlingualen und interkulturellen Kontakt*. Maribor: Zora. ISBN 9789616930031, pp. 317-330.

Scheffler, Gabriele. 2000. *Schimpfwörter im Themenvorrat einer Gesellschaft*. Marburg: Tectum Verlag. ISBN 3828881726.

Segura, Blanca. 1998. *Kontrastive Idiomatik, Deutsch-Spanisch: eine textuelle Untersuchung von Idiomen anhand literarischer Werke und ihrer Übersetzungsprobleme*. Frankfurt am Main: Peter Lang. ISBN 9783631327678.

Toury, Gideon. 1995. *Descriptive Translation Studies - and beyond*. Amsterdam/Philadelphia: John Benjamins. ISBN 9781556194955.

Toury, Gideon. 2012. *Descriptive Translation Studies - and beyond*. Revised edition. Amsterdam/Philadelphia: John Benjamins. ISBN 9789027224484.

Uribarri, Ibon. 2009. Übersetzung deutscher Literatur ins Baskische. @ C. Jarillot, ed. *Bestandaufnahme der Germanistik in Spanien: Kulturtransfer und methodologische Erneuerung*. Bern: Peter Lang. ISBN 9783034300032, pp. 859-870.

Utka, Andrius (2004). Phases of translation corpus: Compilation and analysis. @ *International journal of corpus linguistics*, 9/2. Disponible en <http://donelaitis.vdu.lt/~andrius/sites/default/files/files/PTC-corpus-Utka.pdf>. [Última consulta 27/5/2014].

van Lawick, Heike. 2006. *Metàfora, fraseologia i traducció. Aplicació als somatismes en una obra de Bertolt Brecht*. Aachen: Shaker Verlag. ISBN 3832247785.

Oster, Ulrike y Heike van Lawick. 2013. Análisi dels somatismes del subcorpus alemany-català. @ L. Bracho, ed. *El corpus COVALT: un observatori de fraseologia traduïda*. Aachen: Shaker Verlag. ISBN 9783844014945.

Preußler, Otfried. 1958. *Bei uns in Schilda*. Stuttgart: Thienemann.

Preußler, Otfried. 1987. *Markako eroak* (traductor: Pello Zabaleta). Madrid: Grupo SM. ISBN 9788434822986.

Schemann, Hans, Carmen Mellado, Patricia Buján, Nely Iglesias, Juan P. Larreta y Ana Mansilla. 2013. *Idiomatik Deutsch-Spanisch*. Hamburg: Helmut Buske Verlag. ISBN 9783875486285.

Xiao, Richard y Ming Yue. 2009. Using Corpora in Translation Studies: The State of the Art. @ P. Baker, ed. *Contemporary Corpus Linguistics*. London/New York: Continuum. ISBN 9780826496102, pp. 237-261.

Zabaleta, Pello y Koldo Biguri. 1995. Pello Zabaletarekin solasean. @ *Senez*, 10. Disponible en <http://www.eizie.org/Argitalpenak/Senez/19901131/pello>. [Última consulta 27/5/2014].

Zubillaga, Naroa. 2013. Übersetzung deutschsprachiger Kinder- und Jugendliteratur ins Baskische: Vergleich direkter und indirekter Übersetzungen mithilfe eines Corpus (versión resumida en alemán de las tesis original en euskera). Disponible en <http://www.ehu.es/argitalpenak/images/stories/tesis/Humanidades/8670ZubillagaDE.pdf> [Fecha de última consulta 27/5/2014].

Construcción de corpus virtuales comparables deslocalizados (DE/ES): Análisis y comparación de recursos

[Building virtual delocalized comparable corpora (DE/ES). Analysis and contrast of resources]

MARÍA TERESA SÁNCHEZ NIETO
Universidad de Valladolid (España)
maysn@lia.uva.es

Abstract: In this paper we set out to analyze two reference corpora of the German and two of the Spanish language, with the aim of evaluating to what extent they can be used to build virtual delocalized comparable corpora for corpus-based contrastive or translation studies in the language pair mentioned above, be it on its own or as part of a broader palette of resources. After briefly describing the nature and compilation aims of the four selected corpora, we compare them with respect to the metadata included in their annotation system, the statistical information on and of the selected subsets of data and the basic features of their search interface. This methodology or resource comparison, which draws on Rojo's (2010) proposal but adds new comparison variables to it, allows us to locate important differences among the resources under study.

Keywords: virtual delocalized comparable corpus; on-line reference corpus; corpus comparison; corpus analysis; German, Spanish

1. Motivación y objetivo del estudio

Tras el advenimiento de los corpus a los estudios de traducción (Laviosa 1998), y la particular sintonía encontrada entre aquellos y los estudios descriptivos de traducción (Laviosa 2004), hoy en día las metodologías basadas en corpus – *corpus based*– o guiadas por corpus –*corpus-driven*– (Tognini- Bonelli 2001:17, v. también Marco y Van Lawick 2009:11, Zanettin 2012) asisten a una parte nada despreciable de los estudiosos de esta área de conocimiento. La importancia de los corpus como base para el estudio de la traducción y para el contraste de lenguas ha desembocado en la compilación de importantes corpus de diferente naturaleza, de utilidad para el traductor o para el investigador de la lengua o de la traducción (v. Borja Albi, 2008: 250 y ss). Tras muchas de estas compilaciones hay fuertes inversiones monetarias y en recursos humanos y de investigación. Algunos de estos corpus están disponibles en línea, y la cuestión de su aprovechamiento y de su accesibilidad cobra cada vez mayor importancia. En los últimos años, en consonancia con el epíritu de las humanidades digitales, se está haciendo un esfuerzo por homogeneizar y reunir diferentes recursos lingüísticos en centros de servicios con el fin de aprovecharlos de manera combinada y de construir con ellos y con las tecnologías lingüísticas que los respaldan nuevas aplicaciones accesibles para toda la comunidad científica, como se pone de manifiesto en el ejemplo paradigmático de CLARIN (CLARIN 2014, Hinrichs 2013, Wynne 2014).

Ante este panorama, es factible iniciar estudios de traducción o estudios contrastivos basados o motivados en corpus apoyándose en estos recursos disponibles en la red. El investigador puede construir su propio corpus comparable (con datos de diferentes lenguas de estudio), virtual (a partir de datos disponibles en servidores) y deslocalizado (a partir de datos disponibles en los *diferentes* servidores que alojan *diferentes* corpus, ya sea utilizando técnicas de búsqueda federada de contenidos o con búsquedas individuales en diferentes corpus). Ello exigirá, ciertamente, un conocimiento detallado de la naturaleza y organización de los recursos de los que se trate.

Tanto en los Estudios de traducción como en los Estudios contrastivos basados en corpus (ETBC / ECBC) se recurre con frecuencia a los denominados *corpus de referencia*, p. ej. para la observación directa de fenómenos en contraste (ECBC) o para la extracción de subconjuntos que sirvan como corpus de control para comparar hallazgos en otros corpus paralelos o comparables *ad hoc* existentes (ETBC). Los corpus de referencia son colecciones muy amplias de testimonios de uso de la lengua, diseñadas para atender todo tipo de consultas de la lengua de la que se trate (Rojo 2010:13, Briz y Albelda 2009: 208). Suelen contar con un importante respaldo institucional y financiero y están en constante evolución tecnológica, aprovechando los avances en informática y en lingüística del corpus. Según Rojo (2010:11), estos corpus se encuentran actualmente «sometidos a las tensiones que producen la explotación directa de lo que se puede encontrar en la red ([…] 'web as corpus') por un lado, y los conjuntos pequeños, centrados en un tipo determinado de textos […], por otro». Es a los corpus de referencia a los que está dedicado este trabajo, que tiene un doble objetivo:

- Explorar las posibilidades que ofrecen diferentes **corpus de referencia** de la lengua española y alemana para definir **corpus virtuales comparables y deslocalizados**.
- Definir y poner a prueba un modelo de análisis dinámico, aplicable a corpus en línea de diferente naturaleza, ya sean de referencia o no (objetivo metodológico).

2. Metodología

En primer lugar, hemos seleccionado los corpus de referencia que someteremos a estudio, teniendo en cuenta tres criterios: autoría, accesibilidad y existencia de documentación en línea. Los corpus de referencia seleccionados han nacido en el seno de instituciones dedicadas al estudio y a la promoción de la lengua[1], son accesibles gratuitamente en línea (previo registro o sin él)[2] y disponen de una documentación en su sitio web que permite entender su uso hasta un nivel avanzado. Se trata de *CorpesXXI* y *Corpus del Español* (*CdE*) para nuestra lengua y *DeReKo* y los *Kernkorpora* de la plataforma *DWDS* para la lengua alemana.

En segundo lugar, hemos estudiado la documentación disponible para cada recurso, con el fin de comprender la naturaleza y el objetivo de compilación de cada uno de estos cuatro corpus. Aunque a los cuatro se les pueda aplicar la misma etiqueta («corpus»), existen importantes diferencias de escopo entre los proyectos que les dan cobertura.

Como tercer paso, hemos definido el método de comparación, adaptando y ampliando el modelo que utiliza Rojo (2010) para la comparación de *CREA / CORDE* y *Corpus del Español*. Proponemos que un usuario que quiera definir conjuntos comparables de datos en dos corpus diferentes en línea ha de tener en cuenta los siguientes aspectos:

- Los subconjuntos en los que está organizada la base textual de cada corpus, reflejados en la anotación de la misma (anotación no lingüística o codificación).
- El modo de calcular el número de palabras de cada subconjunto seleccionado por el usuario.

---

[1] Ello nos lleva a dejar de lado los corpus editoriales. Ver Borja Albi (2008): división tripartita de autorías en instituciones dedicadas al estudio y promoción de la lengua, corpus editoriales y corpus de facultades de traducción.

[2] Ello nos lleva a excluir corpus como el *Spanish Web Corpus* de la herramienta *SketchEngine* (<http://www.sketchengine.co.uk/>), de Lexical Computing, Ltd.

- El modo de acceder a los subconjuntos, que implica, a su vez conocer el funcionamiento básico del motor de búsquedas: si hay posibilidad de combinar en la búsqueda la anotación no lingüística (codificación) y anotación lingüística y tipo de interfaz (máscara de búsqueda o ventana).

Como resultado, hemos fijado una serie de parámetros de comparación, divididos en generales (objetivo de la compilación, historia, tamaño y cobertura cronológica) y específicos. Los parámetros específicos atañen a la codificación (áreas geográficas cubiertas, medios y soportes, géneros literarios o temas, tipos textuales, cronología / actualización e información sobre actualización, datos bibliográficos e información sobre números de formas de subconjuntos estáticos y dinámicos) y a la aplicación de búsquedas (tipo de interfaz y utilidades del motor de búsquedas)[3].

3. Análisis comparado de los recursos

3.1. Naturaleza y objetivo de la compilación

Los cuatro recursos analizados encajan en la definición de Briz y Albelda (2009: 208) de *corpus de referencia*, puesto que fueron creados con fines generales «con el propósito de ponerse a disposición de la comunidad científica como conjunto de materiales» para realizar sobre ellos investigaciones lingüísticas con los más variados fines. También cumplen otros dos criterios adicionales que señala Rojo (2010: 13) para este tipo de corpus, a saber: (i) permiten encontrar «diferencias existentes entre lo que contiene ese corpus y lo que se puede obtener de otros o bien las que se dan entre distintos subcorpus (temporales, geográficos, tipológicos) del mismo corpus» y (ii) tener un tamaño grande (ver apartado 3.3). No obstante, cada una de las compilaciones, con unos objetivos particulares, muestra un perfil propio con respecto al resto de las estudiadas.

CorpesXXI, proyecto conjunto de la Asociación de Academias de la Lengua Española (ASALE) con financiación parcial del Banco de Santander (Santander 2012), se entiende como una ampliación del Corpus de Referencia del Es-

---

[3] V. Ahmad (2008) para una comparación de varios corpus de referencia de la lengua inglesa (Brown Corpus, Bank of English, LOB Corpus entre otros), en la que se ponen en valor otros interesantes parámetros como el género de los autores, el nivel de dificultad de los textos, que pueden resultar de utilidad en la comparación de otros corpus de naturaleza diferente a la de los aquí estudiados.

pañol Actual o *CREA* (v. Briz y Albelda 2009: 209, nota 21), en la que se ha apostado sobre todo por un sistema de codificación muy sofisticado, que facilita al investigador la extracción selectiva de la información no solo sobre «la totalidad del corpus, sino para cualquiera de los subconjuntos que se pueden configurar en su interior de forma dinámica» (Real Academia Española, 2013a:7).

El *Corpus del Español* (*CdE*), de Mark Davies, nace también con fines de investigación de la lengua española, como se deduce del hecho de que el registro en el corpus implique la creación de un perfil de diferentes niveles, los últimos de los cuales corresponden al de «investigador». La presencia de los perfiles de los investigadores que han utilizado el corpus para generar investigación, junto con las referencias de las publicaciones correspondientes, permite al usuario saber cómo y con qué fines se usa el corpus[4]. Sin embargo, el autor del *CdE* también prevé usos comerciales para el mismo (v. Davies, 2014).

El *Kernkorpus des 20. Jahrhunderts* y su complemento, el *Kernkorpus des 21. Jahrhunderts*, forman parte del proyecto Digitales Wörterbuch der Deutschen Sprache (DWDS), financiado por la Deutsche Forschungsgemeinschaft (Geyken 2013d). Este proyecto nace con un objetivo doble. Por una parte, recopilar y actualizar el saber léxico de tres grandes diccionarios académicos: el *Wörterbuch der deutschen Gegenwartssprache* (WDG), el *Deutsches Wörterbuch* de Jacob Grimm y Wilhelm Grimm (1DWB) y su reelaboración (2DWB) y el *Etymologisches Wörterbuch des Deutschen* de Wolfgang Pfeifer. El segundo objetivo, paralelo al anterior, consiste en

> [...] desarrollar un sistema léxico digital flexible, ampliable, corregible, útil para fines científicos y no científicos y, sobre todo, en el que una serie de corpus bien explotados permitan relacionar los usos de una palabra con una descripción científicamente fiable de las características de dicha palabra (Geyken 2013c, nuestra traducción).

En la plataforma de consultas de *DWDS* se combinan de forma modular diferentes fuentes de información léxica interconectadas entre sí por un potente motor de búsquedas[5] que devuelve simultáneamente resultados de todas ellas. Estos recursos son, a su vez, de distinto tipo: corpus (divididos a su vez en corpus de

---

[4] Consultables por país, palabra clave, apellido, etc.
[5] El motor de búsqueda DDC-Suchmachine es un proyecto de software libre y se puede descargar en Sourceforge.net: <http://sourceforge.net/projects/ddc-concordance/>.

referencia o *Referenzkorpora*, corpus de periódicos o *Zeitungskorpora* y corpus especiales o *Spezialkorpora*), diccionarios (*DWDS, WDG* –generales–, *eWB* – etimológico–, *DW-Grimm* y *OpenThesaurus*) y estadísticas (el generador de perfiles léxicos *Wortprofil*, el generador de curvas léxicas *Wortverlaufskurve* y el panel de estadísticas *Korpusstatistiken*). En la interfaz, el usuario puede añadir, quitar y reorganizar módulos según sus necesidades de consulta o intereses investigadores.

Por su parte, el *Deutscher Referenzkorpus* (*DeReKo*) se entiende como una «empirical basis for linguistic research» para la lengua alemana (Kupietz et al. 2010: 1848). El carácter de muestra primaria (*primordial sample*) de *DeReKo* implica que sus diseñadores intentan proporcionar una cantidad de datos lo más amplia posible para que el investigador luego, a partir de esa muestra, cree sus propios corpus virtuales para investigaciones concretas.

Así pues, estamos ante recursos de muy diferente naturaleza: *CorpesXXI* y *CdE* son corpus en sentido estricto, mientras que *DeReKo* y *DWDS* son recursos más complejos: *DeReKo* es un conjunto «moldeable» de colecciones de datos para formar corpus y *DWDS* es un conjunto de recursos entre los que figuran corpus, pero no solo. Por otra parte, tanto *Corpes XXI* como *CdE* y los corpus de la plataforma *DWDS* son corpus del tipo que Kupietz et al. (2010) denominan *ready-to-use*, es decir una base de datos textual y una aplicación de búsquedas que permite extraer información de la misma de manera selectiva recurriendo a los metadatos con los que se ha codificado dicha base textual. Por el contrario, *DeReKo*, al ser una muestra primaria, exige del usuario o investigador que él mismo diseñe su propio corpus virtual.

3.2. Historia

En el siguiente gráfico podemos observar los principales hitos temporales de cada proyecto. *DeReKo* es el proyecto más antiguo y el que ha tenido más tiempo de evolucionar:

Construcción de corpus virtuales comparables deslocalizados (DE/ES)

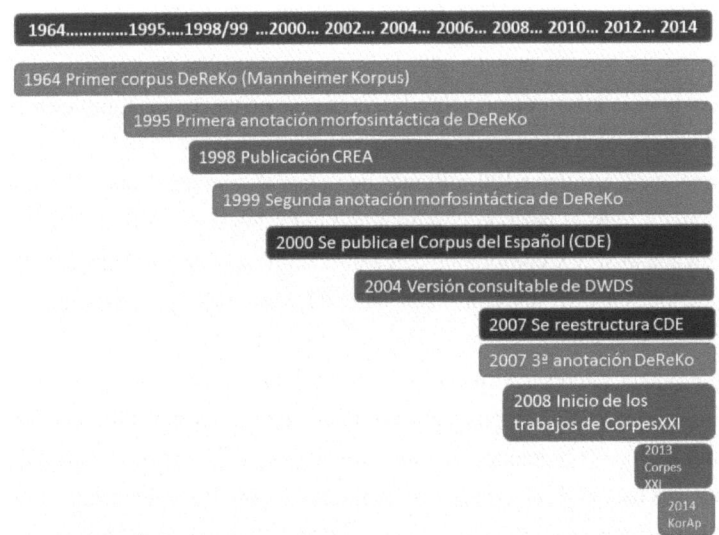

Gráfica 1. Hitos en la historia de *DeReKo*, *DWDS*, *CdE* y *CorpesXXI*

3.3. Tamaño y tasa de crecimiento

El objetivo final de *CorpesXXI* es «reunir, en el 2014, un total de 300 millones de formas y palabras de la lengua común de 450 millones de hispanohablantes», creciendo a una tasa de 24 millones de formas por año (Agencia EFE 2012). Sin embargo, en su versión (0.7 beta[6]) el número de formas era de 174.156.994 (Real Academia Española 2013b: 1).

En 2014, *DeReKo* contenía 24.000 millones de formas o aproximadamente 60 millones de páginas de libros (a aproximadamente 400 palabras por página) en más de cien corpus (Eichinger & Trabold 2014b, Kupietz & Lüngen, 2014:2378). Este recurso crecía hasta ahora a una media de 300 millones de formas al año[7]. Al ser una muestra primaria, el objetivo de sus diseñadores es maximizar el tamaño de la misma (Kupietz et al. 2010: 1848). *DeReKo* se versiona dos veces al año; la crónica de los lanzamientos de las versiones está disponible en Eichinger y Trabold (2014c).

---

[6] La versión 0.7 beta de CorpesXXI es de julio de 2014.
[7] En la gráfica disponible en Eichinger & Trabold (2014b) puede observarse el enorme crecimiento del archivo de *DeReKo* entre los años 2013 y 2014, que es evidentemente superior a la cifra mencionada de 300 millones de formas anuales. Para más detalles sobre la razón de este crecimiento exponencial v. Kupietz & Lüngen (2014).

El *Kernkorpus* del proyecto *DWDS* contiene 125 millones de formas y crece a 10 millones de formas por década. Este corpus también se versiona (Geyken 2013a), si bien la información sobre las versiones no estaba disponible en la web al cierre la redacción de este trabajo.

Por último, *CdE* contiene 100 millones de palabras, aunque estas corresponden, no obstante, a todo el periodo comprendido entre los siglos XIII y XX. La sección dedicada al s. XX comprende cerca de 23 millones de palabras. Las últimas incorporaciones a *CdE* tuvieron lugar en 2007, y no están previstas nuevas adiciones a la base textual.

Algo que puede interesar al usuario es tener información actualizada sobre los momentos en los que el corpus aumenta de tamaño, así como sobre el contenido de las nuevas incorporaciones. De los proyectos que estudiamos, solo *DeReKo* informa a sus usuarios registrados de las nuevas incorporaciones (cada 6 meses).

De los datos anteriores se desprende que el *Kernkorpus* de *DWDS* y *CorpesXXI* tienen actualmente un tamaño comparable, si bien la tasa de crecimiento que se declara en la documentación para *CorpesXXI* es mucho más rápida que la del recurso alemán. En cuanto a *CdE*, el tamaño de la sección dedicada al siglo XX, comparable en cobertura cronológica al *Kernkorpus des 20. Jh.* de *DWDS*, supone apenas un cuarto del tamaño de este último. Finalmente, *DeReKo* tomado en su conjunto no es comparable en tamaño al resto de los recursos, aunque, como bien sabemos, este último recurso no está construido para trabajar sobre toda su base textual, sino sobre una parte seleccionada por el usuario.

3.4. Cobertura cronológica

Los recursos objeto de estudio se diferencian notablemente entre sí en su cobertura cronológica. La sección del siglo XX de *CdE*[8] es comparable al *Kernkorpus des 20. Jh.* de *DWDS*, pero no a los dos *Kernkorpora* tomados conjuntamente (*Kernkorpus des 20. Jh.* y *Kernkorpus des 21. Jh.*, al que irán destinadas las nuevas incorporaciones). Por otra parte, mientras que *CdE* es un recurso cerrado, el *Kernkorpus* de *DWDS* es un recurso abierto hacia el futuro. También lo son *DeReKo* y *CorpesXXI*. Este último sería directamente comparable, en cuanto a

---

[8] CdE contiene testimonios desde el S. XIII hasta el XX, sin embargo en este trabajo nos limitaremos a observar las características de la parte de la base textual que cubre el periodo comprendido entre 1900 y 1999.

cobertura cronológica, al *Kernkorpus des 21. Jh.* de *DWDS*. Por su parte, *DeReKo* es comparable a los dos anteriores en lo que respecta al siglo XXI, pues también va incorporando testimonios del siglo actual. Sin embargo, en lo que respecta al siglo XX, *DeReKo* solo contiene testimonios a partir de 1945.

3.5. Zona lingüística y país

La codificación de estos datos reviste importancia, dado que tanto el español como el alemán son lenguas pluricéntricas, esto es, lenguas para las que, por razón de su extensión geográfica, existen varios centros nacionales y diferentes variedades estándar codificadas en dichos centros (Hägi 2007:6). El investigador interesado en observar contrastivamente fenómenos asociados a variedades diatópicas o interesado en aislar fenómenos asociados a cierta variedad, para posteriormente comprobar en corpus paralelos el tratamiento de la misma en la traducción, tiene en los metadatos con los que se ha codificado el país y la zona lingüística sus principales aliados. En este sentido, dos de los cuatro recursos estudiados se oponen a los otros dos, y resultarán, por tanto, de mayor utilidad para el tipo de investigaciones que acabamos de insinuar. *CorpesXXI* y *DeReKo* codifican el país, mientras que el *Kernkorpus* de *DWDS* y *CdE* no lo hacen[9].

Aun así, estos metadatos distan mucho de tener una organización similar en *CorpesXXI* y *DeReKo*, debido a las particularidades de la extensión geográfica del español y del alemán, respectivamente. Mientras que en este último recurso se codifica el origen directamente como país (Alemania, Austria, Suiza), en *CorpesXXI* el origen tiene cuatro divisiones iniciales, correspondientes a las áreas lingüísticas del mundo hispánico (España, América, Guinea Ecuatorial y Filipinas) y, para el caso de América, otros dos niveles ulteriores: la zona lingüística y el país. La selección de una zona lingüística americana concreta (Antillas, Caribe, etc.) posibilita la selección de uno o más países de la zona. Así, el metadato «zona andina» abre la posibilidad de seleccionar Bolivia, Ecuador y Perú, la zona «Antillas» permite seleccionar Cuba, Puerto Rico y República Dominicana, etc. Estados Unidos es a la vez zona lingüística y país. Otra diferencia que llama la atención es que la documentación de *CorpesXXI* ofrece in-

---

[9] No obstante, el *Kernkorpus des 20. Jh.* forma parte a su vez del proyecto *C4-Korpus*, junto con el el *Austrian Academy Corpus* (*AAC*), el *Korpus Südtirol* y el *SCHWEIZER TEXT KORPUS* (*CHTK*), v. <www.korpus-c4.org>.

formación sobre los porcentajes que conforman los testimonios del español de cada área lingüística (Guinea Ecuatorial 0,49%, España 36,34%, América 63,13% y Filipinas 0,03%), mientras que *DeReKo* no ofrece porcentajes de los testimonios de las tres áreas lingüísticas del alemán recogidos en él hasta que el usuario ha compuesto su propio corpus virtual a partirde la muestra primaria. Estos datos se ofrecerían en la vista «Länderansicht», v. columna izquierda en la ilustración 2, pág. 252).

El *CdE*, al igual que el *Kernkorpus de DWDS*, no codifica la zona lingüística. También como este, el origen del testimonio está registrado y puede recuperarse tras la búsqueda, esto es, a posteriori, pero no puede utilizarse para construir esta.

3.6. Datos bibliográficos

Cuando estos metadatos, que suelen formar parte de la cabecera de cada uno de los documentos que constituyen el corpus, estan desarrollados, permiten aislar conjuntos de datos muy variados. Investigados con respecto a este criterio, los recursos analizados aquí también muestran diferencias importantes. De entrada, *CdE* no los incluye en su codificación, sino en una ficha aparte, a la que se accede pinchando en cada una de las concordancias que devuelve la aplicación de búsquedas. Así pues, en *CdE* no puede formularse una búsqueda con criterios bibliográficos. Por lo que respecta a *CorpesXXI* y a los *Kernkorpora* de *DWDS*, los metadatos bibliográficos se utilizan para construir las búsquedas de concordancias y para, una vez generada la búsqueda, ordenar y mostrar los datos y filtrarlos. Finalmente, en *DeReKo* algunos de estos metadatos (año, país) se utilizan para *componer* el corpus y, una vez compuesto, ordenar y mostrar las concordancias obtenidas; el autor no está codificado, pues en muchos de los textos es desconocido, debido a su origen periodístico[10].

3.7. Medio

Si un investigador quiere aislar fenómenos específicos de la lengua oral o de la lengua escrita sólo podrá trabajar con corpus que permitan seleccionar los ejemplos del medio correspondiente. Para los corpus aquí analizados hemos determi-

---

[10] En Eichinger & Trabold (2014d) encontramos más información sobre el modelo textual de *DeReKo*. En Real Academia Española (2013a) encontramos información sobre el sistema de codificación de *CorpesXXI*.

nado en primera instancia (i) si el medio (oral o escrito) está codificado o no y (ii) en caso de no estarlo, si al menos se pueden reconocer subconjuntos de textos orales / escritos y qué volumen tienen esos subconjuntos.

Así, observamos que en *DeReKo* no se ha codificado específicamente el medio, puesto que en principio solo recoge textos escritos. Se define como «die weltweit größte linguistisch motivierte Sammlung elektronischer Korpora mit *geschriebenen* deutschsprachigen Texten aus der Gegenwart und der neueren Vergangenheit» (Eichinger & Trabold 2014 - *DeReKo*)[11]. No obstante, *DeReKo* incluye corpus específicos de textos que tienen cierto componente de oralidad, bien porque están escritos para ser leídos en voz alta o bien porque están escritos a partir de textos que se producen en situación de oralidad. Es el caso del corpus *REI* (*Reden und Interviews*, con 6 millones de formas) o IKO (*Interviewkorpus*, con algo más de 700.000 formas). Así, estos rasgos de oralidad se codifican indirectamente en *DeReKo* a través del género textual: «entrevista» (*Interview*), «conversación» (*Gespräch*), o «discurso» (*Rede*), etc.

Por otra parte, *CdE* y *CorpesXXI* sí que codifican el medio. En el primer caso el medio está indirectamente codificado como *tipo de discurso* (*oral* por oposición a los textos marcados como *académicos, de ficción* o *noticias*) en los testimonios pertenecientes al bloque del siglo XX. El conjunto de los datos marcados como *oral* suma 4,2 millones de formas. En el caso de *CorpesXXI* existe una etiqueta específica para el medio (con los atributos «oral» o «escrito», v. Real AcademiaEspañola 2013a:18)[12].

Finalmente, el *Kernkorpus* de *DWDS* contiene solo ejemplos de textos escritos. No obstante, en la página antigua de *DWDS* (<http://retro.dwds.de>) aún puede consultarse un corpus específico de textos orales, denominado *Gesprochene Sprache*, que contiene testimonios de uso pertenecientes a diferentes géneros orales como discursos, alocuciones radiofónicas, extractos de actas de los par-

---

[11] La cursiva es nuestra.

[12] En la versión 0.6 beta, el conjunto de los datos marcados como *oral* sumaba 15,8 millones de formas. En el documento de datos estadísticos de formas y lemas de la versión 0.7 beta, de julio de 2014 (Real AcademiaEspañola 2013b), no hemos encontrado los datos correspondientes a los subconjuntos *oral* y *escrito*, al contrario de lo que ocurría con el documento correspondiente a la versión 0.6.

lamentos austriaco y alemán, entrevistas, debates televisivos, entre otros. Su tamaño es de 2,5 millones de formas (Geyken, 2013b)[13].

3.8. Soporte y fecha

Encontramos también importantes diferencias con respecto a estos dos parámetros entre los recursos estudiados. Sólo *CorpesXXI* incluye en las cabeceras una etiqueta referida al soporte, que puede tener los atributos «libro», «prensa», «internet» o «miscelánea»[14]. En el resto de los recursos este parámetro no se encuentra en la cabecera, pero podemos obtener información sobre el soporte al que pertenecen los textos seleccionados indirectamente de diferentes maneras: en el caso de *DeReKo* a partir del nombre del corpus en el sistema de búsquedas *Cosmas-II* (p. ej. deducimos que los textos del corpus «BRZ13/JUN Braunschweiger Zeitung» están en soporte prensa, gracias al componente *Zeitung*). En el caso del *Kernkorpus* de *DWDS* solo podemos cerciorarnos del soporte del texto al que pertenece determinada concordancia pinchando sobre la misma y observando los datos bibliográficos[15]. Por su parte, *CdE* tiene una determinada cantidad de textos marcados como «prensa», pero no por oposición a «libro», «internet», etc., sino a otras etiquetas que indicarían más bien un macrogénero textual («académico», «ficción, v. 3.9) o el medio («oral», v. 3.7). Así pues, *DeReKo* sí que nos permitiría, aunque indirectamente, definir corpus virtuales con textos de determinados soportes, y en *CdE* y el *Kernkorpus des 20. Jh.* esta operación estaría restringida a textos en soporte prensa.

La fecha está también codificada de diferentes maneras en estos recursos. En un extremo se sitúan *CorpesXXI* y *DeReKo*, que codifican el año (en este último caso incluso el mes, en los corpus de textos de prensa). En el otro extremo se encuentra *CdE*, que únicamente codifica el siglo, y que, por tanto, incluye todos

---

[13] En el sitio web indicado no se indica exactamente cuánto tiempo permanecerá disponible dicho corpus.

[14] V. Real Academia Española, 2013b) para la distribución entre los diferentes soportes de las formas incorporadas. Esta información se va actualizando a medida que el corpus incorpora formas y sube de versión.

[15] En la documentación en línea (Geyken 2013a) no podemos contrastar esta afirmación, pero tras sucesivas catas deducimos que los subconjuntos *Wissenschaft* (textos académicos), *Belletristik* (textos literarios) y *Gebrauchsliteratur* (textos cotidianos) están en soporte «libro».

los textos del siglo XX en un solo bloque (v. la discusión sobre los inconvenientes que este hecho genera para la investigación en Rojo, 2010: 20-21). Los *Kernkorpora* de *DWDS* también codifican el año.

3.9. Género textual

Si entendemos género textual como «formas convencionalizadas de 'textos' que reflejan tanto las funciones y metas asociadas a determinadas ocasiones sociales como los propósitos de quienes participan en ellas» (Hatim & Mason 1994:91), entonces tenemos que concluir que no todos los recursos incluyen exactamente o consecuentemente este parámetro en su codificación. Observamos una convivencia, en proporción variable, de etiquetas que remiten a géneros textuales junto con otras que remiten a macrogéneros textuales o a dominios temáticos. Por otra parte, la diferente naturaleza de los recursos impone diferentes praxis de asignación y la presencia de listas cerradas y no cerradas de etiquetas.

DeReko constituye en este sentido una excepción. Si bien en su documentación se indica, de manera muy general, que contiene «belletristische, wissenschaftliche und populärwissenschaftliche Texte, eine große Zahl von Zeitungstexten sowie eine breite Palette weiterer Textarten» (Eichinger & Trabold 2014a), los atributos del metadato *Textsorte* se refieren indudablemente a géneros textuales. La lista, en el momento de la redacción de este trabajo, comprendía 78 etiquetas diferentes (desde *Abstract, Analyse, Anzeigetext* hasta *Umfrage, Veranstaltungsinformation, Vorspann* o *Zitat*), y su carácter no es cerrado. La asignación de la etiqueta de género textual viene dada en algunos casos por las editoriales (sobre todo en el caso de los textos de la prensa), y el sistema de gestión de *DeReKo* la detecta automáticamente, aunque los responsables advierten de que puede haber errores y lagunas en la asignación (Eichinger & Seubert 2013).

CorpesXXI codifica en la cabecera el metadato «tipo de texto» (Real Academia Española, 2013a:10), cuyos atributos son de naturaleza heterogénea: «ficción» (que comprende a su vez los subtipos «novela», «relato», «guion», «teatro», esto es, géneros textuales literarios), «biografía», «memoria», «libro de texto», «carta al director», «crónica», «editorial», «entrevista», «noticia», «opinión», «reportaje», «varios», así como «académico», «divulgación» y «jurídico-administrativo» (estos tres últimos atributos, en nuestra opinión, etiquetan más bien dominios temáticos o conjuntos de géneros textuales y no tanto géneros textuales concretos). La asignación no es automática y la lista de atributos es cerrada.

CdE utiliza los atributos «oral» y «académico» (que parecen etiquetar, respectivamente, un tipo de comunicación y un macrogénero textual), «ficción» (una macroetiqueta para géneros literarios narrativos) y «noticias», que sí parece etiquetar un género textual propiamente dicho. Como el corpus no prevé nuevas incorporaciones, la lista ha de entenderse como cerrada.

Finalmente, en el *Kernkorpus* de *DWDS*, las etiquetas *Belletristik* (textos literarios) *Zeitung* (textos periodísticos) *Gebrauchsliteratur* (textos cotidianos) *Wissenschaft* (textos académicos) parecen más bien etiquetas para macrogéneros textuales. Observamos la misma clasificación en géneros textuales en el *Kernkorpus des 20. Jh.* y en el *Kernkorpus des 21. Jh.*, con lo que entendemos que se trata de una clasificación cerrada.

Sabemos que el criterio *Textsorte* (género textual) desempeña un papel esencial en la consecución del equilibrio de los *Kernkorpora* de *DWDS*. En *CorpesXXI*, a juzgar por las cifras, que muestran una clara tendencia a favor del macrogénero «ficción» (v. Real Academia Española 2013b: 1, 3), no parece que se busque el equilibrio en este sentido. *DeReKo*, por su parte, no aspira a ningún tipo de equilibrio sino a maximizar tamaño. Por fin, sí que se observa equilibrio entre los subcorpus del *CdE*, puesto cada uno constituye aproximadamente el 15% de los testimonios de uso contenidos en la sección del siglo XX.

3.10. Tema

Con respecto a este criterio, los cuatro recursos estudiados se dividen en dos bloques. Mientras que *CdE* y el *Kernkorpus* de *DWDS* no codifican el tema, *CorpesXXI* y *DeReKo* sí lo hacen, aunque con diferentes procedimientos y estructuras de clasificación. *Corpes XXI* tiene una estructura temática de un nivel, sin embargo, la estructura de los datos temáticos de *DeReKo* es de dos niveles[16], con 12 categorías principales y 52 secundarias. Por otra parte, en *DeReKo* solo se codifica el tema de los corpus de periódicos y de comunicaciones de prensa, mientras que en *CorpesXXI* todos los textos contienen este metadato.

La manera en la que se asigna el metadato «tema» difiere en cada uno de estos dos recursos. En el caso de *CorpesXXI* existe primero una lista de temas, que se confeccionó en el momento de diseñar el corpus (Real Academia Española 1998, 2013a). Esa lista, en un segundo paso, se aplica de manera manual a los

---

[16] Al igual que en el caso de *CREA*, predecesor de *CorpesXXI*.

textos adquiridos. Sin embargo, en *DeReKo*, debido a la gran masa de datos que entra regularmente a formar parte de él, la clasificación es automática, mediante el recurso a un clasificador bayesiano ingenuo (Eichinger & Seubert 2013)[17]. Las categorías principales en *DeReKo* son «ocio y entretenimiento», «país y sociedad», «política», «ciencia», «economía y finanzas», «deportes», «naturaleza y medio ambiente», «cultura», «tecnología e industria», «salud y nutrición», «ficción» y «resto». Las categorías secundarias están detalladas en Eichinger & Seubert (2013). En el caso de *CorpesXXI* observamos que el tema depende del bloque al que pertenezcan los textos. A los textos del bloque «ficción» se les asigna una de las siguientes etiquetas temáticas –que, a nuestro entender, remiten más bien a géneros textuales literarios–: «guion», «novela», «relato» o «teatro». Los textos del bloque «no ficción» pueden recibir una de las siguientes etiquetas: «actualidad, ocio y vida cotidiana», «artes, cultura y espectáculos», «ciencias sociales, creencias y pensamiento», «ciencias y tecnología», «política, economía y justicia» o «salud». Solo en su primer nivel, la clasificación temática en *DeReKo*, aunque coincide parcialmente con la de *CorpesXXI*, reviste una complejidad mayor que la de este. La construcción de un corpus paralelo comparable con datos de estos dos recursos requerirá, por tanto, un cuidadoso diseño.

3.11. Información sobre el número de palabras de los subconjuntos generados por el usuario

En los apartados 3.5 a 3.10 hemos ido analizando comparativamente los principales parámetros con los que cada recurso codifica sus textos, información necesaria para que el investigador de las lenguas alemana y española diseñe la estructura de su corpus comparable virtual y pueda proceder a aislar subcorpus dentro de cada recurso. Sin embargo, en los estudios basados o motivados en corpus el investigador necesita además conocer el número de formas de cada uno de esos subconjuntos, ya sea con el fin de construir los argumentos o de aislar un corpus virtual comparable deslocalizado que esté equilibrado, en caso de

---

[17] Este sistema descansa sobre la elaboración previa de una taxonomía mediante técnicas que incluyen la minería de datos de los textos adquiridos y la comparación de la taxonomía obtenida con una taxonomía externa, en este caso la proporcionada por el Open Directory (<www.dmoz.org>). Para una motivación, descripción y evaluación de todo este proceso técnico, véase Weiß (2005).

que este criterio sea relevante para su investigación. En lo que sigue, analizamos la manera en la que cada recurso ofrece información sobre este particular.

En algunos recursos la documentación ofrece información sobre lo que denominamos subconjuntos *estáticos*, esto es, sobre los subconjuntos existentes en el corpus fruto del proceso de codificación, p. ej. tomando como referencia el parámetro «país de origen» (¿cuántas palabras suma el conjunto de textos con «Argentina» en el parámetro *origen*, cuántas con «España», cuántas con «Filipinas», etc.?). Otra información no menos importante para el investigador es la referida a los subconjuntos *dinámicos*, esto es, los que surgen de una búsqueda en la que el usuario ha cruzado dos o más parámetros, p. ej.: ¿Cuántas palabras suman los textos con «política y sociedad» en el parámetro *tema* y «Argentina» en el parámetro *origen*?

Los cuatro recursos estudiados ofrecen información sobre los subconjuntos *estáticos*. En *CdE* la codificación clasifica los textos únicamente por siglos (XIII-XX), con la excepción de los textos del siglo XX, que también vienen clasificados por lo que hemos denominado *tipo de discurso* (v. 3.9). Si al buscar seleccionamos la opción «gráfico», y, en el gráfico resultante, pasamos el ratón por las barras correspondientes a cada subconjunto, el sistema nos ofrece para cada bloque la frecuencia normalizada de la expresión buscada, pero además también el número de palabras que contiene cada bloque de *tipo de discurso*. En el extremo derecho de la Ilustración 1 observamos que el sistema ofrece información estadística para el bloque FIC (ficción) de los resultados de una búsqueda para la la forma «extrañamente». Como dentro del conjunto de datos del s. XX no hay más codificación, no hay posibilidad de combinar más parámetros para formar subconjuntos dinámicos.

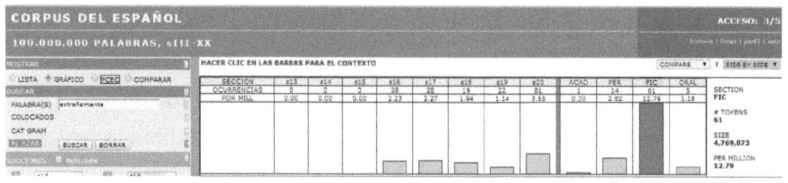

Ilustración 1. Información de número de palabras según tipo de discurso en *CdE*

A diferencia de lo visto en el caso de *CdE*, *CorpesXXI* ofrece información sobre el número de palabras de sus subconjuntos *estáticos* en un documento titulado «Datos estadísticos de formas y lemas» (Real Academia Española 2013b),

Construcción de corpus virtuales comparables deslocalizados (DE/ES)

e información sobre el número de palabras de los subconjuntos *dinámicos* a través del botón «estadística» una vez formulada la búsqueda (número de palabras del subconjunto aislado por zona, país, periodo, tema y tipología), v. Ilustración 2.

Ilustración 2. Información estadística en CorpesXXI

En *DeReKo*, al tratarse de una muestra primaria a partir de la cual el investigador construye su propio corpus, el investigador siempre trabaja con subconjuntos *dinámicos*. Una vez que este ha definido y cargado el corpus, en la opción *Korpusansichten* se muestra el número de palabras de su corpus por fuente, subcorpus que lo integran (en este caso corpus de periódicos: A09, BRZ09, etc.), décadas, años, meses, días, países, género textual y tema, v. Ilustración 3.

Finalmente en el *Kernkorpus* de *DWDS* encontramos información en forma de tabla sobre los subconjuntos *estáticos*. Se ofrece para cada macrogénero textual el número de palabras por década del siglo XX y del s. XXI (Geyken 2013a). A partir de esta información, combinada con la ofrecida por el panel *Wortverlauf* (frecuencia absoluta de la expresión de búsqueda por género y década) se puede calcular manualmente la frecuencia normalizada de dicha expresión por y género/s y década/s[18]. v. Ilustración 4.

---

[18] Esta información puede descargarse como archivo CSV, v. ilustración 4. La información de la frecuencia total y normalizada de una expresión buscada en todo el corpus se ofrece a través del panel *Korpusfrequenzen*, donde el usuario podrá encontrar además esas mismas frecuencias en otros corpus de la plataforma (corpus de periódicos como el *Zeit-Korpus*, el *Berliner-Zeitung-Korpus* o el *Bild-Korpus* entre otros).

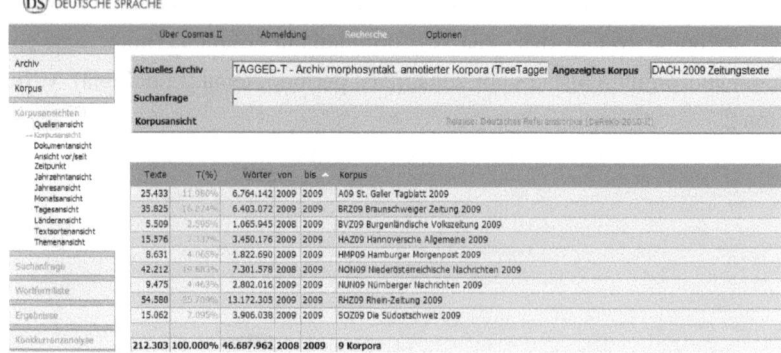

Ilustración 3. Información de número de palabras según diferentes parámetros de un corpus formado a partir del archivo Tagged-T de $DeReKo^{19}$

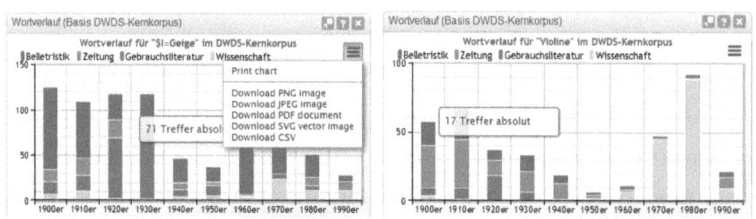

Ilustración 4. Evolución de los sustantivos *Geige* y *Violine* por décadas y macrogénero textual a lo largo del siglo XX, según *Kernkorpus des 20. Jahrhunderts*

3.12. Las aplicaciones de búsquedas

Una comparación exhaustiva de las aplicaciones de búsquedas de los cuatro recursos estudiados al estilo de la que realiza Rojo (2010) para *CREA/CORDE* y *CdE* excedería los límites de este trabajo. No obstante, sí queremos dejar constancia de las principales semejanzas y diferencias que plantean los motores de búsqueda de estas aplicaciones cuando el usuario quiere interactuar con los metadatos del corpus.

Observamos dos tipos de interfaz para interactuar con los datos: la máscara y la ventana de texto. En la máscara de búsqueda existen campos de selección, botones o casillas de activación que permiten al usuario ir especificando las condiciones de su búsqueda (y en ocasiones de la recuperación de los ejemplos),

---

[19] Corpus integrado por textos de periódicos generados en 2009 de origen suizo (19,07%), austriaco (22,47%) y alemán (58,46%).

mientras que en una ventana de texto el usuario especifica esas condiciones con ayuda de unas etiquetas que se combinan según las reglas de la sintaxis de búsqueda. Las condiciones pueden referirse a la anotación no lingüística (denominada aquí «codificación», siguiendo a Rojo, 2010:18) o a la anotación lingüística (lematización, POS-tagging –anotación de la clase de palabra– y anotación sintáctica, así como la tokenización –o marcado de los límites de la palabra–, marcado de oraciones y párrafos, etc., v. Zanettin 2012: 94).

CorpesXXI y *CdE* utilizan máscara para la búsqueda de concordancias, si bien la máscara de *CorpesXXI* es muy compleja, pues permite especificar condiciones tanto de la anotación como de su rica codificación[20]. La máscara de *CdE* es necesariamente más sencilla, y, además, ciertas condiciones han de introducirse manualmente en una ventana contenida en la máscara (p. ej. la búsqueda de sinónimos, encerrando el lema entre corchetes). En *DeReKo*, al *construir* un corpus virtual el usuario interactúa con una máscara, pero para *buscar concordancias* en dicho corpus interactúa con una ventana. No obstante, si el investigador está trabajando con un corpus construido con datos de uno de los conjuntos (*Archive*) que contienen anotación lingüística (TAGGED-C, TAGGED-M, TAGGED-T), existe un «asistente morfológico» en forma de máscara que ayuda a introducir en la ventana las etiquetas correctas. En los *Kernkorpora* de *DWDS*, para buscar concordancias se interactúa con la codificación a través de una ventana general, que lanza la búsqueda en todos los módulos de la plataforma, pero también a través las diferentes máscaras propias de cada panel de corpus[21].

Merece también la pena prestar atención a los operadores de distancia disponibles en cada aplicación para la recuperación de concordancias, puesto que existen notables diferencias entre las posibilidades de las aplicaciones estudiadas. Los operadores de distancia permiten búsquedas conjuntas de más de un elemento dentro de ciertos límites. *CdE* actualmente permite buscar los dos elementos en un intervalo determinado por el usuario. Los operadores de *Corpe-*

---

[20] Si bien actualmente (versión 0.7, beta) los metadatos que pueden usarse en la búsqueda de *coapariciones* son solo una selección de los que pueden usarse en la búsqueda de *concordancias*, concretamente la clase de palabra y la zona geográfica (origen y zona lingüística).

[21] En *DWDS* las coapariciones de una palabra se investigan con ayuda de la anotación lingüística en un panel aparte, denominado *Wortprofil*. Este panel trabaja no solo con los datos de los *Kernkorpora*, sino también con datos de los *Zeitungskorpora* (v. 3.1).

sXXI, más complejos, permiten buscar dos elementos no solo por el intervalo de palabras que les separa sino también a una distancia exacta (si bien en ambos casos el límite es 5). Esta doble funcionalidad está presente también en las aplicaciones de *DeReKo* y *DWDS*, que, además, permiten especificar intervalos aún más complejos, con un límite anterior diferente del propio pivote (p. ej., para generar concordancias en las que el segundo elemento de búsqueda está a una distancia de entre 2 y 6 del pivote). Las aplicaciones de búsquedas de *DeReKo* y *DWDS* disponen igualmente de operadores para buscar palabras en el entorno de la oración (p. ej. en posición inicial o final de la oración, en segunda posición, en (ante)penúltima posición, etc.). Finalmente, sólo la aplicación de *DeReKo* tiene operadores que permiten buscar el segundo elemento más allá de los límites de la oración o más allá de los límites del párrafo.

Un último aspecto de esta breve comparación de las aplicaciones de búsqueda son las opciones de guardado y exportación de los resultados de las búsquedas. Los recursos difieren en gran medida en lo que se refiere a esta prestación. *CdE* no permite exportar los resultados pero sí guardar listas de palabras obtenidas en una búsqueda para posteriormente utilizarlas en otra búsqueda. La plataforma *DWDS* permite justo lo contrario. Actualmente no se pueden guardar ejemplos seleccionados por el usuario en una cuenta de la plataforma[22], pero sí exportar un máximo de 5000 ejemplos con un máximo de 3 oraciones de contexto; la anotación lingüística no se exporta, pero sí la referencia bibliográfica de cada línea de concordancia. El formato de exportación es un archivo de texto plano sin saltos de línea que requiere de considerable reelaboración si se quiere importar p. ej. en una base de datos. *DeReKo* permite en principio exportar todas las concordancias encontradas y es muy flexible a la hora de exportar contexto (se pueden pedir tantas palabras, frases o párrafos como se quiera), y también exportar la referencia bibliográfica de cada ejemplo e incluso la anotación. Los formatos de exportación son TXT o RTF. Por último, *CorpesXXI* permite actualmente exportar los resultados de la búsqueda de concordancias, en formato TXT, con un contexto mínimo, sin anotación pero con referencia bibliográfica e información de la cabecera (atributos de los metadatos de la codificación).

---

[22] Hasta febrero de 2014 sí era posible guardarlos a través de la función "Mein Korpus". Esta función ha quedado temporalmente desactivada tras la reestructuración de los paneles llevada cabo en dicho mes (Edmund Pohl, comunicación personal).

4. Conclusiones

Tanto si se utiliza una metodología basada en corpus (para validar una teoría preexistente) como una metodología guiada por corpus (para crear una teoría a partir de los datos presentes en el corpus), una adecuada selección del material textual es esencial a la hora de confeccionar el corpus que permitirá al investigador estudiar cierto fenómeno, pues los resultados pueden verse sesgados en algunos casos si no tiene en cuenta determinadas características de los textos. Por ello, es imprescindible que, como usuario, aquel esté familiarizado con la codificación de los textos del corpus del que va a extraer datos. No obstante, si la perspectiva de su estudio es comparable o contrastiva, el investigador ha de ser capaz además de reconocer las intersecciones existentes en las codificaciones de los (al menos) dos corpus de los que va a extraer información. En este trabajo hemos puesto a prueba una metodología para este tipo de exámenes (v. apartado 2), que, aplicada a los cuatro recursos considerados aquí (*CdE, CorpesXXI,* los *Kernkorpora* de *DWDS* y *DeReKo*), nos ha permitido localizar importantes similitudes y diferencias en su codificación, con lo que cumplimos con el primero de los objetivos que nos proponíamos en este estudio. Las diferencias nos permiten concluir que el investigador que construye un corpus virtual deslocalizado accede fácilmente a grandes bases textuales preparadas por expertos, pero a la vez asume la desventaja de que han sido otros los que han seleccionado y codificado dicha base textual. Cada corpus habla su idioma, y el investigador tiene que entenderlos todos e interpretar entre ellos.

La construcción de corpus virtuales comparables a partir del criterio de la autoría resulta particularmente complicada, pues solo *CorpesXXI* codifica el autor, si bien es cierto que *DeReKo,* con algunas limitaciones, permite extraer datos de ciertos autores (Thomas Mann, Siegfried Lenz, Martin Walser, etc.) a partir de las siglas de los nombres de ciertos corpus. Por otra parte, hay categorías, como el *tema,* que, al estar presentes en un recurso español (*CorpesXXI*) y otro alemán (*DeReKo*), parecen mostrarse especialmente propicias para el diseño de un corpus comparable; no obstante, un estudio detallado de este metadato pone de manifiesto que la articulación interna de la misma es bastante diferente en cada uno de dichos recursos, con lo que hay que ser especialmente cuidadoso con la selección de datos sobre la base de esta categoría. Otras categorías como el *género textual* o *tipo textual* (*Textart* en *DeReKo*, *Textsorte* en *DWDS*) exigirán la misma prudencia al investigador, en este caso porque los recursos parecen apoyarse en conceptos diferentes, con lo que su articulación interna muestra también una importante variación entre recursos.

Queremos destacar que la mayor o menor facilidad con la que los recursos estudiados informan sobre datos cuantitativos (tamaño de subcorpus seleccionado, frecuencias normalizadas de las expresiones de búsquedas en el subcorpus seleccionado o en la totalidad del corpus) puede convertirse en una gran ventaja o una gran desventaja a la hora de manejar datos numéricos, imprescindibles en estudios de corte cuantitativo.

Finalmente, deseamos hacer hincapié en las destacables diferencias observadas en las prestaciones de exportación de las aplicaciones de búsqueda de los cuatro recursos estudiados. La exportación es un factor crítico si el investigador quiere seguir analizando datos del corpus desde una perspectiva cualitativa. En el momento de la redacción de este trabajo, el espectro varía desde aplicaciones que permiten incluir la anotación lingüística, la referencia bibliográfica y determinar el tamaño del contexto de la concordancia y el formato del archivo de exportación (entre otros factores), hasta aplicaciones que no dejan personalizar ningún factor de la exportación y que funcionan con formato y datos fijos. Por otra parte, ninguna de las aplicaciones de los recursos estudiados permite la anotación manual de ejemplos del corpus por parte del usuario dentro de la propia aplicación (*in-corpus-tool annotation*, Smith, Hoffman y Rayson, 2008:168-170), aunque es de suponer que al menos alguno de los proyectos subyacentes desarrolle esta prestación en los años venideros.

5. Bibliografía

Agencia EFE. 2012. El Corpus del Español del Siglo XXI tendrá 300 millones de formas en el 2014. Disponible en <http://www.fundeu.es/noticia/el-corpus-del-espanol-del-siglo-xxi-tendra-300-millones-de-formas-en-el-2014-6933/>. [Última consulta: 20/04/2014].

Ahmad, Khurshid. 2008, Being in Text and Text in Being: Notes on Representative Texts. @ G. Anderman y M. Rogers, eds. *Incorporating Corpora. The linguist and the translator*. Toronto: Multilingual Matters. ISBN 9781853599859, pp. 60-94.

Banski, Piotr et al. 2014. KorAP: The New Corpus Analysis Platform at IDS Mannheim, @ N. Calzolari et al., eds. *Proceedings of the Ninth International Conference on Language Resources and Evaluation (LREC'14)*. European Language Resources Association (ELRA), Disponible en: <http://korap.ids-mannheim.de/wp-content/uploads/2013/12/ltc-demo-126-banski.pdf≥ [Última consulta: 03/05/2014]. ISBN 9782951740884, s/p.

Borja Albi, Anabel. 2008. Corpora for Translators in Spain. The CDJ-GITRAD Corpus and the GENTT Project. @ G. Anderman y M. Rogers, eds. *Incorporating Corpora. The linguist and the translator*. Toronto: Multilingual Matters. ISBN 9781853599859, pp. 253-265.

Briz Gómez, Antonio y Marta Albelda Marco. 2009. Estado actual de los corpus de lengua española hablada y escrita: I+D. @ *El español en el mundo. Anuario del Instituto Cervantes 2009*. Madrid: Instituto Cervantes. ISBN 9788492632022, pp. 165-226.

CLARIN 2014. CLARIN ERIC. Disponible en: <http://www.clarin.eu/>. [Última consulta: 22/06/2014].

Eichinger, Ludwig M. y Eric Seubert. 2013. Textklassifikation unter COSMAS II. Disponible en: <http://www.ids-mannheim.de/cosmas2/projekt/referenz/textklassifikation.html> [Última consulta: 30/05/2014].

Eichinger, Ludwig M. y Anette Trabold. 2014a. Das Deutsche Referenzkorpus - DeReKo. Disponible en: <http://www1.ids-mannheim.de/kl/projekte/korpora.html>. [Última consulta: 24/05/2014].

Eichinger, Ludwig M. y Anette Trabold. 2014b. Aktuelles Korpusarchiv. Disponible en: <http://www1.ids-mannheim.de/kl/projekte/korpora/archiv.html>. [Última consulta: 24/05/2014].

Eichinger, Ludwig M. y Anette Trabold. 2014c. Chronik der DeReKo-Freigaben seit 2005. Disponible en: <http://www1.ids-mannheim.de/kl/projekte/korpora/releases.html>. [Última consulta: 30/05/2014].

Eichinger, Ludwig M. y Anette Trabold. 2014d. Das IDS-Textmodell. Disponible en: <http://www1.ids-mannheim.de/kl/projekte/korpora/textmodell.html>. [Última consulta: 25/10/2014].

Geyken, Alexander. 2013a. DWDS - Digitales Wörterbuch der deutschen Sprache - Kernkorpus. Disponible en: <http://dwds.de/ressourcen/kernkorpus/>. [Última consulta: 30/05/2014].

Geyken, Alexander. 2013b. DWDS - Digitales Wörterbuch der deutschen Sprache - Korpus Gesprochene Sprache. Disponible en: <http://www.dwds.de/ressourcen/gesprsprache/>. [Última consulta: 23/03/2014].

Geyken, Alexander. 2013c. DWDS - Digitales Wörterbuch der deutschen Sprache - Projekt - Hintergrund. Disponible en: <http://www.dwds.de/projekt/hintergrund/>. [Última consulta: 30/05/2014].

Geyken, Alexander. 2013d. DWDS - Digitales Wörterbuch der deutschen Sprache - Ressourcen - Korpora. Disponible en: <http://www.dwds.de/ressourcen/korpora/>. [Última consulta: 30/05/2014].

Hägi, Sara. 2007. Bitte mit Sahne / Rahm / Schlag: Plurizentrik im Deutschunterricht. @ *Fremdsprache Deutsch* 37 / 2: 5-13.

Hatim, Basil e Ian Mason. 1990. *Discourse and the Translator*. Londres: Longman ISBN 9780582021907 [*Teoría de la traducción*. Una aproximación al discurso, Barcelona, Ariel, 1994, ISBN 9788434481145].

Hinrichs, Erhard. 2013. CLARIN: Ressourcen, Werkzeuge und Dienste für die eHumanities. Disponible en: <http://www.oeaw.ac.at/icltt/sites/default/files/uploads/hinrichs_2013_10_24_2_a.pdf>. [Última consulta: 25/06/2014].

Institut für Deutsche Sprache. Das Deutsche Referenzkorpus – DeReKo. Consultable en < https://cosmas2.ids-mannheim.de/cosmas2-web/>. [Ultima consulta 30/10/2014].

Kupietz, Marc et al. 2010. The German Reference Corpus DEREKO: A Primordial Sample for Linguistic Research. @ N. Calzolari et al., eds. *Proceedings of the seventh conference on International Language Resources and Evaluation (LREC 2010)*. ISBN 9782951740860, pp. 1848-1854.

Kupietz, Marc y Harald Lüngen. 2014. Recent Developments in DeReKo. @ Proceedings of the Ninth International Conference on Language Resources and Evaluation (LREC'14), Reykjavic, Iceland, May 26-31th. N. Calzolari et al., eds. Reykjavik, Iceland: European Language Resources Association (ELRA). ISBN 9782951740884, pp. 2387-2385.

Laviosa, Sara. 2004. Corpus-based translation studies: Where does it come from? Where is it going? @ *Language Matters* 35 / 1: 6-27.

Laviosa, Sara. 1998. The Corpus-based Approach: A New Paradigm in Translation Studies. @ META 43 / 4: 474-479.

Marco, Josep y Heike van Lawick. 2009. Using corpora and retrieval software as a source of materials for the translation classroom. @ A. Beeby, P. Rodríguez-Inés y P. Sánchez-Gijón, eds. *Corpus Use and Translating: Corpus Use for Learning to Translate and Learning Corpus Use to Translate*. Ámsterdam y Filadelfia: John Benjamins. ISBN 9789027224262, pp. 9-28.

Real Academia Española. Banco de datos (CREA): Corpus de referencia del español actual [en línea]. Disponible en: <http://www.rae.es>. [Última consulta: 05/06/2014].

Real Academia Española. Banco de datos (CorpesXXI): Corpus del español del siglo XXI [en línea]. Disponible en: <http://www.rae.es>. [Última consulta: 30/10/2014].

Real Academia Española 2013a. Corpus del español del siglo XXI (CORPES). Descripción del sistema de codificación. Libros y prensa [Recurso de Internet]. Madrid: Real Academia Española. Disponible en <http://www.rae.es/sites/default/files/CORPES_Sistema_de_codificacion2014.pdf>. [Última consulta: 01/07/2014].

Real Academia Española 2013b. Datos estadísticos de formas y lemas. Disponible en: <http://web.frl.es/CORPES/org/publico/pages/ayuda/informacion.view>. [Última consulta: 30/05/2014].

Real Academia Española. 1998. Banco de datos del Español. Manual de consulta. Disponible en: <http://corpus.rae.es/ayuda_c.htm#_Toc30228224>. [Última consulta: 03/06/2014].

Rojo, Guillermo. 2010. Sobre la codificación y explotación de corpus textuales: Otra comparación del Corpus del Español con el CORDE y el CREA. @ *Lingüística* [Online] 24: 11-50.

Santander - Sala de comunicación. 2012 La RAE y Banco Santander renuevan su colaboración para culminar el CORPES XXI y digitalizar el archivo académico. Disponible en: <http://bit.ly/1kcim8P>. [Última consulta: 26/04/2014].

Tognini-Bonelli, Elena. 2001. Corpus Linguistics at Work. Ámsterdam y Filadelfia: John Benjamins. ISBN 9789027222763.

Weiß, Christian. 2005. Die thematische Erschließung von Sprachkorpora. @ *OPAL - Online publizierte Arbeiten zur Linguistik* 1: 1-14.

Wynne, Martin. 2014. CLARIN for beginners. Disponible en: <http://blogs.it.ox.ac.uk/martinw/2014/04/11/clarin-for-beginners/>. [Última consulta: 24/06/2014].

Zanettin, Federico. 2012. *Translation-Driven Corpora: Corpus Resources for Descriptive and Applied Translation Studies*. Manchester / Kinderhook: St. Jerome. ISBN 9781905763290.

TRANSÜD. Arbeiten zur Theorie und Praxis des Übersetzens und Dolmetschens

Die Bände 1 bis 5 sind bei der Peter Lang GmbH erschienen und dort zu beziehen.

Bd. 6 Przemysław Chojnowski: Zur Strategie und Poetik des Übersetzens. Eine Untersuchung der Anthologien zur polnischen Lyrik von Karl Dedecius. 300 Seiten. ISBN 978-3-86596-013-9

Bd. 7 Belén Santana López: Wie wird *das Komische* übersetzt? *Das Komische* als Kulturspezifikum bei der Übersetzung spanischer Gegenwartsliteratur. 456 Seiten. ISBN 978-3-86596-006-1

Bd. 8 Larisa Schippel (Hg.): Übersetzungsqualität: Kritik – Kriterien – Bewertungshandeln. 194 Seiten. ISBN 978-3-86596-075-7

Bd. 9 Anne-Kathrin D. Ende: Dolmetschen im Kommunikationsmarkt. Gezeigt am Beispiel Sachsen. 228 Seiten. ISBN 978-3-86596-073-3

Bd. 10 Sigrun Döring: Kulturspezifika im Film: Probleme ihrer Translation. 156 Seiten. ISBN 978-3-86596-100-6

Bd. 11 Hartwig Kalverkämper: „Textqualität". Die Evaluation von Kommunikationsprozessen seit der antiken Rhetorik bis zur Translationswissenschaft. ISBN 978-3-86596-110-5

Bd. 12 Yvonne Griesel: Die Inszenierung als Translat. Möglichkeiten und Grenzen der Theaterübertitelung. 362 Seiten. ISBN 978-3-86596-119-8

Bd. 13 Hans J. Vermeer: Ausgewählte Vorträge zur Translation und anderen Themen. Selected Papers on Translation and other Subjects. 286 Seiten. ISBN 978-3-86596-145-7

Bd. 14 Erich Prunč: Entwicklungslinien der Translationswissenschaft. Von den Asymmetrien der Sprachen zu den Asymmetrien der Macht. 442 Seiten. ISBN 978-3-86596-146-4 (vergriffen, siehe Band 43 der Reihe)

Bd. 15 Valentyna Ostapenko: Vernetzung von Fachtextsorten. Textsorten der Normung in der technischen Harmonisierung. 128 Seiten. ISBN 978-3-86596-155-6

Bd. 16 Larisa Schippel (Hg.): TRANSLATIONSKULTUR – ein innovatives und produktives Konzept. 340 Seiten. ISBN 978-3-86596-158-7

Bd. 17 Hartwig Kalverkämper/Larisa Schippel (Hg.): Simultandolmetschen in Erstbewährung: Der Nürnberger Prozess 1945. Mit einer orientierenden Einführung von Klaus Kastner und einer kommentierten fotografischen Dokumentation von Theodoros Radisoglou sowie mit einer dolmetsch-wissenschaftlichen Analyse von Katrin Rumprecht. 344 Seiten. ISBN 978-3-86596-161-7

F Frank & Timme

TRANSÜD. Arbeiten zur Theorie und Praxis des Übersetzens und Dolmetschens

Bd. 18   Regina Bouchehri: Filmtitel im interkulturellen Transfer. 174 Seiten.
ISBN 978-3-86596-180-8

Bd. 19   Michael Krenz/Markus Ramlow: Maschinelle Übersetzung und XML im Übersetzungsprozess. Prozesse der Translation und Lokalisierung im Wandel. Zwei Beiträge, hg. von Uta Seewald-Heeg. 368 Seiten. ISBN 978-3-86596-184-6

Bd. 20   Hartwig Kalverkämper/Larisa Schippel (Hg.): Translation zwischen Text und Welt – Translationswissenschaft als historische Disziplin zwischen Moderne und Zukunft. 700 Seiten. ISBN 978-3-86596-202-7

Bd. 21   Nadja Grbić/Sonja Pöllabauer: Kommunaldolmetschen/Community Interpreting. Probleme – Perspektiven – Potenziale. Forschungsbeiträge aus Österreich. 380 Seiten. ISBN 978-3-86596-194-5

Bd. 22   Agnès Welu: Neuübersetzungen ins Französische – eine kulturhistorische Übersetzungskritik. Eichendorffs *Aus dem Leben eines Taugenichts*. 506 Seiten. ISBN 978-3-86596-193-8

Bd. 23   Martin Slawek: Interkulturell kompetente Geschäftskorrespondenz als Garant für den Geschäftserfolg. Linguistische Analysen und fachkommunikative Ratschläge für die Geschäftsbeziehungen nach Lateinamerika (Kolumbien). 206 Seiten. ISBN 978-3-86596-206-5

Bd. 24   Julia Richter: Kohärenz und Übersetzungskritik. Lucian Boias Analyse des rumänischen Geschichtsdiskurses in deutscher Übersetzung. 142 Seiten. ISBN 978-3-86596-221-8

Bd. 25   Anna Kucharska: Simultandolmetschen in defizitären Situationen. Strategien der translatorischen Optimierung. 170 Seiten. ISBN 978-3-86596-244-7

Bd. 26   Katarzyna Lukas: Das Weltbild und die literarische Konvention als Übersetzungsdeterminanten. Adam Mickiewicz in deutschsprachigen Übertragungen. 402 Seiten. ISBN 978-3-86596-238-6

Bd. 27   Markus Ramlow: Die maschinelle Simulierbarkeit des Humanübersetzens. Evaluation von Mensch-Maschine-Interaktion und der Translatqualität der Technik. 364 Seiten. ISBN 978-3-86596-260-7

Bd. 28   Ruth Levin: Der Beitrag des Prager Strukturalismus zur Translationswissenschaft. Linguistik und Semiotik der literarischen Übersetzung. 154 Seiten. ISBN 978-3-86596-262-1

Bd. 29   Iris Holl: Textología contrastiva, derecho comparado y traducción jurídica. Las sentencias de divorcio alemanas y españolas. 526 Seiten. ISBN 978-3-86596-324-6

F Frank & Timme

TRANSÜD. Arbeiten zur Theorie und Praxis des Übersetzens und Dolmetschens

Bd. 30   Christina Korak: Remote Interpreting via Skype. Anwendungsmöglichkeiten von VoIP-Software im Bereich Community Interpreting – Communicate everywhere? 202 Seiten. ISBN 978-3-86596-318-5

Bd. 31   Gemma Andújar/Jenny Brumme (eds.): Construir, deconstruir y reconstruir. Mímesis y traducción de la oralidad y la afectividad. 224 Seiten. ISBN 978-3-86596-234-8

Bd. 32   Christiane Nord: Funktionsgerechtigkeit und Loyalität. Theorie, Methode und Didaktik des funktionalen Übersetzens. 338 Seiten. ISBN 978-3-86596-330-7

Bd. 33   Christiane Nord: Funktionsgerechtigkeit und Loyalität. Die Übersetzung literarischer und religiöser Texte aus funktionaler Sicht. 304 Seiten. ISBN 978-3-86596-331-4

Bd. 34   Małgorzata Stanek: Dolmetschen bei der Polizei. Zur Problematik des Einsatzes unqualifizierter Dolmetscher. 262 Seiten. ISBN 978-3-86596-332-1

Bd. 35   Dorota Karolina Bereza: Die Neuübersetzung. Eine Hinführung zur Dynamik literarischer Translationskultur. 108 Seiten. ISBN 978-3-86596-255-3

Bd. 36   Montserrat Cunillera/Hildegard Resinger (eds.): Implicación emocional y oralidad en la traducción literaria. 230 Seiten. ISBN 978-3-86596-339-0

Bd. 37   Ewa Krauss: Roman Ingardens „Schematisierte Ansichten" und das Problem der Übersetzung. 226 Seiten. ISBN 978-3-86596-315-4

Bd. 38   Miriam Leibbrand: Grundlagen einer hermeneutischen Dolmetschforschung. 324 Seiten. ISBN 978-3-86596-343-7

Bd. 39   Pekka Kujamäki/Leena Kolehmainen/Esa Penttilä/Hannu Kemppanen (eds.): Beyond Borders – Translations Moving Languages, Literatures and Cultures. 272 Seiten. ISBN 978-3-86596-356-7

Bd. 40   Gisela Thome: Übersetzen als interlinguales und interkulturelles Sprachhandeln. Theorien – Methodologie – Ausbildung. 622 Seiten. ISBN 978-3-86596-352-9

Bd. 41   Radegundis Stolze: The Translator's Approach – Introduction to Translational Hermeneutics. Theory and Examples from Practice. 304 Seiten. ISBN 978-3-86596-373-4

Bd. 42   Silvia Roiss/Carlos Fortea Gil/María Ángeles Recio Ariza/Belén Santana López/Petra Zimmermann González/Iris Holl (eds.): En las vertientes de la traducción e interpretación del/al alemán. 582 Seiten. ISBN 978-3-86596-326-0

Frank & Timme

TRANSÜD. Arbeiten zur Theorie und Praxis des Übersetzens und Dolmetschens

Bd. 43   Erich Prunč: Entwicklungslinien der Translationswissenschaft. 3., erweiterte und verbesserte Auflage (1. Aufl. 2007. ISBN 978-3-86596-146-4). 528 Seiten. ISBN 978-3-86596-422-9

Bd. 44   Mehmet Tahir Öncü: Die Rechtsübersetzung im Spannungsfeld von Rechtsvergleich und Rechtssprachvergleich. Zur deutschen und türkischen Strafgesetzgebung. 380 Seiten. ISBN 978-3-86596-424-3

Bd. 45   Hartwig Kalverkämper/Larisa Schippel (Hg.): „Vom Altern der Texte". Bausteine für eine Geschichte des interkulturellen Wissenstransfers. 456 Seiten. ISBN 978-3-86596-251-5

Bd. 46   Hannu Kemppanen/Marja Jänis/Alexandra Belikova (eds.): Domestication and Foreignization in Translation Studies. 240 Seiten. 978-3-86596-470-0

Bd. 47   Sergey Tyulenev: Translation and the Westernization of Eighteenth-Century Russia. A Social-Systemic Perspective. 272 Seiten. ISBN 978-3-86596-472-4

Bd. 48   Martin B. Fischer/Maria Wirf Naro (eds.): Translating Fictional Dialogue for Children and Young People. 422 Seiten. ISBN 978-3-86596-467-0

Bd. 49   Martina Behr: Evaluation und Stimmung. Ein neuer Blick auf Qualität im (Simultan-)Dolmetschen. 356 Seiten. ISBN 978-3-86596-485-4

Bd. 50   Anna Gopenko: Traduire le sublime. Les débats de l'Église orthodoxe russe sur la langue liturgique. 228 Seiten. ISBN 978-3-86596-486-1

Bd. 51   Lavinia Heller: Translationswissenschaftliche Begriffsbildung und das Problem der performativen Unauffälligkeit von Translation. 332 Seiten. ISBN 978-3-86596-470-0

Bd. 52   Claudia Dathe/Renata Makarska/Schamma Schahadat (Hg.): Zwischentexte. Literarisches Übersetzen in Theorie und Praxis. 300 Seiten. ISBN 978-3-86596-442-7

Bd. 53   Regina Bouchehri: Translation von Medien-Titeln. Der interkulturelle Transfer von Titeln in Literatur, Theater, Film und Bildender Kunst. 334 Seiten. ISBN 978-3-86596-400-7

Bd. 54   Nilgin Tanış Polat: Raum im (Hör-)Film. Zur Wahrnehmung und Repräsentation von räumlichen Informationen in deutschen und türkischen Audiodeskriptionstexten. 138 Seiten. ISBN 978-3-86596-508-0

Bd. 55   Eva Parra Membrives/Ángeles García Calderón (eds.): Traducción, mediación, adaptación. Reflexiones en torno al proceso de comunicación entre culturas. 336 Seiten. ISBN 978-3-86596-499-1

F Frank & Timme

TRANSÜD. Arbeiten zur Theorie und Praxis des Übersetzens und Dolmetschens

Bd. 56   Yvonne Sanz López: Videospiele übersetzen – Probleme und Optimierung. 126 Seiten. ISBN 978-3-86596-541-7

Bd. 57   Irina Bondas: Theaterdolmetschen – Phänomen, Funktionen, Perspektiven. 240 Seiten. ISBN 978-3-86596-540-0

Bd. 58   Dinah Krenzler-Behm: Authentische Aufträge in der Übersetzerausbildung. Ein Leitfaden für die Translationsdidaktik. 480 Seiten. ISBN 978-3-86596-498-4

Bd. 59   Anne-Kathrin Ende/Susann Herold/Annette Weilandt (Hg.): Alles hängt mit allem zusammen. Translatologische Interdependenzen. Festschrift für Peter A. Schmitt. 544 Seiten. ISBN 978-3-86596-504-2

Bd. 60   Saskia Weber: Kurz- und Kosenamen in russischen Romanen und ihre deutschen Übersetzungen. 256 Seiten. ISBN 978-3-7329-0002-2

Bd. 61   Silke Jansen/Martina Schrader-Kniffki (eds.): La traducción a través de los tiempos, espacios y disciplinas. 366 Seiten. ISBN 978-3-86596-524-0

Bd. 62   Annika Schmidt-Glenewinkel: Kinder als Dolmetscher in der Arzt-Patienten-Interaktion. 130 Seiten. ISBN 978-3-7329-0010-7

Bd. 63   Klaus-Dieter Baumann/Hartwig Kalverkämper (Hg.): Theorie und Praxis des Dolmetschens und Übersetzens in fachlichen Kontexten. 756 Seiten. ISBN 978-3-7329-0016-9

Bd. 64   Silvia Ruzzenenti: «Präzise, doch ungenau» – Tradurre il saggio. Un approccio olistico al *poetischer Essay* di Durs Grünbein. 406 Seiten. ISBN 978-3-7329-0026-8

Bd. 65   Margarita Zoe Giannoutsou: Kirchendolmetschen – Interpretieren oder Transformieren? 498 Seiten mit CD. ISBN 978-3-7329-0067-1

Bd. 66   Andreas F. Kelletat/Aleksey Tashinskiy (Hg.): Übersetzer als Entdecker. Ihr Leben und Werk als Gegenstand translationswissenschaftlicher und literaturgeschichtlicher Forschung. 376 Seiten. ISBN 978-3-7329-0060-2

Bd. 67   Ulrike Spieler: Übersetzer zwischen Identität, Professionalität und Kulturalität: Heinrich Enrique Beck. 340 Seiten. ISBN 978-3-7329-0107-4

Bd. 68   Carmen Klaus: Translationsqualität und Crowdsourced Translation. Untertitelung und ihre Bewertung – am Beispiel des audiovisuellen Mediums *TEDTalk*. 180 Seiten. ISBN 979-3-7329-0031-1

Bd. 69   Susanne J. Jekat/Heike Elisabeth Jüngst/Klaus Schubert/Claudia Villiger (Hg.): Sprache barrierefrei gestalten. Perspektiven aus der Angewandten Linguistik. 276 Seiten. ISBN 978-3-7329-0023-7

F Frank & Timme

TRANSÜD. Arbeiten zur Theorie und Praxis des Übersetzens und Dolmetschens

Bd. 70　Radegundis Stolze: Hermeneutische Übersetzungskompetenz. Grundlagen und Didaktik. 402 Seiten. ISBN 978-3-7329-0122-7

Bd. 71　María Teresa Sánchez Nieto (ed.): Corpus-based Translation and Interpreting Studies: From description to application / Estudios traductológicos basados en corpus: de la descripción a la aplicación. 268 Seiten. ISBN 978-3-7329-0084-8

Bd. 72　Karin Maksymski/Silke Gutermuth/Silvia Hansen-Schirra (eds.): Translation and Comprehensibility. 296 Seiten. ISBN 978-3-7329-0022-0

Bd. 73　Hildegard Spraul: Landeskunde Russland für Übersetzer. Sprache und Werte im Wandel. Ein Studienbuch. 360 Seiten. ISBN 978-3-7329-0109-8

Bd. 74　Ralph Krüger: The Interface between Scientific and Technical Translation Studies and Cognitive Linguistics. With Particular Emphasis on Explicitation and Implicitation as Indicators of Translational Text-Context Interaction. 482 Seiten. ISBN 978-3-7329-0136-4

Bd. 75　Erin Boggs: Interpreting U.S. Public Diplomacy Speeches. 154 Seiten. ISBN 978-3-7329-0150-0

Bd. 76　Nathalie Mälzer (Hg.): Comics – Übersetzungen und Adaptionen. 404 Seiten. ISBN 978-3-7329-0131-9

Bd. 77　Sophie Beese: Das (zweite) andere Geschlecht – der Diskurs „Frau" im Wandel. Simone de Beauvoirs *Le deuxième sexe* in deutscher Erst- und Neuübersetzung. 264 Seiten. ISBN 978-3-7329-0141-8

Bd. 78　Xenia Wenzel: Die Übersetzbarkeit philosophischer Diskurse. Eine Übersetzungskritik an den beiden englischen Übersetzungen von Heideggers *Sein und Zeit*. 162 Seiten. ISBN 978-3-7329-0199-9

Bd. 79　María-José Varela Salinas/Bernd Meyer (eds.): Translating and Interpreting Healthcare Discourses/Traducir e interpretar en el ámbito sanitario. 266 Seiten. ISBN 978-3-86596-367-3

Bd. 80　Susanne Hagemann: Einführung in das translationswissenschaftliche Arbeiten. Ein Lehr- und Übungsbuch. 360 Seiten. ISBN 978-3-7329-0125-8

Bd. 81　Anja Maibaum: Spielfilm-Synchronisation. Eine translationskritische Analyse am Beispiel amerikanischer Historienfilme über den Zweiten Weltkrieg. 144 Seiten mit CD. ISBN 978-3-7329-0220-0

Bd. 82　Sybille Schellheimer: La función evocadora de la fraseología en la oralidad ficcional y su traducción. 356 Seiten. ISBN 978-3-7329-0232-3

F Frank & Timme

TRANSÜD. Arbeiten zur Theorie und Praxis des Übersetzens und Dolmetschens

Bd. 83   Franziska Heidrich: Kommunikationsoptimierung im Fachübersetzungsprozess. 276 Seiten. ISBN 978-3-7329-0262-0

Bd. 84   Cristina Plaza Lara: Integración de la competencia instrumental-profesional en el aula de traducción. 222 Seiten mit CD. ISBN 978-3-7329-0309-2

Bd. 85   Andreas F. Kelletat/Aleksey Tashinskiy/Julija Boguna (Hg.): Übersetzerforschung. Neue Beiträge zur Literatur- und Kulturgeschichte des Übersetzens. 366 Seiten. ISBN 978-3-7329-0234-7

Bd. 86   Heidrun Witte: Blickwechsel. Interkulturelle Wahrnehmung im translatorischen Handeln. 274 Seiten. ISBN 978-3-7329-0333-7

Bd. 87   Susanne Hagemann/Julia Neu/Stephan Walter (Hg.): Translationslehre und Bologna-Prozess: Unterwegs zwischen Einheit und Vielfalt / Translation/Interpreting Teaching and the Bologna Process: Pathways between Unity and Diversity. 434 Seiten. ISBN 978-3-7329-0311-5

Bd. 88   Ursula Wienen/Laura Sergo/Tinka Reichmann/Ivonne Gutiérrez Aristizábal (Hg.): Translation und Ökonomie. 274 Seiten. ISBN 978-3-7329-0203-3

Bd. 89   Daniela Eichmeyer: Luftqualität in Dolmetschkabinen als Einflussfaktor auf die Dolmetschqualität. Interdisziplinäre Erkenntnisse und translationspraktische Konsequenzen. 144 Seiten. ISBN 978-3-7329-0362-7

Bd. 90   Alexander Künzli: Die Untertitelung – von der Produktion zur Rezeption. 264 Seiten. ISBN 978-3-7329-0393-1

Bd. 91   Christiane Nord: Traducir, una actividad con propósito. Introducción a los enfoques funcionalistas. 228 Seiten. ISBN 978-3-7329-0410-5

Bd. 92   Fabjan Hafner/Wolfgang Pöckl (Hg.): „... übersetzt von Peter Handke" – Philologische und translationswissenschaftliche Analysen. 294 Seiten. ISBN 978-3-7329-0443-3

Bd. 93   Elisabeth Gibbels: Lexikon der deutschen Übersetzerinnen 1200–1850. 216 Seiten. ISBN 978-3-7329-0422-8

Bd. 94   Encarnación Postigo Pinazo: Optimización de las competencias del traductor e intérprete. Nuevas tecnologías – procesos cognitivos – estrategias. 194 Seiten. ISBN 978-3-7329-0392-4

Bd. 95   Marta Estévez Grossi: Lingüística Migratoria e Interpretación en los Servicios Públicos. La comunidad gallega en Alemania. 574 Seiten. ISBN 978-3-7329-0411-2

F Frank & Timme

TRANSÜD. Arbeiten zur Theorie und Praxis des Übersetzens und Dolmetschens

Bd. 96   Ivana Havelka: Videodolmetschen im Gesundheitswesen. Dolmetschwissenschaftliche Untersuchung eines österreichischen Pilotprojektes. 346 Seiten. ISBN 978-3-7329-0490-7

Bd. 97   Maria Mushchinina (Hg.): Formate der Translation. 340 Seiten. ISBN 978-3-7329-0506-5

Bd. 98   Zehra Gülmüş: Übersetzungsverfahren beim literarischen Übersetzen. Ahmet Hamdi Tanpınars Roman „Das Uhrenstellinstitut". 196 Seiten. ISBN 978-3-7329-0498-3

Bd. 99   Peter Sandrini: Translationspolitik für Regional- oder Minderheitensprachen. Unter besonderer Berücksichtigung einer Strategie der Offenheit. 524 Seiten. ISBN 978-3-7329-0513-3

Bd. 100 Aleksey Tashinskiy/Julija Boguna (Hg.): Das WIE des Übersetzens. Beiträge zur historischen Übersetzerforschung. 248 Seiten. ISBN 978-3-7329-0536-2

Bd. 101 Heike Elisabeth Jüngst/Lisa Link/Klaus Schubert/Christiane Zehrer (eds.): Challenging Boundaries. New Approaches to Specialized Communication. 228 Seiten. ISBN 978-3-7329-0524-9

Bd. 102 Chuan Ding: „Peterchens Mondfahrt" in chinesischer Übersetzung. Eine Kritik. 124 Seiten. ISBN 978-3-7329-0528-7

Bd. 103 Changgun Kim: Übersetzen von Videospieltexten. Nekrotexte lesen und übersetzen. 164 Seiten. ISBN 978-3-7329-0379-5

Bd. 104 Guntars Dreijers/Agnese Dubova/Jānis Veckrācis (eds.): Bridging Languages and Cultures. Linguistics, Translation Studies and Intercultural Communication. 338 Seiten. ISBN 978-3-7329-0429-7

Bd. 105 Madeleine Schnierer: Qualitätssicherung. Die Praxis der Übersetzungsrevision im Zusammenhang mit EN 15038 und ISO 17100. 286 Seiten. ISBN 978-3-7329-0539-3

Bd. 106 Lavinia Heller/Tomasz Rozmysłowicz (Hg.): Translation und Interkulturelle Kommunikation / Translation and Intercultural Communication. Beiträge zur Theorie, Empirie und Praxis kultureller Austauschprozesse / Theoretical, Empirical and Practical Perspectives on Cultural Exchanges. 178 Seiten. ISBN 978-3-7329-0351-1

Bd. 107 Brita Dorer: Advance Translation as a Means of Improving Source Questionnaire Translatability? Findings from a Think-Aloud Study for French and German. 554 Seiten. ISBN 978-3-7329-0594-2

Bd. 108 Annegret Sturm: Theory of Mind in Translation. 334 Seiten. ISBN 978-3-7329-0492-1

TRANSÜD. Arbeiten zur Theorie und Praxis des Übersetzens und Dolmetschens

Bd. 109 Akkad Alhussein: Vom Zieltext zum Ausgangstext. Das Problem der retroflexen Wirksamkeit der Translation. 290 Seiten. ISBN 978-3-7329-0679-6

Bd. 110 Ursula Stachl-Peier/Eveline Schwarz (Hg./eds.): Ressourcen und Instrumente der translationsrelevanten Hochschuldidaktik / Resources and Tools for T&I Education. Lehrkonzepte, Forschungsberichte, Best-Practice-Modelle / Research Studies, Teaching Concepts, Best-Practice Results. 308 Seiten. ISBN 978-3-7329-0685-7

Bd. 111 Guntars Dreijers/Jānis Sīlis/Silga Sviķe/Jānis Veckrācis (eds.): Bridging Languages and Cultures II. Linguistics, Translation Studies and Intercultural Communication. 258 Seiten. ISBN 978-3-7329-0705-2

Bd. 112 Anu Viljanmaa: Professionelle Zuhörkompetenz und Zuhörfilter beim Dialogdolmetschen. 580 Seiten. ISBN 978-3-7329-0719-9

Bd. 113 Johan Franzon/Annjo K. Greenall/Sigmund Kvam/Anastasia Parianou (eds.): Song Translation: Lyrics in Contexts. 498 Seiten. ISBN 978-3-7329-0656-7

Bd. 114 Anna Wegener: Karin Michaëlis' *Bibi* books. Producing, Rewriting, Reading and Continuing a Children's Fiction Series, 1927–1953. 400 Seiten. ISBN 978-3-7329-0588-1

Bd. 115 Gesa Büttner: Dolmetschvorbereitung digital. Professionelles Dolmetschen und DeepL. 130 Seiten. ISBN 978-3-7329-0750-2

Bd. 116 Jutta Seeger-Vollmer: Schwer lesbar gleich texttreu?. Wissenschaftliche Translationskritik zur *Moby-Dick*-Übersetzung Friedhelm Rathjens. 530 Seiten. ISBN 978-3-7329-0766-3

Bd. 117 Katerina Sinclair: TranslatorInnen als SprachlehrerInnen: Eignung und Einsatz. 346 Seiten. ISBN 978-3-7329-0739-7

Bd. 118 Nathalie Thiede: Qualität bei der Lokalisierung von Videospielen. 116 Seiten. ISBN 978-3-7329-0793-9

Bd. 119 Iryna Kloster: Translation Competence and Language Contrast – A Multi-Method Study. Italian – Russian – German. 416 Seiten. ISBN 978-3-7329-0761-8

Bd. 120 Kerstin Rupcic: Einsatzpotenziale maschineller Übersetzung in der juristischen Fachübersetzung. 252 Seiten. ISBN 978-3-7329-0782-3

Bd. 121 Rocío García Jiménez/María-José Varela Salinas: Aspectos de la traducción biosanitaria español–alemán / alemán–español. 94 Seiten. ISBN 978-3-7329-0812-7

F Frank & Timme